The Partnership

The Voyage of the Century
Lusitania
The Ship that Hunted Itself
Emma: The Life of Lady Hamilton

With David Smith
Mugabe: a Biography

With Phillip Knightley
The Secret Lives of Lawrence of Arabia

With Lewis Chester and David Leitch
The Cleveland Street Affair

COLIN SIMPSON

The Partnership

The Secret Association of
Bernard Berenson and Joseph Duveen

THE BODLEY HEAD
LONDON

British Library Cataloguing
in Publication Data
Simpson, Colin, *1931*–
The partnership: the secret association
of Bernard Berenson and Joseph Duveen.
1. Duveen, Joseph   2. Berenson, Bernard
I. Title
338.7′617   N8660.D8
ISBN 0–370–30585–X

© C. & J. Simpson Ltd 1987
Printed in Great Britain for
The Bodley Head Ltd
32 Bedford Square, London WC1B 3EL
by St Edmundsbury Press Ltd,
Bury St Edmunds, Suffolk
First published 1987

Contents

CONTENTS

Illustrations

ILLUSTRATIONS

'The Madonna of the Eucharist', by Botticelli

'Portrait of a Lady', by Sebastiano Mainardi: (left) as 'restored' and sold by Duveen to Andrew Mellon; (right) the original as revealed after cleaning

'Madonna and Child', by Crivelli

The Allendale 'Nativity', by Giorgione

Introduction

The secret partnership between Bernard Berenson and Joseph Duveen was not such an unlikely alliance as some of the more sensitive members of the art world would have us believe. Duveen is remembered as the most successful art broker of the twentieth century; this trade—thanks to his undoubted charisma and his gift for salesmanship, laced with lavish doses of corruption—made him immensely rich and earned him the title of Lord Duveen of Millbank.

Berenson was a genius who early in life channelled his gifts into the study of that finest flower of Christian art: Italian Renaissance painting. By the age of thirty-five he had become the world's leading authority. He was, so it was believed, that rare bird of scholarship, a high priest with no contact with Mammon.

The curators of many of the world's great museums were either his former pupils or his disciples. Until his death in 1959, aged ninety-four, scholars, socialites, princes and students flocked to I Tatti, his magnificent hill-top villa on the outskirts of Florence. They came to hear his opinions, take his advice, and pay homage to his scholarship and his intellectual integrity.

A small minority saw him as a disgustingly rich, opinionated, spiteful tyrant—a man who reviled those who disagreed with him and who was tainted with more than a whiff of financial duplicity. But only a handful were aware that it was Berenson, not Duveen, who was probably the most successful and unscrupulous art dealer the world had ever seen.

René Gimpel, the Paris picture dealer and Duveen's brother-in-law, was one of the few. He was an occasional partner in some of Berenson's more lucrative deals, but both disliked and mistrusted him. Gimpel wrote:

> If small, lithe tigers could speak, they would have the voice and intelligence of this feline Pole. Behind that calculating sweetness a high old roaring goes on . . . He knows the whole gamut of society and its milieux, but everywhere he has only enemies. The hatred he expends he gets back in full measure.

Berenson began to deal covertly in 1891, three years after his arrival in Europe from the United States as a student. By the time he accepted Duveen's offer of a secret partnership in 1906, he had already had several similar 'arrangements' with dealers of the calibre of Colnaghis of London, Seligman of Paris, the German collector-dealer J. P. Richter, and one of Italy's master 'improvers' of second-rate paintings, the Baron Lazzaroni.

The thirty-year partnership was immensely profitable to both men. Duveen Brothers kept several sets of accounts and misled Berenson with the same insouciance that they meted out to the revenue and customs inspectors. Nevertheless, during their association, Berenson always received at least $100,000 a year; and in the twenty-six years between 16 December 1911 and 31 December 1937 his share of the profits, with no outlay, was $8,370,000—in today's values almost $150 million.

Duveen needed Berenson for his scholarship; Berenson needed the money, though he came to despise himself for allowing Duveen to compromise, and eventually to corrupt, him.

In his old age Berenson jotted down some notes for the biography he knew was inevitable. It would, he conceded, be a scandalous chronicle. Then the mostly straightforward if somewhat introspective memories and reflections erupted into bitter remorse as he hoped that his regrettable behaviour over the years in and out of art dealing would not be remembered against him.

It is clear from the papers of both Berenson and Duveen that they disliked and distrusted each other from the beginning. Duveen despised Berenson but Berenson hated his partner, even more than he hated himself.

This account is in five parts. The first two attempt to place each man in his correct historical context and to explain the circumstances and the pressures which brought such highly disparate characters into uneasy relationship. Parts three and four detail some of their more profitable and occasionally outrageous 'coups', made first as individuals, then as partners. The fifth and final part unravels the mystery of the dispute which led to their bitter break-up and generated Berenson's venomous epitaph on his former partner: 'Duveen stood at the center of a vast circular nexus of corruption that reached from the lowliest employee of the British Museum, right up to the King'.

There have been biographies of both men, in Berenson's case several, of which I have found three most useful, though not always reliable. The first of these is Sylvia Sprigge's *Bernard Berenson*, written with the sensitivity of a devoted former mistress, which the late Lord Clark denounced as a 'deplorable book'. Perhaps it was too perceptive?

I have also found much of value in *Being Bernard Berenson* by Meryl Secrest, a detailed if rather over-psychological study. Ms Secrest has since acknowledged that her book could not have been written without the enthusiastic if slightly mischievous assistance of the late Lord Clark. She devotes two chapters to Berenson's relationship with Duveen, with which I was able to give her some guidance. In particular I introduced her to the widow of Edward Fowles, the man to whom Duveen left his business in his will. Fowles' book, *Memories of Duveen Brothers*, was a major source for many of Ms Secrest's revelations.

Here I have a confession to make. I was introduced to the Fowles family when I began to research this book during 1969. They very kindly offered me all their material, including the use of the Duveen archives. Edward Fowles had intended to write his own account, but a combination of glaucoma and infirmity had hampered his plans. It was agreed that I would 'ghost' his notes and first drafts into publishable form and arrange publication, before my own study appeared. This I did. My name appeared on the copyright page of *Memories of Duveen Brothers*, though the title page very properly carries Edward's name alone. Mr Thomas Hoving and Mr Ashton Hawkins of the Metropolitan Museum, New York, endorsed the Fowleses' permission to use the Duveen archives and allowed me unrestricted access to them, subject to three conditions: first, that I would not publish while certain of the characters I wrote about were still alive; second, that I would not preempt a study of Berenson's attributions which was being prepared by the late Mrs Elizabeth Gardner, a member of the curatorial staff of the Metropolitan, who was the only other person to whom Mr and Mrs Fowles had granted access (sadly, Mrs Gardner died prematurely before she could publish, but I was privileged to read her draft manuscript: many of my sager comments on the authorship of certain paintings stem from her discriminating eyes and meticulous research); third, that I would not reveal how I had gained access to the archives if, in the opinion of her legal advisers, it would—during her lifetime—prejudice Mrs Fowles' relationship with the United States Internal Revenue Service.

Lord Duveen had left his business, lock, stock and barrel, to Edward Fowles and two others. In due course Edward acquired the interests of both other parties. He ran the firm until 1964 when he sold it to Mr Norton Simon. The archives were specifically excluded from the sale. They were valued at $750,000, and were deeded to the Metropolitan Museum in exchange for an equitable income tax concession. Fowles stipulated that they were to be embargoed—save for the personal permission he and his wife gave to Ms Gardner and myself—until the year 2002. The Fowles' embargo was primarily for fiscal reasons, plus a wish not to embarrass their many colleagues in the art trade and museum world. They had also learned that many of Berenson's former pupils, led by Lord Clark and John Walker, then Director of the Washington National Gallery, formed a powerful lobby, jealous of their master's and their own reputations: during the five-year period leading up to the publication of Edward's book there was a constant barrage of anxious inquiries and lawyers' threats.

Edward Fowles was eminently well qualified to assess the relationship between Duveen and Berenson. He joined Duveens in 1898, and early in the century was appointed manager of the Paris branch of the company. He watched Joseph Duveen grow from a precocious youth into a seasoned manipulator of the art market. He became not only his second-in-command in Europe, but his confidant and his heir. He knew Berenson from the early days of this century, was present at the negotiations which led to the secret partnership agreement of 1906, and was witness to the numerous contracts between the two men.

As they mutually disliked and distrusted each other, Edward became the conduit between them. Berenson never wrote to Duveen. He wrote to Edward who passed on the letter and then drafted Duveen's reply. Edward settled their numerous quarrels, sorted out their complicated financial affairs, and held their trust until they died. 'My main job', he said while preparing his memoir, 'was to keep Joe honest and BB sweet'.

Late in his life, by a curious coincidence, Edward Fowles married Jean Langton Douglas, the widow of Berenson's one-time arch-rival, Robert Langton Douglas, who, though Berenson was never told, had been responsible for his employment by Duveen in the first place. Jean had been her first husband's researcher and secretary and had kept his papers. This book is therefore the fruit of my research into the combined archives of Duveens and Langton Douglas, supplemented by the memories, diaries, and notes of Jean and Edward Fowles, with whom I had many long and detailed conversations.

This is the appropriate place for me to acknowledge the Fowleses' unstinting help and generosity. I have been immensely fortunate to have enjoyed access to these archives, when scholars such as Sir John Pope-Hennessy, Lord Clark, and Mr John Walker were refused.

The most important scholar to have suffered under the embargo is Professor Ernest Samuels of Harvard University, the official biographer of Berenson. Samuels' first volume, *Bernard Berenson, The Making of a Connoisseur*, was the third and most valuable of my principal published sources; it is a masterpiece of discretion and friendly scholarship. Because of the Fowles embargo, it ends in the year before Duveen and Berenson became acquainted. I have accepted Professor Samuels' views on disputed facts up to 1895.

I have also had access to Berenson's letters to Edward Fowles; to Duveens' files, ledgers and accounts, including the 'X' book maintained by the firm of chartered accountants, Westcott Maskall; to the Berenson-Richter correspondence in Zurich; to the Huntington archives in Pasadena, and to Edward Fowles' copious personal files on all of Duveens' major clients. Mr John Allen of New York, the former financial comptroller of Duveens, Mr William Oelshlager of New Jersey, who spent his entire working life with the firm of Duveens, and the executors of the late Bertram Boggis have also been extremely helpful, as was Mr R. Langdon Douglas' eldest daughter, Mrs Claire Salinger.

In addition, I had a series of long interviews with the late Lord Clark before his death. Lord Clark had originally been invited to become Berenson's official biographer. At first he accepted, but after discussing the matter with Edward Fowles, withdrew. This was a prime reason why Fowles was determined to publish. Lord Clark's executors and publishers have generously allowed me to quote at length from his autobiography *Another Part of the Wood*. I am also grateful to Mr David Ekserdjian, the Christie's Fellow in Italian Renaissance Art at Balliol College, Oxford, who checked my manuscript where painters and paintings were concerned.

Mary Berenson began a biography of her husband which covered his life until 1926. This has never been published, but her family have allowed several would-be biographers access. My own copy was given to me by Berenson's first biographer, Mrs Sylvia Sprigge. While I have drawn upon it for facts, I have not quoted from it.

Much of the early material on Duveens comes from another member of the family, Lord Duveen's brother-in-law, the late Mr J. Hangjas Duveen. The English edition of his two-volume auto-biography, *Confessions of an Art Dealer*, was bowdlerized and eventually bought up by Lord Duveen. The second volume of this work was translated into six languages; it was serialized in France in the magazine *Gringoire* from October to December 1936.

Shortly after Lord Duveen's death in 1939, his younger brother Edward asked J. Hangjas Duveen to compile a history of the firm which would do something to correct the impression that it was solely the creation of his older brother. J. Hangjas Duveen had finished the first fifteen chapters when Edward Fowles assumed full control of the company in 1944. He was opposed to the project, as was Lord Duveen's daughter, the Hon. Mrs Burns: between them they persuaded J. Hangjas Duveen to abandon the project and place his manuscripts in the Duveen archives. He was, however, allowed to use some of the material up to the date of Joel's death. This was published in 1957 under the title *The Rise of the House of Duveen*. I have read the unpublished fifteen chapters.

There has been only one study of Lord Duveen, and that is the often quoted and immensely readable *Duveen* by the *New Yorker* humorist, the late Sam Behrman. The jokes and anecdotes flow so fast that facts bend or disappear in the current. The history of this book needs explanation. In its original form it was not written by Behrman, but by the late Mr Louis Levy, a New York lawyer who acted both for Duveen and for Berenson until he was disbarred from the state and federal courts for dishonesty and unprofessional conduct. Mr Levy steered both his clients through some very murky waters, and, in partnership with Berenson, attempted to acquire control of Duveen Brothers when Lord Duveen was terminally ill. Their plan was discovered by Edward Fowles, and Lord Duveen dispensed with both men's services.

Levy's original manuscript, which I have read, was a spiteful personal apologia, so prolix and spattered with legal jargon that it was unpublishable. He took it to Behrman, who attended the same synagogue, for advice. Levy's professional disgrace then made it unwise to publish under his own name as he could have been sued for breach of his clients' confidence. By agreement Behrman used much of the material in a series of articles in the *New Yorker*, which were then expanded into the book as we know it today. Behrman spent his publisher's advance on a trip to I Tatti. He carefully turned Levy's spite into jokes, which showed Duveen as a lovable scallywag and Berenson as the patient guru, good-humouredly trying to keep his patron reasonably honest.

Behrman showed a copy of the manuscript to Edward Fowles before publication, asking for his endorsement. Fowles, who admired Behrman and knew him well—they were golfing partners—replied, listing numerous inaccuracies, and sportingly explained that he could only endorse the book if they were corrected, 'when', he wrote, 'it would not be so funny. As it is, I am sure it will do very well'. It did.

However, Behrman's book gives a totally misleading account of the operation of Duveen Brothers and credits the establishment of the business almost entirely to Joseph. This was not the case, as will be seen from the opening chapter of the present account, which tells the story of the rise of the House of Duveen.

PART ONE

Duveen

❧ 1 ❧

The House of Duveen

The name Duveen was adopted by a penniless Jewish refugee from Paris in 1810. His name was Henoch Joseph. Bankrupted by the Napoleonic Wars, he moved to northern Holland, settling in the town of Meppel where he started up business as a blacksmith. Partly to escape his creditors and partly due to the Napoleonic edict that Jewish families had to adopt surnames by which they could be registered, he took the name of Du Vesne, which had belonged to one of his wife's ancestors. This was pronounced Duvane, but in Flemish was written Duveen.

At first the business prospered and Duveens of Meppel became the leading manufacturers of weights and measures to the Dutch government. Henoch Duveen retired in 1860 and handed over the business to his son Joseph. Joseph (Lord Duveen's grandfather and namesake) was no businessman, and his problems were compounded in 1864 when his wife died leaving him with three children, Joel, Betsy and Henry. He shut down his forge and, after a disastrous attempt to start a cotton wool factory in Amsterdam, he abandoned commerce and married the forty-year-old daughter of a wealthy neighbour.

She was an excellent wife but an unenthusiastic stepmother, with little time for her three stepchildren. The eldest, Joel (Lord Duveen's father), then aged twenty-three, was found a position as a travelling salesman with the firm of Dumouriex and Gostschalk of Hull, who were wholesale importers of Dutch vegetable produce. Betsy, the sixteen-year-old daughter, went to Haarlem to stay with her Hangjas cousins, who owned a wholesale antique and scrap metal business, while Henry, the youngest, then aged eleven, was packed off to the Burgher High School in Amsterdam, where he was given board and lodging by distant relatives.

Joel lodged with a family called Barnett, who lived above their jewellery and pawnbroking business at 49 Waterworks Street in Hull. He fell in love with their daughter Rosetta, but, as he had few prospects and little money, the family opposed the match. However, he had a supporter in her brother Barney, who acted as a buyer for his father, and it was agreed that Rosetta and Joel could marry if and when Joel acquired a capital sum of £1,000 free of all indebtedness. It was a dismal prospect.

During the Easter holiday of 1868, Barney Barnett and Joel crossed to Holland to spend a short holiday with Joel's sister, Betsy, and the antique-dealing Hangjas cousins. Henri Hangjas, the eldest son, took the two young visitors off to see around the family warehouse. In one corner were rows of Chinese blue and white cups and saucers of the Nankin pattern, priced at fivepence each. Barney was adamant that they would sell well in England; in his enthusiasm he ordered a case and persuaded Joel to do the same, proposing that Joel should take them with him on his sales round. Joel was more cautious, and to hedge his bets he also ordered a case of Delft jars. Henri Hangjas then persuaded both of them to increase their order, offering two months' credit against their post-dated cheques.

On his return to England, Joel Duveen stuffed his bags with samples of Nankin patterned china and Delftware and added antique dealers to his round of greengrocers on his weekly produce-selling trips, which ranged from Hull to Manchester and Liverpool. Two weeks later he was back in Haarlem for more; by midsummer Joel and Barney were full-time importers of antique porcelain.

It was a steady business. Barney sold through his father's shop while Joel, cutting out the dealers, travelled the north of England, giving monthly exhibitions in hotel rooms. His displays, particularly at the Stork Hotel in Liverpool, became well-known, and through them he was introduced to a number of wealthy collectors who asked not only for the blue and white ware with which he had started, but for many other types of oriental porcelain, such as Famille Rose, Verte and Jaune.

In the autumn of 1868 Barney and Joel entered into a formal partnership as importers of porcelain and works of art. Betsy Duveen came over to Hull from Haarlem to sort out the crateloads of cups, saucers, tea bowls, scent bottles and other items which her brother was importing, and Joel was now accepted by the Barnetts as a future son-in-law. The wedding was arranged for February 1869. Joel might have spent the rest of his life in Hull as an importer if it had not been for two coups which he pulled off, shortly before his marriage, which deserve rather more than a footnote in the history of art dealing.

The first was the purchase of the remarkable Hawthorn Ginger Jar, now in the Victoria and Albert Museum. Coloured in a rare shade of cobalt blue, hawthorn jars were produced just once at the imperial porcelain factory at King-Te-Chin during the reign of the Emperor Ching-Tsou (1662-1722). Against the blue background an unknown artist painted a pattern of white prunus sprays. He gave his jars a unique crackled background which possessed remarkable depth and seemed iridescent when seen in daylight. The vase belonged to a Dutch nobleman, and Henri Hangjas learned that it was for sale. He telegraphed Barney and Joel, and between them they bought it for £470, payable in gold.

Barney was initially against the purchase, arguing that they had no customers prepared to pay that sort of money, but Joel insisted that he could sell it in London. He was right, and the then leading collector, James Orrock, paid him £1,200 without a murmur.

Joel had had to pay a number of commissions to other dealers just to obtain an interview with Orrock, and from that moment on he determined to open his own showrooms in London. Barney demurred at the expense, saying that they had just had a lucky break, but only a week later Henri Hangjas found Joel a further and even more profitable bargain.

Count von der Goltz of Schlangenburg Castle had a magnificent collection, which included a famous set of tapestries. Hangjas arranged for Joel to call and admire the collection on the off-chance that the Count might care to sell some of his porcelain. In fact, he had nothing for sale, but Joel noticed that, though the pictures and porcelain were all antique, the furniture was modern mahogany. He learned that, when the Count had succeeded to the estate, the furniture had been inherited by a distant relative. Joel and Henri traced it and purchased the lot for £2,500. Joel described what he found in a memorandum written many years later:

As we entered the room, we thought it looked more like a warehouse. There was an unbroken row of furniture against the walls, and the centre of the room was stacked with settees and chairs; everything was covered in dust sheets . . . in a few minutes we had uncovered them all. There were two large settees and two small, six bergeres, six armchairs and twelve singles, all Louis XVth, carved and gilt. Every piece covered in the same tapestry as the Schlangenburg hangings . . . There were fourteen other pieces of furniture, apart from a pair of threefold screens which matched the tapestry chairs. There were two pairs of commodes, one Louis XV pair with mounts by Caffieri, the other Louis XVI by Reisener, with Ormulu mounts by Gouthiere.

Then there was a small escritoire and a matching chiffoniere, also by Reisener, a pair of red lacquered tric trac tables and a bonheur du jour all by Martin Carlin with mounts by Gouthiere, a matching set of two bookcases and two library cabinets by David Roentgen. All the pieces were signed by their makers, but I knew nothing about French furniture at that time. I was stunned. Without asking Henri's advice I asked how much for the lot. He replied £2,500 and I heard myself saying 'I'll take them'.*

Joel's problem was that he did not have £2,500. However, he managed to borrow the money and loaded the furniture onto the Paris train at nearby Arnhem. In Paris, in his haste to cover his debt, he let the lot go for £8,000, though he later discovered that he could have asked and obtained £40,000.

The profits, which were shared out with Barney and Henri Hangjas, not only gave Joel a useful start to his own marriage but gave Henri Hangjas the capital and the courage to propose to Betsy Duveen, who accepted him. After a long engagement they were married and Henri Hangjas, following the Dutch custom, added his wife's name to his own and became Henri Hangjas Duveen. Both men's marriages prospered. Each had a child a year, and Joel's first-born, Joseph, later to become Lord Duveen, was born on 14 October 1869. Barnett and Duveen continued in prosperous partnership but, at the former's insistence, stuck to im-

* J. H. Duveen, *The Rise of the House of Duveen*.

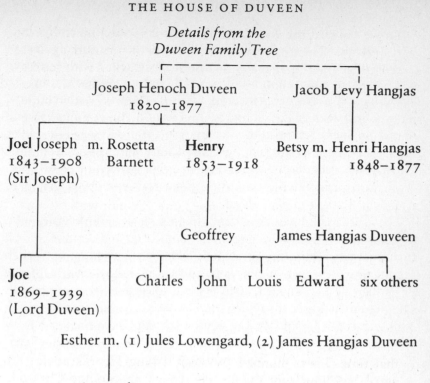

Details from the
Duveen Family Tree

porting. Joel also entered into a separate arrangement with Henri Hangjas whereby they bought in partnership, offering their purchases firstly to Barnett and Duveen at cost plus 5 per cent plus carriage. If Barnett demurred, Joel was then free to sell elsewhere, usually through the London auction house of Robinson and Fisher.

It was an arrangement that was bound to lead to friction. Joel was impetuous, always after the finer pieces and desperate to open in London. Barnett found it difficult to hold his ebullient partner in check and preferred to stick to items he understood such as silver and jewellery. The partnership was dissolved by mutual agreement in 1876 but, as is often the case where tortuous legal discussions take place, the outcome was far from what either partner wished. Barnett finished up with a lump sum, and, to Joel's chagrin, promptly opened a jeweller's shop at the junction of Holborn and Gray's Inn Road in London. Joel was left with the lease of the Hull shop, a wife, six children, and stock and cash totalling

£8,000. A final condition of the dissolution was that neither would trade within ten miles of the other for a period of three years.

Characteristically, Joel was not to be thwarted. He was advised that selling by auction in London would not constitute trading, so he proposed a fresh partnership with his other brother-in-law, Betsy's husband, Henri Hangjas. Joel would run the English end of the business, selling only by auction until 1879, while Henri Hangjas Duveen would visit the United States and choose a suitable location for a wholesale warehouse in either Boston or New York. Their European buying would be done for them by a group of friends in Paris and The Hague.

The principal buyer was Jan Theunissen of The Hague, who offered twelve months' credit if he could be sole supplier of all furniture, porcelain, tapestries and silver, except those of French manufacture. French items were to be the responsibility of the Paris firm of Lowengard, who offered all goods on a six-month sale-or-return basis, provided that at least 10 per cent of each consignment was sold or the equivalent sum of money paid, by way of a penalty. Pictures were to be supplied on a similar basis by Messrs Gimpel and Wildenstein of Paris.

The new partnership papers were drawn up and ready for signature early in January 1877. Henri Hangjas Duveen had booked his passage to Boston when two tragedies intervened. Henri contracted typhoid and was dead within a week, and Joel's father died a few days later.

Joel was now not only the head of the family but the guardian and trustee of his sister Betsy's five children by Henri Hangjas, who ranged from five years old to three months. To add to his problems he was now responsible for the future of his youngest brother, Henry Duveen.

Henry had graduated from the Amsterdam Burghers School but, finding his stepmother difficult to live with, had made a brief and financially disastrous trip to the newly discovered diamond fields in Cape Province, South Africa. He was twenty-three and of a feckless nature, having complicated matters still further by forming a close attachment to a neighbour's daughter who was not quite sixteen.

Joel sorted out the problems with characteristic speed, even if he did not think out the likely consequences. He packed his brother off to Hull and, after a three-day course in the details of his stock, handed him Henri Hangjas' ticket to Boston, two trunks of samples and a priced stocklist.

The young Henry Duveen sailed for the United States. On 3 July 1877, he wrote a prophetic letter home to his brother. It was in a mixture of Dutch, Yiddish and English and merits quotation in full. (The Dutch and Yiddish have been translated; the syntax has only been corrected where the original meaning is unclear.)

Boston. 3 July 77

Dear Brother

Today I have worked and walked hard, and want to tell you the following:

I have been to various people in the business and to my amazement I have so far seen little Delftware here. You must know that a lot of copies are getting sold here, but nothing genuine, but they [dealers] are all willing to buy genuine Delft but have to see the goods first—it is no good just telling and talking. They must see the stuff.

There is surely a good business to be carried on here in antiques. They are mad on Gobelin tapestries, especially the smaller square pieces. There are also buyers for chairs, sideboards, and oak Friesian cupboards, provided they are in good condition and ready for sale, looking as new, so let's have some made in advance. Marquetries will also sell well, principally in chairs with cushions. Nice pieces sell at a good price. It is possible to build a good business in antiques, but you have to push and chat a lot.

With goods there is a wide open market for us. They are all anxious to do business, but would rather wait until September as at present there are not many gentlemen in town—they are all at the seaside now, but business is improving in all branches every day.

I have been in lots [of shops] today and could not really sell [on description] but I had to promise each one on my word that they should have first sight of the stuff you will ship to Boston. I must let them know 14 days beforehand when I know what is coming and when it will arrive.

Put these addresses away and do not lose them, we shall

want them again, for they also buy old oak and loose pieces.

But can you expect much to be done by me of all people who does not understand the trade very well as yet? You must remember that you cannot sell articles you cannot show. I believe that I have done quite well so far. I have done my utmost best and you have nothing to grumble about. If you came yourself you could judge better, but I am sure that there is a nice business to be done here, but you want to be in New York and have a wholesale business only for the trade.

I am getting quite a hand in antiques for a greenhorn.

I am off tomorrow for New York and will call on all the dealers and make connections for you. Do not send anything off yet. I shall probably return to Europe to see you and then we could return here together in September to make arrangements for establishing ourselves. Save all my letters and the addresses. I like America very well. It is a fine rich country. It beats England in everything, and you will be astonished at what it is like, it is A.1.

✿ 2 ✿

Uncle Henry

New York in 1877 was the capital of the world for expensive furniture and porcelain masquerading as antique. For the most part these were reproductions, and Henry Duveen quickly realized that he was offering goods of a far higher quality for a much lower price, even though this included shipment from Europe by passenger steamer. He therefore doubled, then tripled, his prices. The wholesalers to whom he showed his stock were not, however, interested in the excellence of his wares and gave him a brusque reception, for few had either the knowledge or the taste to appreciate them. After a fruitless fortnight he decided to try to sell direct to the public.

He persuaded the owner of a shop selling artist's and draughtsman's materials in John Street, near the Battery, to rent him a corner of an upper floor. Joel had by now sent him a few fine pieces of porcelain and silver, several hundred Delft tiles packed into an Italian credenza or large cupboard to prevent them from breaking, some Dutch oak tables, and a set of Dutch marquetry chairs. Henry laid the Delft tiles on the floor and arranged the furniture on them with great care. As a final touch, he added a pair of brand-new reproduction French carved and gilt armchairs in the style of Louis XV which Joel had included, taking his brother's letter literally: 'ready for sale, looking as new, so let's have some made in advance'.

Collectors and connoisseurs were not the usual customers of the premises, but Henry had not realised this: the artist's easels, palettes and paints in the window had made him think that it was some form of art gallery. His upstairs pitch was in the department that specialised in pencils and drawing paper, where the majority of the customers were architects and architectural draughtsmen. Almost his first customer was a man who was well on his way to becoming legendary, as the *New York Times* put it, as 'the Benvenuto Cellini of American architecture'—Stanford White.

White had originally wanted to be a painter, but architecture claimed him, and he was a partner in the reputable and already well-known firm of McKim, Mead and White, who specialised in designing public buildings and large Italianate town and country houses. White preferred the Renaissance period, while McKim borrowed his themes from ancient Rome. Their design for Pennsylvania Station in New York, for example, was taken from Bernini's colonnade in front of St. Peter's, Rome, while the doors of Boston's public library derive from those of Ghiberti for the Baptistry in Florence.

White bought Duveen's Italian credenza for his office and both he and McKim were entranced by the tiles. On learning that unlimited supplies were available by fast steamer, they ordered twenty thousand for a mansion they were designing on Fifth Avenue. They were also impressed by the workmanship of the French chairs and, after some negotiation, ordered a substantial quantity. They inquired if copies could be made of other European styles and periods.

These chairs had been made by the Paris firm of Carlhian and Beaumetz, who were specialists in making copies of the finer examples of French furniture. Anatole Beaumetz, brother-in-law to the French Minister for the Arts, had access to almost anything that a Duveen client might want copied. The firm employed their own carvers, gilders, tapestry weavers and brass founders, and their workmanship was superb. Most specialists agree that a Carlhian replica is almost as good as the original, and today they are frequently mistaken for the genuine article.

Joel now found Beaumetz fine examples of Chippendale furniture to copy, including several items in the designer's Chinese manner, dining tables and chairs and library furniture, and the two firms entered into a partnership which lasted for thirty-three years, until Paul Carlhian's death in 1914. From 1881 until 1914, Duveen Brothers never spent less than $2.5 million a year with their gifted French partners, a fact which the French government recognized in 1902 when Henry received the Légion d'Honneur for his services to the arts.

Once McKim and White had learnt to trust Henry, they had no hesitation in introducing him to their clients, who included such millionaires as J. Pierpont Morgan, Collis Huntington, P. A. B. Widener and George Jay Gould, who soon became close friends. There was something about Henry Duveen's rotund little figure and drooping walrus moustache that they found rather endearing. He was moreover young, enthusiastic, and filled with integrity; he had consciously set himself to learn all he could about his wares and never attempted to bluff, freely confessing when he would prefer a second opinion.

In the spring of 1879, Joel came to New York for the first time. He wanted to discuss future plans with Stanford White and to urge Henry to find larger premises in a better quarter of the city and to lease a warehouse for the reproduction furniture. When Joel returned to England, he decided that as his three-year embargo on trading within ten miles of Barney Barnett was almost up, he would open in London. Joel took a lease of a former pottery showroom at 181 Oxford Street, redecorated it in sumptuous style and, unheard of at the time, illuminated his windows at night with the newly introduced electric light.

Joel felt that he had now arrived. Although Henry wrote saying he had secured two new sets of premises, one at 11 East 30th Street and another at 262 Fifth Avenue, Joel made no mention of his brother on his writing paper, simply stating that J. J. Duveen of Oxford Street, London, and Fifth Avenue, New York, was an Importer of Antique and Decorative Furniture, China, Bronzes, Old Tapestries and Silks.

The tapestries were an idea of Stanford's. He wanted to cover vast walls in his mansions, and tapestries were not only relatively cheap compared with pictures, but there was a surfeit of them in Europe as a result of the craze for William Morris wallpaper. White specified them for J. Pierpont Morgan's new house, scheduled for completion in 1882, which Henry Duveen was asked to furnish throughout.

Henry returned to England for a conference with Joel. Together they planned a major public relations exercise. While Joel amassed what Henry required for Morgan's house, he also gathered together what was probably the most mouth-watering collection of fine furniture, silver, armour and tapestries that any dealer had ever had under one roof. A great deal of this was on sale-or-return, but in order to make a show Joel issued bills of exchange that exhausted his available capital and agreed overdraft.

When the goods and Joel eventually arrived in New York, he found that Fifth Avenue was the address of the warehouse and that East Street was too small to display all that he had brought. Joel was understandably angry with Henry for failing to plan ahead. What Joel found difficult to realize was that, although Henry loved his porcelains, he preferred to spend his time with his clients and cared not a jot for the ostentatious display techniques favored by his brother. Henry was content to put a boy in to mind the store while he visited his customers, who were also his friends.

Joel speedily found larger premises at 827 Broadway and spent all their joint funds in New York on decorating them to look as he wished. By the time he had finished, both brothers were desperate for money. Their credit was exhausted and Henry refused to approach any of his richer customers for assistance. 'Money', he told Joel, 'is what America is all about, and the rich will never deal with us if they suspect that we are hard pressed'.

Henry recalled that Collis Huntington, the Pacific Coast railway tycoon, had asked him to look out for the finest French furniture, so a message was sent inviting him to a private view. He kept them waiting a week, and then arrived, accompanied by Arabella Wortham, a widow whom he was later to marry and who was, in Joel's opinion, a 'showy girl'. Joel left the selling to Henry and watched from the rear of the shop.

Henry showed off the furniture and the porcelain, but Huntington took no notice, not even bothering to ask the price of anything. Joel later recounted what happened next.

'Show me something worthwhile', he growled, using one of our best oriental rugs as a spittoon. I realized the sort of mentality we had to deal with so I came forward and introduced myself and said, 'I think I can show you something which is as fine as anything you will have ever seen, but I am keeping it for another customer so you must give me your word that you will not tell anyone that you have seen it'.

As I intended, he thought it was being reserved for Morgan, but agreed to my request. I took him upstairs and showed him a set of four tapestries each with [François] Boucher panels from the Manufacture Royale des Gobelins. I had bought them on impulse shortly before I left England for £12,000.

Huntington asked me how much I was asking, I dodged the question by saying that they were reserved. 'I am not asking you to sell them to me', he rumbled, 'I want to know what you hope to get for them'. I replied that I was asking £30,000. Huntington promptly offered me £35,000 but I demurred. Then he demanded to know if my fictitious customer had a written option on them. I had to confess that he did not and so reluctantly allowed myself to be persuaded to sell. He wrote a cheque immediately and demanded they be delivered to Mrs Wortham's house at 4 West 54th Street before anyone else saw them.*

Huntington's cheque solved the brothers' problem for the time being, but Henry's unconcealed disapproval of his brother's ideas on presentation and sales technique irritated Joel. A coolness developed between them which, apart from one brief *rapprochement*, lasted until Joel's death twenty-five years later. Between 1883 and 1889 they continued to work together on an informal basis, but it was an uneasy association. No formal partnership was drawn up, which led to constant financial quarrels, for each took a percentage of the business introduced by the other. Joel kept the words 'New York' on his letterheading, while Henry traded more specifically as H. J. Duveen of 262 Fifth Avenue, New York. He also opened a small retail gallery out at Newport, Rhode Island, where he displayed his finest porcelain.

Many of Henry's richer clients made lengthy annual visits to Europe, so he would arrange his own year around theirs, making sure that he ran into them at the various spas and luxurious hotels they frequented. He encouraged several of them to purchase houses in Paris and London, which he then furnished. But he left the day-to-day supervision of these European mansions and estates to Joel when he returned to New York. Not unnaturally this led many people to regard Joel as the single-minded driving force behind

* Joel Duveen in J. Hangjas Duveen's unpublished manuscript in the Edward Fowles archives.

the firm. Nothing could have been further from the truth, for Joel had many other interests, Henry only one.

Joel was a speculative builder, with a housing estate at Sutton and a row of terraced shops in the Finchley Road, and the owner of the freeholds of 67 and 68 New Bond Street. He had also purchased the Duke of Cambridge's London residence on the corner of Piccadilly and Park Lane, shipped the Grinling Gibbons carvings, the fireplaces and the numerous architectural fittings to Henry in New York, demolished the house and built in its place the first modern block of flats in London with bricks supplied from his own brick works.

Henry, on the other hand, had only one passion apart from his business: he was an enthusiastic stamp collector. Because of this interest, J. Pierpont Morgan introduced him to Lord Esher (private secretary to Edward, Prince of Wales), who in turn introduced him to the Prince's son George (the future King George V), who was also an avid stamp collector. The art dealer and the Prince became regular correspondents, and whenever Henry was in London he would be asked to Buckingham Palace. Henry Duveen eventually amassed the third finest stamp collection in the world, which was valued at his death in 1919 at $5 million; only George V and the Czar of Russia had better.

Lord Esher also introduced Henry to Sir Horace, soon to be Lord Farquhar, who advised the Prince of Wales on his complicated financial affairs. Farquhar was also a director of Parrs, bankers to the Duveen brothers. Farquhar now arranged to discount the sums owed by Morgan and other clients of Henry's in order to free the brothers from their dependence upon Lowengard and other European suppliers, but in return he insisted that they should organise their affairs on a formal basis, setting up companies in London, New York and Paris.

Joel and Henry were each to have 50 per cent of the London operation and 35 per cent of the New York company, with 30 per cent of the shares in the latter unissued. Henry wholly owned a second American company which, on paper at least, imported from the London company and sold on to the jointly owned American enterprise. The French company, which was purely a buying operation, was arranged slightly differently with 50 per cent of the shares owned by Joel, 35 per cent by Henry and the remaining 15 per cent by Lowengard. Once this corporate structure had been established Parrs granted the two brothers a credit line of $6 million, secured against nothing more than their personal guarantees.

Parrs' credit line enabled the two brothers, though they were constantly at loggerheads even after 1889, to dominate—and almost monopolize—the business of redecorating the houses of the rich. As they did so, they found a ready market, amongst their own clientele, for the discarded pieces their new furnishings replaced.

Royal patronage also helped. Many people have assumed that it was Lord Esher who brought the Duveen family to the notice of the future Edward VII, but it was Lord Farquhar. The Prince of Wales was always short of money, but managed to find it from the ready pockets of such *nouveaux riches* as the Monds, Cassels and Sassoons and the various branches of the Rothschild family. They in turn were anxious for honours and titles, and Farquhar became the conduit for many an otherwise inexplicable 'elevation', the Prince increasingly using him as a go-between for some of his more colourful financial dealings. Farquhar lost no time in acquiring honours for himself, first a knighthood, then a baronetcy and a peerage, and finally an earldom. As his dignities increased he began to furnish his houses with the help of Duveen Brothers, who tactfully never sent him a bill. In turn he passed to them the names of those whom he knew to be financially embarrassed, as often as not those who had lost substantial sums playing cards with his master.

When Edward succeeded to the throne he found both Windsor Castle and Buckingham Palace to be furnished like 'a Scottish funeral parlour'. It was Farquhar, recently appointed as Master of the Households, who suggested to the King that Duveens redecorate them. The King agreed but asked Esher to convey his wishes to Duveens. When the time came for the Coronation, Duveens were asked to 'smarten up the Abbey', which they did with a prodigious display of oriental carpets, French and Flemish tapestries, and a pair of specially made thrones which are still used to this day.

The fraternal reconciliation did not last long. Joel by now had eight sons and four daughters and was planning a dynasty that worried Henry, who naturally saw himself in an ever-diminishing role. He had already had Joel's two eldest sons, Joseph and Charles, for brief visits, to learn how the American end of the operation worked. He regarded Joseph as too hasty and brash and Charles as an idle spendthrift, and believed that both his nephews had been sent to New York to see how he could be squeezed out of the firm. This view was reinforced when Joel announced that he had arranged for his eldest daughter, Esther, to marry Jules, the only son of Marcel Lowengard, who had been such a help to them in the beginning.

In the past, by siding with Lowengard, Henry had managed to curb Joel's buying excesses in France, but the marriage would mean that Joel and his children would dominate the buying operations of the firm, which still relied on France to supply almost 90 per cent of their stock. Henry accepted an invitation to the wedding, which was to take place at the Savoy Hotel, London, on 9 March 1891; at the same time he wrote to his solicitor, Mr Charles Mylne Barker of Bedford Row, asking for an appointment for 12 March as he wished him 'to devise a way to extricate myself from the clutches of my relations who have come to dominate *my business*'.

The formation of the various companies into a proper corporate structure had briefly stabilized the relationship between the Duveen brothers. Their finances now on a firmer footing, they moved their New York premises further up Fifth Avenue to Number 302, premises found for them by the department store magnate Benjamin Altman. Altman had become a customer of Henry's in 1888 when he had stopped by one evening and bought a pair of enamelled oriental jugs for $35, thus starting the world-famous Altman Collection, now in the Metropolitan Museum, which was largely formed by Henry Duveen.

Again the brothers staged a major exhibition for the opening of the new premises, and by coincidence it was Collis Huntington who, once more, purchased their star attraction: a splendid set of tapestry covers by François Boucher, his *scènes d'enfants* series. The set, which was adapted to fit ten chairs, two sofas, two fire-screens and two bergeres, cost Collis $150,000, plus the cost of making a set of chair and sofa frames to suit them.*

---

* The work was carried out in Paris by Carlhian and Beaumetz, but before they could be shipped to New York, Huntington changed his mind and they remained in Paris. Eventually they were sold to Messrs Seligman. In 1909, Arabella, Collis Huntington's widow, saw them at Seligman's and, unaware of their history, bought them. Today they are in the Huntington Art Collection at Pasadena, inventory number 154–166.

Henry was right in believing that his brother had dynastic ideas, for Joel insisted that all his sons enter the business as soon as possible. Joseph, the eldest, was allowed to stay at Brighton College until he was seventeen, but the others started work at fourteen. For the first year they worked out of sight of the customers as cleaners, porters, packers and stock-room assistants. Those who wrote a legible copperplate hand worked as ledger clerks, letter writers and copyists: new-fangled typewriters and carbon papers had no place in a business committed to personal attention.

After a year below stairs they spent a further year as either doorboys or receptionists, opening the doors of the customers' carriages and learning how the showrooms operated. Here they were under the watchful eye of their mother, Rosetta, who kept the books and sat behind what can only be described as a banker's counter and grille at the back of the showroom.

Only Joel and Joseph were allowed to quote prices or discuss the merits of an item with a customer. If they were busy then the sons' task was to engage the client in polite and deliberately evasive conversation until their father or eldest brother was free. Nothing was priced but everything carried a number, and the key to the numbers was a series of folders, bound on morocco leather, which Rosetta kept. These gave the original cost plus whatever proportion of overheads or repair work had been assigned to each item. They also noted to whom it had been shown and what price had been quoted at the time.

It was the job of the younger sons to determine the identity and interests of the client, collect the appropriate folder, and introduce him to Joel or Joseph. They would then stand respectfully in the background ready to operate Joel's artfully designed lighting switchboard.

Joel believed in spotlights and each item of merit was discreetly illuminated. With the exception of the lobby and the window facing the street, a display was only lit when being shown to a customer. It was a younger son's task to follow Joel's or Joseph's progress round the showrooms, throwing the switches on cue. The only exceptions were the tapestries and the finest blue and white porcelain, which were displayed in a large studio room at the rear of the building which had a fine north light. Electric light kills the subtleties of the blue glazes, making the finest look almost black, while it turns the delicate dyes of tapestry wools, particularly the soft rose pinks, into garish reds.

Joel and Joseph wore deep blue lounge suits, with silk shirts, starched cuffs, four-inch-high double collars and patent leather shoes. The younger sons wore frock coats and top hats, while the rest of the staff were dressed in grey alpaca jackets and bowler hats. There was one other way of recognizing a member of the family: only they were permitted to wear a fob watch and chain.

Discipline was strict as Joel was a stickler for appearances and operated a firm timetable. The day began at 8 A.M. when the goods were cleaned and polished, the windows washed, and fresh sand laid and raked on the cobbles outside the door, where the horses and carriages would stand. At 8.45 Joel would arrive in his carriage and pair and inspect premises and staff like an old-fashioned sergeant-major. When he found fault he operated a system of fines which were levied regardless of whether the offender was a member of the family or not. This was to the disadvantage of the sons as they were only allowed pocket money until they were twenty-one, when Joel transferred a small percentage of his shareholding in the London company to them.

In October 1890, on the occasion of Joseph's twenty-first birthday, Joel insisted that 10 per cent of the unissued shares of the New York company be allocated to his eldest son. Henry agreed reluctantly to this on condition that a further 10 per cent be held in trust for his only son, Geoffrey, who was but four years old. However, Joel so arranged it that young Geoffrey's trustees had no vote in the running of the New York company, thus effectively securing Joel voting control of the American operation.

It was the suspicion that his brother would eventually oust him that led to Henry's appointment with his solicitor, Charles Mylne Barker, immediately after his niece's wedding. Mylne Barker advised against precipitate action. To unscramble the various companies would involve a voluntary winding up and liquidation and precise values would have to be agreed on the stocks. The accounts of any liquidation would be available to their trade creditors who, in many cases, were rivals. Clients would have their debts to the firm revealed and, as their banking arrangements were somewhat special, he felt that to ask Lord Farquhar to testify might well lead to a lack of respect for, and confidence in, the firm. There could also be a possibly unhealthy interest from the revenue authorities in both London and New York.

Henry agreed to hold his hand, and the following week he was to be glad of his decision. While he had been meeting his lawyers, Joel had hastened to Manchester, despite having a bad cold, for discussions with a major client, Mr W. H. Lever, later Lord Leverhulme, whose houses he furnished and whose collections he formed. He had then travelled on to Brussels by boat where he had gone down with a near fatal bout of double pneumonia.

Although he eventually recovered he was left a shadow of his former self. His doctors ordered a strict regime which involved leaving England every year before the autumn set in. In mid-October he would leave for Biarritz or the French Riviera; there then followed a leisurely progress from Rome to Naples and Palermo, thence to Cairo and Aswan where he would spend January and February. As spring came to Europe he would retrace his route, spending Easter in Monte Carlo, take a quick early summer cure at Bad Vittel, and be home in England in time for the Derby and Ascot week.

Joel started his first tour shortly after Joseph's twenty-second birthday. It was a reluctant departure for, although he retained a controlling interest in the London business and wrote almost daily with advice and querulous demands for details as to what his brother and thrusting eldest son were up to, he was absent for nearly eight months so there were long periods when Joseph was in sole control of Duveens' London operation.

Joseph revelled in the role, and his first action was to insist that his staff call him Mr Joseph. Hitherto it had been Mr Joel and Master Joseph. His second was to make it plain to his younger brothers, Charles and John, now aged twenty-one and twenty respectively, that there was no place for them in the Oxford Street gallery. He increased their allowances and told them they would be better off on the road, visiting country dealers and auction rooms, but he forbade them to purchase anything without consulting him by telegraph first. In fact, he didn't really care what they got up to as long as they stayed off the premises. From the beginning he was determined to be the only 'Duveen', at least in London and during his father's absence abroad.

Joseph was a thickset young man with a luxuriant black moustache, a weakness for wearing overcoats in all but the hottest weather, and a decided taste for the good life. He began to have his cigars made for him personally, took a regular private room for his lunches at nearby Claridge's, then a genteel chophouse with a few letting rooms for travelling businessmen, and persuaded the reluctant management of that establishment to stock such delicacies as the gulls', plovers' and quails' eggs of which he was inordinately fond. He spent every third weekend in Paris, liaising with Anatole Beaumetz at Carlhians and checking the inventory of the Paris branch, which was then on the rue de Rivoli.

Supervising Uncle Henry's American furnishing contracts kept him and his brothers busy. Joseph would receive such lordly cables as 'Send set 12 gilt salon chairs preferably 18th century fastest steamer', and would then initiate a frenzied hunt through the galleries and auction rooms. He alone dealt with Paris and the leading London dealers while Charles and John scoured the provinces.

It was during these high-speed forays that Joseph came to meet the most go-ahead of the Paris picture dealers, Nathan Wildenstein, who was then thirty-seven. Originally from Alsace, Wildenstein had started in Paris in a small way on the Left Bank. In 1890 he had taken the plunge and opened a gallery, rather than a shop, on the fashionable Faubourg St. Honoré, where he specialised in paintings of the finest quality.

He also had an encyclopaedic knowledge of the antique milieu, and this he cheerfully shared with the ebullient Joseph, believing—falsely as it turned out—that Duveens had no interest in pictures except as items for decoration. At first they worked well together. Nathan had an exclusive clientele who frequently paid for their paintings with furniture or other *objets d'art*. Styles were changing and the Parisians, ever sensitive to fashion, were happy to sell their gilt-encrusted furniture for the handsome prices Nathan offered on Joseph's behalf.

Joseph in his turn was fascinated by Nathan's picture dealing expertise and was anxious to copy him. Uncle Henry disagreed. 'Pictures', he said, 'are the last thing a man buys'. Henry and Joel were united in their opposition to young Joseph entering the picture market, but in 1894 he saw his chance.

That year, Joel decided to buy the old Robinson and Fisher auction rooms in Bond Street, to transfer most of the Oxford Street stock there, and to fill the place with his favourite wares: the porcelain, silver and bronzes so dear to his heart, and all the dozens of smaller items which he had purchased on his winter travels— Persian tiles, oriental rugs, Egyptian terra-cottas, Italian majolica, French faience and Eastern ivories. Any remaining space was filled with oriental vases, converted into table lamps, for he was still enchanted by electricity. Behind Joel's back, Henry and Joseph referred to all this clutter as 'The Bazaar'.

This left the Oxford Street premises nearly empty though the lease still had two years to run, so Joseph asked if he could show a few pictures there; reluctantly, the brothers agreed. Joseph obtained a consignment from Nathan Wildenstein and René Gimpel of Paris but the pictures were neither important nor expensive. He had little success but early in 1895 he thought he saw an opportunity to establish himself as a major force in the picture market.

A few minutes' stroll from Joseph's Oxford Street premises was the New Gallery, a fashionable venue renowned for its important exhibitions. That spring the New Gallery decided to ask leading collectors and stately home owners to loan them their best works of Venetian art, and the organizers asked Joseph if he would help them approach the owners of likely paintings. This he did with considerable energy, and at the time of the private view he held his own reception in his premises for those clients whom he had persuaded to lend pictures and for those who wished to visit the New Gallery.

The exhibition, which opened on 2 February 1895, was a great social occasion. From every castle, landed seat and great house came works of art attributed by tradition and their owners to painters of the calibre of Giorgione and Titian. Most had been bought a century or two before by forebears on their 'Grand Tour' of Europe and had hung in their respective ancestral homes ever since. Others, loaned by the newly rich, had been purchased from leading London dealers over the previous thirty years. The pictures were catalogued by the labels they bore, and the cataloguers wisely inserted a qualification that neither they nor the New Gallery were responsible for the attributions.

Two days after the exhibition opened a second catalogue appeared which caused fury and dismay amongst the owners of the pictures concerned and exploded the beliefs of the self-styled *cognoscenti* of the London art world. The author of this bombshell—for such it was—was a young American student called Bernhard Berenson.

PART TWO

Berenson

3

The Scholar Gipsy

Bernhard was born on 26 June 1865 in Butrymanz, a small Jewish ghetto some twelve miles from Vilno, the capital of Lithuania, in the northern section of the Pale of Settlement. This was a slice of Europe running from the Baltic to the Black Sea which the Russian Empress Catherine the Great had designated as the only area in her empire in which Jews could live and work. They were, however, forbidden to own land, to travel outside the Pale, to enter most of the professions, or to attend Christian universities. At the age of twelve they were liable to conscription into the Russian army, where they were expected to serve for fifteen years. Only eldest sons, theological students and sole supporters of a family were exempt, but even these exemptions were ignored if the community failed to provide its regular annual quota of conscripts. In 1863 the Poles had rebelled against the Tsar and, as a handful of Jews had supported the rebellion, further humiliating measures were taken against the entire Jewish community.

Bernhard's father, Albert Valvrojenski, was a victim of these measures. He came from a town called Troki and his first inclination had been to become a rabbi. His family had encouraged him and in 1861, at the age of fifteen, he was accepted as a student at a seminary in Vilno. Two years later, his college was closed down as a result of the Polish uprising and the students were ordered to return to their home districts. Butrymanz was within the Troki administrative area and, as it was the closest village to Vilno, he settled there, shortly afterwards marrying seventeen-year-old Julie Mieliszanski, who was a year younger than himself. The following year, Bernhard was born.

Butrymanz had a population of around two thousand, most of

whom earned an exiguous living from the nearby forests. It was a life of unending hard work, leavened only by a profound and deeply introspective devotion to the study of Judaism. Albert was warmly welcomed in Butrymanz as it was well-known in the area that his family was both cultured and devout. He had completed part of his rabbinical training and spoke French and Russian as well as High German and Yiddish, which was the day-to-day language. He was a Hebrew scholar and had read such forbidden authors as Voltaire, Dickens and Darwin. He soon found work as a forestry contractor, tendering for the timber as it stood, and spending each autumn and winter in the forest with a logging gang of Polish Christian peasants, remaining there with them until the spring thaw came and floated the logs down to Riga.

It was a stern life, with few compensations. Bernhard would see much of his father during the summer, perhaps visiting the woods to assess and bid for the forthcoming season's timber, but during the long winter months when the men were away, the village became a semi-matriarchy. The influence of the womenfolk was diluted only by the presence of men too old to work, the village rabbi and the schoolmaster—though the prestige of these latter was immense. The author Smolenskin has left a graphic cameo of the Lithuanian Jews of that time:

> The land is steeped in poverty and the Jews who dwell there are paupers . . . White bread and meat grace their tables on Sabbath only. But take heed of those papers, for the *Torah* goes forth from them. The Lithuanian Jews have the greatest regard for Study. There is not a town whose house of learning is not crammed with scholars young and old, nor is there a man, no matter how poor, who will not contribute to their maintenance, sharing his crust with them and hurrying to their aid. For they are all scrupulously pious, cherishing the traditions of their fathers and clinging to their old customs with unyielding tenacity.

In an intellectual atmosphere which was devoid of any form of visual stimulation, sculpture, paintings or even illuminated manuscripts, excessive value was placed on the written word: books were read and re-read, discussed and argued over, until a state of great academic sterility was reached. Chaim Weizmann, the first president of Israel who also came from the Lithuanian Pale, recalled that in his youth, Thackeray's *Vanity Fair* was distributed page by page, and that a fresh chapter took upwards of three months to circulate within the community. The arrival of the travelling bookseller, with another installment, was an eagerly awaited event. By this time everyone knew their *Vanity Fair* by heart and had exhausted themselves discussing the style in which it was written, the characterisation, the motivation of the participants, and possible developments of the plot.

The practise of learning by rote dominated the village school or *Chede* in which Bernhard was enrolled on his fifth birthday. First he had to master the Hebrew alphabet and then learn by heart substantial sections of the scriptures. After several years he was expected to be able to recite a set passage in public. Bernhard was chosen to make his recitation shortly before his seventh birthday, a remarkable achievement, doubtless due to the encouragement and stimulation he received from his father. That Passover he announced to his parents that he had grown up and expected to be treated as such.

When his father next left for the forest, Bernhard took his place at the head of the table and supervised the family's religious rituals. He soon became the favourite of the rabbi and the village elders, who encouraged his precocity. At home his mother let him read the foreign books which arrived for his father for she felt that every effort must be made to give this, her eldest and favourite child, all the opportunities for educational advancement that had been denied to his father. She hoped that Bernhard would eventually escape from the political and cultural straitjacket that life in the Pale of Settlement entailed.

She thrashed him for following the military band when the soldiers came to enforce conscription. She knew all too well that neighbours were quite capable of kidnapping someone else's child and sending it into the army in place of their own. There were well-documented cases of children as young as ten disappearing in this way, and she had no desire to lose Bernhard.

Despite his precocity, he was not a prig. He was a cheerful, happy little boy who relished all those escapades that small boys of all ages and nationalities enjoy. He climbed trees, went for picnics in the woods, swam in the local lake, and larked about with the other village children.

On one of these personal forays into the countryside, he underwent an experience that was to mould his life. It must be remembered that he was unaware of the visual arts, that he had no knowledge of botany or contemporary science, that so far his progress had been through his ability to absorb much of what he had read and heard. To date, his sensibilities were slightly finer than those of a well-trained parrot. Now he became aware of physical beauty and relished the effect that it had upon him.

Much later in life, Berenson recalled that his years as a young boy were the happiest of his life. The beauty of the world revealed itself to the five-year-old ugly duckling as 'It-ness', and young Bernhard realised that he wanted to be an aesthetic swan. 'It'—the union with the 'It-ness' of life—became the goal in life, the source of his only real happiness. At his worst moments later in life, Berenson would find solace in 'It'.

From this early time on his sense of awareness, his ability to absorb a visual effect, be it a beautiful woman, a painting or a sunset, to sift and refine the physical pleasure and translate it into words, became his most precious and private aim. It was this boyhood fusion of the mental and physical disciplines dinned into him at the feet of the elders of Butrymanz with his own sudden discovery of natural beauty that lit the flame of scholarship which burned, despite the winds of prejudice, avarice and arrogance, for the remainder of his life.

There were many in Butrymanz who were now well aware that Albert Valvrojenski was not only more opinionated than most, but, as his son sagely remarked some thirty years later, his opinions were those of a nihilist. At the same time, the regulations regarding conscription were drastically tightened up. Henceforth there would be far fewer exceptions and far fewer vacancies in the government schools for promising children. Once again, the chance of a university education was to be denied to them. Albert decided to emigrate.

Every few months a travelling bookseller visited Butrymanz. He had a small sideline selling tickets to the United States. The fare was payable in two stages. A deposit of one third would take the emigrant as far as a British port. Once there, payment of the remaining two thirds bought a ticket to America. Those who could not afford the second installment stayed in England. In Albert Valvrojenski's case he raised the money to pay for two tickets direct to Boston.

The tickets, which for security's sake were bought under a pseudonym, were, according to Bernhard, in the names of Ber und sohn, the Yiddish diminutive for Albert and son, hence the new surname. Bernhard said that he was originally to have accompanied his father but his mother had vetoed the idea so an adult cousin of his father's took his place. This would seem a plausible explanation for the change of name were it not for the fact that the family already had two distant cousins in North Boston who had called themselves Berenson some five years previously. Perhaps their father had also been called Albert?

Whatever the original plan may have been, what actually occurred was that Albert and his cousin left home in the autumn of 1874. They travelled to Berlin, and from there to Bremen where they shipped steerage class for Boston. On arrival they were welcomed by their 'Berenson' cousins.

Albert, at twenty-eight, appears to have been as impressed with America as Henry Duveen was to be three years later. Perhaps the place gave him a heady sense of freedom from persecution. It cannot have been for commercial reasons for he could find no skilled employment. Swallowing his pride he was reduced to buying and selling old pots and pans for a local tinsmith. Each dawn he would set off for the villages surrounding Boston, pushing his barrow. But he must have been good at his job, for he lost no time in buying tickets for his wife and three children, who joined him in June 1875.

The family's first home, at 32 Nashua Street, was a tiny cottage backing on to the railway shunting yards. Here, amidst the clatter from the trucks and the smuts from the locomotives, the Berensons tried to find their feet. Bernhard went to the local free school. His mother took in washing and then opened their front room as a lunch place for railway workers. Two more daughters were born, Elisabeth in 1878 and Rachel two years later. For a brief period Albert abandoned his peddler's cart and opened a dry goods store around the corner at 11 Minot Street. In 1880 the project ended in financial disaster and the family gave up the lease of the Nashua Street house and moved in above the shop. Albert reapplied for his peddler's license while his wife turned the former shop into a slightly larger lunch room and, abandoning the laundry business, took in sewing instead.

Boston's archives detail the moves from house to house, and the application for, and reissue of, the peddler's license, but in later life Bernhard would never refer to those early days. Other members of the family who made somewhat greater headway than poor Albert recall what are probably apocryphal stories of a proud father avoiding embarrassing encounters with his children when they met him wheeling his cart around the city. The fact was that the academically minded Albert was totally unable to come to terms with nineteenth-century industrialised America. But this was no cause for shame, and it is most unlikely that Bernhard felt any. He developed a remarkable insight into his father's commercial limitations, then swept the matter from his mind until he could do something positive about it. It is to his credit that his first act when he became financially independent was to purchase his parents a decent suburban home and settle sufficient money upon them to enable them to live out their lives in comfort.

The move to Minot Street occurred when Bernhard was fifteen. He had set his heart on entering Boston Latin School, from which, provided he could master the classics, he could qualify for a university education. His progress at school had been satisfactory. He had easily mastered English and, since the little house was grotesquely overcrowded, had adopted Boston Public Library as his second home.

The library was undoubtedly his salvation and the reading lists he set himself were remarkable. His mother, impressed by her bookish son, scraped up the fees to send him to the Latin School for eight months. From there he went through a crammer's course at a small private institution (called the Myers Richardson School) and, at the age of seventeen, he qualified for a free place at Boston University.

At this time he was a startlingly attractive youth, a fact of which he was well aware. He still wore his hair in ritual locks but brushed and curled it so that he looked almost Byronic. He dressed fastidiously and was known as a grave-voiced, sensitive young man who never pushed his opinions and yet was pleasant company, often to be found amongst the numerous undergraduates who spent their leisure hours browsing in the Old Corner Bookstore. He also possessed what some contemporaries described as a 'mysterious quality', as though he had a personal secret which he would never share with anyone else. He had exactly that. He still retained his personal goal of a sense of 'It-ness'. He still believed that life was to be lived as a sacrament in search of this personal goal, and the hours in the Boston library had shown him various routes by which his goal might be achieved.

'It-ness', as it affected him so far, was a state when his physical antennae were alerted or stretched to their finest pitch. It was a purely physical reaction to a given set of circumstances or stimuli. The first such stimulus had been a delight in colour, sunlight and the pure lime-scented air of the Lithuanian plain. He had often repeated the sensations to himself in walks in the countryside outside Boston, but adolescence and the hours in the library had introduced him to more cerebral delights.

He recalled almost the precise moment of his discovery. He had been reading deeply about astronomy, had even drafted a speculative essay on the mysteries of interstellar space, borrowing heavily from the works of Edward Young, the English eighteenth-century divine who exercised an undeserved influence at the time. Young tended to overwrite, drowning his originality in purple rhetoric. Nevertheless, he was heady and impressive stuff for a teenager.

Young's basic message, when stripped of platitudes, was one of despair. He foretold an ultimate apocalypse, based on the relentless logic of higher mathematics, riding roughshod over the mysteries and subtleties of both divine creation and human creativity. In short, his message was the nineteenth-century literary equivalent of the nuclear threat. Bernhard had been reading perhaps the most suicidal of Young's works, his *Night Thoughts*, and then, deeply depressed, had continued with his self-imposed programme by reading George Eliot's critical essay on Young.

In one dose, George Eliot convinced Bernhard that the values of art were as important as those of life and morality. Eliot explained that Young's wasteful and pointless blank verse concealed what he was trying to say. His art, she argued, translating the Latin tag, conceals his art. The real art of life is the art of doing things well.

This tag, *'ars celare artem'*, immediately became Bernhard's motto, and thereafter his book lists reflected his planned campaign: Cowper's *Discipline and Art*, Carlyle, Ruskin, New England's own recent heritage of Thoreau, Longfellow, Emerson and Nathaniel

Hawthorne. The monthly magazines contained the latest from Greenleaf Whittier and Walt Whitman, while Boston's resident sages, James Russell Lowell, Oliver Wendell Holmes and Charles Elliot Norton were available to anyone who cared to attend the public meetings of the debating societies and the free lectures which they gave at regular intervals. Of these three men it was Norton to whom Bernhard gave his most respectful attention.

Charles Elliot Norton was almost sixty when Bernhard first heard him lecture. He had had a strange career for an academic. Having trained as a clergyman, he then spent some years as a merchant in the Far East, and subsequently lived in India, Italy, Egypt and France. From each he absorbed those facets of their culture that appealed to him and bought all that his ample private income could afford. In Rome, for example, he discovered Dante and spent two years making himself an internationally recognised authority on the poet and, more significantly, a collector of his manuscripts and the bibliography relating to them. Norton numbered among his friends Ruskin, Carlyle, Burne-Jones, Matthew Arnold, Whistler, Sargent and a host of writers and critics.

In 1873, Norton's uncle and namesake Charles Elliot, who was president of Harvard, appointed Norton to the chair of the History of Fine Art, a post he held for a quarter of a century. On years of even date Norton delivered a weekly public lecture on Dante; on years of uneven date he spoke on the Italian medieval Church: never once did he mention painting or the Italian Renaissance.

When Bernhard heard Charles Elliot Norton lecture, he was in his freshman year at Boston University, supporting himself by coaching backward members of his own class and a few freshmen from Harvard. Two young Harvard men who benefited from this coaching were Charles Loeser and George Santayana. These two, together with the worldly charm of Charles Elliot Norton, fired Bernhard with the ambition to enter Harvard.

❧ 4 ❧

The Young Man from the East

Charles Loeser had introduced Bernhard to the recently graduated Edward (Ned) Warren, who now offered to give Berenson a character reference for Harvard. The son of a prosperous and well-respected paper mill owner who had been a major benefactor of the university, Ned was fascinated by his new acquaintance as they argued long and hard about classical mythology and antiquities.

Ned had secured himself a postgraduate place at Oxford from where he was planning to explore the classical archaeological sites of Italy and Greece. He imbued Bernhard with his own enthusiasm, urged him to follow an identical career, and did what he could to help him. Ned personally sponsored Bernhard for Harvard but did not pay his fees, although he was to come to his financial rescue on many occasions in the future.

Exactly who did pay for Bernhard to go to Harvard in 1884 is not clear, but it was very probably Mr and Mrs Jack Gardner, a prominent Boston couple, who were known to finance students whom Charles Elliot Norton thought particularly promising. The Gardners could not, however, have met Berenson at the time, for they were abroad throughout the academic terms of 1883 and did not return until the summer of 1884 when Bernhard's admission had already been agreed and the Harvard authorities had satisfied themselves that he was both a suitable candidate and able to cover the fees.

Isabella Gardner's father was a prosperous New Yorker called David Stewart, her mother the daughter of the landlady of the Old Ferry tavern and stables. In 1855, when she was sixteen, Isabella's parents decided to send her to school in Paris, taking an apartment there themselves while she finished her education. There were two

other American girls at the school, the sisters Julia and Eliza
Gardner of Boston, whose parents came over to join them during
the long summer vacation of 1856. The Gardner and Stewart
families spent that summer travelling together through France and
Italy, and the friendship did not stop when both families returned
to America. The Gardners stayed with the Stewarts in New York
and Isabella was a frequent guest both at the Gardners' house in
Boston and at their country estates at Brookline and Roque Island
off the coast of Maine.

In 1859 Isabella became engaged to the Gardner's son, Jack,
who was three years older than she was; she married him a year
later on 10 April, four days before her twentieth birthday. It was
undoubtedly a love match, but Jack Gardner came from one of
Boston's best and richest families and his capture by a pert, out-
spoken New Yorker, who had a worldliness of which Boston's
heavily chaperoned younger set jealously disapproved, was deeply
resented. She rapidly acquired a reputation for being 'fast', while
there were unkind remarks aplenty when the matrons of Boston
discovered that her grandmother had been a tavern keeper.

Isabella delighted in being conspicuous. She attended every social gathering wearing the latest Worth creation, with the dia-
monds and pearls her husband lavished on her adorning her auburn
hair. Her husband, though inordinately proud of his wife, was
rarely with her. He worked all day, dined at his club, and often
returned home only on the weekend.

Home was usually an open house, which Isabella filled with the
people she had met on her European travels. Henry James was an
early acquaintance, as were Whistler and F. Marion Crawford,
who dedicated his first novel to her.

Isabella Gardner's reputation was that of an ostentatious and
despotic millionairess, indescribably selfish and seemingly revelling
in the publicity she attracted. The gossip columnists could always
rely upon her for some new excess, and when her father died
leaving her $2 million she became a national celebrity. She was
rumoured to receive her guests perched in the branches of a ceiling-
high mimosa tree installed in her conservatory, while one mid-
western tourist to Boston confessed that the object of her visit east
was 'to see the Atlantic Ocean and Mrs Gardner'.

There was, however, a more serious side to her character. Her only son had died in infancy and a later miscarriage denied her the chance of further children. In 1875 a further tragedy struck the family. Its aftermath probably had a direct bearing on her sponsoring Bernhard and several other young men. Her husband's elder brother died suddenly, aged only forty-six. His wife had died some years previously in childbirth and he left three orphan boys, aged thirteen, eleven, and nine. Isabella promptly adopted them.

Characteristically, she entered wholeheartedly into their education. She planned their curriculum, took them abroad, introduced them to her own idea of what she thought was the discipline and code of honour existing at the great English public schools, and groomed them for Harvard. In many ways she went back to school herself. She spoke some Italian but had no Latin, so now she and her nephews mastered their ablative absolutes together. When Joe, the eldest, entered Harvard, Isabella was with him in spirit. She watched every football game and kept open house for his friends. It was through Joe that she first met Harvard's Professor of Fine Art, Charles Elliot Norton.

Isabella and Charles had much in common. They had both travelled widely and had separately enjoyed many similarly exotic experiences, including breakfast at Angkor Wat. Both had climbed the Pyramids, picnicked at Delphi and been received by the Pope. Both had walked along the Great Wall of China, explored the splendour of the great church of Santa Sofia in Constantinople. Both had been laughed at by their Boston neighbours, largely because they had been born rather larger than life. Isabella admired and respected Norton because he gave her a sense of justification for what she, in her heart, considered a rather wasteful lifestyle. Perhaps more importantly, Norton, who had trained as a clergyman before entering commerce, recognized the sense of emptiness that she still felt over the loss of her only child and, seeing beyond that loss, identified the loneliness and guilt she felt over her inability to have other children.

Charles Norton rapidly gained a curious ascendancy over Isabella. He toned down some of her more wilful extravagances, encouraged her to bring music and art into her life, as opposed to merely musicians and artists, and slowly brought her to realise that there are more important things to collect than Worth gowns or Cartier jewellery. Patiently he explained that there was no merit in collecting unless there was comprehension, that paintings and manuscripts merited more understanding than people and press cuttings. Isabella was a willing pupil and to her joy she found that her husband was becoming equally interested in pictures and furniture and, with his interest aroused, encouraged Norton's visits.

Norton's main accomplishment was to persuade the Gardners to help pay the fees of students whom he thought particularly promising and who were anxious to attend Harvard. They also gave generously towards travelling fellowships for graduates, but in both cases Jack Gardner insisted that there was never to be any publicity. He would sign a cheque which Isabella would give to Norton. They wished for no accounting, no acknowledgement and no embarrassment.

Charles Norton's particular protégés in 1884 were George Santayana, Charles Loeser, Bernhard Berenson and Logan Pearsall Smith, all of whom were to be closely linked for the next decade and whose influence upon each other was to mark them, for better or for worse, for the remainder of their lives. Bernhard was eventually to marry Logan's sister Mary, although they are said not to have spoken to each other while he was at Harvard.

Logan, Mary and Alys were the children of Robert and Hannah Pearsall Smith, ardent Quakers who took themselves very seriously indeed. They had been engulfed by the religious revivalism which had swept America in the early 1870s and had decided to take this new gospel to England. Both were preachers and tract writers: Hannah's pamphlet, 'The Christian Secret of a Happy Life', sold well over a million copies, while Robert became a leading figure in an obscure religious movement called the Harrisites. Hannah was heir to her family's glass business so they lived in considerable style in England while awaiting the day of judgement, which they expected to come at any moment. It came rather too soon for Robert, who was disgraced when the London newspapers exposed a misunderstanding between him and one of his young lady acolytes over his habit of greeting his flock with a holy kiss. Romans XVI: 16 meant little to Fleet Street. Logan, in his second year when Bernhard arrived at Harvard, owed much of his popularity to the fact that his sister, Mary, had abandoned Smith College and together with her friend Gertrude Hitz had established herself in a house on the Harvard campus. They attended lectures as and when the professors allowed them to and called themselves 'The Harvard Annex'. The annex grew and today is Radcliffe College, Harvard's answer to Girton.

Mary was beautiful in a statuesque manner; she had hosts of admirers and was filled with boundless sensuality, becoming deeply emotionally attached to both Gertrude Hitz and the aging, bisexual Walt Whitman. When Edmund Gosse came to stay with her family, he mentioned 'the sacred world of Botticelli', and, as she was later to write, she turned to her brother Logan and explained they were in the middle of something very exciting. Immediately brother and sister plastered their rooms with reproductions of Botticelli. Soon after this, Mary suddenly confused everyone by announcing her engagement to an obscure Irish barrister called Frank Costelloe who happened to be staying with her family on a brief visit to America. When she met Bernhard three years later, she was married to Frank, with two children.

Logan was a proselytising homosexual but fortunately was both open about his interests and able to take no for an answer. He was deeply attached to young Charles Loeser, who regarded Logan as an amusing companion but no more, his own interests being firmly centered on Bernhard Berenson. Bernhard was very happy to coach Loeser but did not reciprocate his affection, astutely managing to avoid becoming emotionally entangled.

In his final year Bernhard became increasingly concerned about his future. His friends, who had no need to earn a living, proposed to spend a few years travelling Europe, while he, at the best, could look forward to little more than a position in government service or perhaps as a librarian. There was one avenue of escape, or at least a means of delaying the choice. Each year the university awarded the Parker Travelling Fellowship, which enabled the holder to globetrot for a year with ample pocket money. Traditionally it was awarded to the applicant with the highest academic averages, provided he had the unanimous support of his professors and tutors. Bernhard qualified on both counts and he applied for it with justifiable confidence.

Bernhard wrote in his application that he hoped to go to Paris in July to study its architecture, art galleries, and great churches. He planned next to visit Berlin to study art and Arabic, then to Italy for the remainder of his journey to study art and Italian literature. Berenson wrote that he felt weakest in art, that he could not really study it in America, and that he planned to devote a great deal of time to solving aesthetic problems. This was hardly an application likely to endear him to Norton, who was responsible for Italian literature and art. He refused to endorse it, and since it did not command the unanimity demanded, Bernhard was not awarded the fellowship.

Norton's action irritated his fellow academics and deeply wounded Bernhard. Many years later, when she had become his wife, Mary Pearsall Smith began a biography of Bernhard; it was never completed but it does throw some light on why Norton denied him the award.

Evidently, during Bernhard's first year at Harvard, Norton had come upon him reading *Studies in the History of the Renaissance* by Walter Pater and Bernhard had lent it to Norton to read. A few days later Norton had returned it with the words: 'My dear boy, it won't do, I don't like it. It's a book you can only read in your bathroom'.

Walter Pater was a shy, scholarly critic, precariously clinging to his fellowship at Brasenose College, Oxford, despite the virulent opposition of that muscular Christian Dr Jowett, Master of Balliol, cultural dictator of Oxford. Jowett's condemnation alone would have been enough for Norton, but Pater had a grossly undeserved reputation as an unhealthy and self-indulgent aesthete whose views were thought to constitute a threat to the then fashionable 'dictats' of art history and art criticism. His book had been 'instantly assailed', wrote Richard Aldington in 1948, 'with that hostility which greets all who run counter to accepted prejudices, particularly those few, who in an English-speaking country, are bold enough to claim an importance for the arts and the intellectual life above mere pastime and idling'.

One of Pater's pupils at Oxford was Oscar Wilde, who totally misunderstood Pater's teachings and philosophy and compounded his ignorance by starting a cult of 'aestheticism' as he misunderstood it. In the hands of Wilde and his cronies, Pater's trained and disciplined perception became a license for self-indulgence and promiscuity which eventually landed Wilde in Reading Jail and effectively consigned Pater and his works to a literary limbo.

Pater's *Studies in the History of the Renaissance* had been published in 1873, so the first waves of criticism had missed Bernhard.

He had found the book by accident in a local bookshop and had relished it for its simple and refreshing approach to the subject. He had lent it in all innocence to Norton, not realizing that to take Pater on to the Harvard campus of the 1880s, when it was still at heart a provincial college for future clergymen, was as great a sin as a novice in a nunnery lending the *Decameron* to her abbess.

Norton now viewed Bernhard with suspicion on two counts: first, as a dangerous potential rival, and second as a possible homosexual. Norton had gained eminence in Boston because his knowledge of European art and culture had been obtained at first hand; he was not therefore enthusiastic for his most brilliant pupil to gain more up-to-date experience than he himself had, but if this pupil were to return endorsing Pater's view of the history of art he would indeed pose problems. Norton saw the cosy nest his uncle had so kindly feathered for him about to be invaded by a vociferous cuckoo.

The second reason for Norton's blackball was more sinister and most probably unfair. Norton suspected Bernhard of being a homosexual, not from any evidence that would stand up to the most elementary investigation, but from a train of circumstances to which the introduction of Pater had been like a match to a haystack. It stemmed from Bernhard's friendship with Charles Loeser and his, at this time, casual acquaintance with Loeser's friend and admirer, Logan Pearsall Smith.

Logan could afford to be open about his sexual proclivities. His family's wealth and his two attractive sisters, who were the admiration of the campus, guaranteed him almost total immunity. His special friend, Charles Loeser, was wealthy in his own right, and there is no doubt that the combination of wealth, intellect and shared interests made the coterie headed by Logan a formidable one.

It will be recalled that Isabella Stewart Gardner had the care of her three orphan nephews, young men whom she tried to bring up in the image of what she imagined was the classic mould of the English gentleman. Their friends were welcome to her house, and when these friends included such protégés as Bernhard and such wits as Logan, she was delighted. Their inclusion particularly delighted the eldest boy, Joe, who was three years older than Bernhard, to whom he was introduced by Logan.

Joe had been causing the Gardners some concern. He had bought himself a remote homestead at Hamilton to the north of Boston. Isabella had speedily put it about that he had done so in order to provide a home for a girl whom he hoped to marry, but that he had been crossed in love.

Logan Pearsall Smith had another version. He said that Joe Gardner had bought himself the Hamilton homestead as a refuge from the censorious eyes of Boston and his aunt's constant urgings to find a 'suitable girl and settle down'.

Logan and his sister Mary had been frequent visitors, but it was Mary who had been the chaperone, for the object of Joe's attentions was Logan himself and it was Logan who had broken Joe Gardner's heart.

Jack Gardner half suspected the truth and he quickly included Joe on his annual European tour. The traditional solution for a broken heart did not work. On 16 October 1886 Joe Gardner committed suicide at a small hotel in Dieppe, while his aunt and uncle were *en route* from Venice to Paris. They learnt of his death from a telegram which was waiting for them in Paris. It was sent from Boulogne and signed with Logan's initials, L. P. S.

The tragedy rocked the Gardners. There must have been recriminations to which Norton would have been privy. Logan had graduated and was not therefore his responsibility, but in Norton's eyes Loeser and Bernhard were suspect. There were still the two younger nephews to consider, and it became Norton's wish to separate Bernhard from the Gardner household. He wanted Bernhard out of Boston, but not at Harvard's expense, so he denied him the Parker Travelling Fellowship.

It was the injustice of Norton's veto that caused Bernhard's professors to rally round and subscribe a purse of $750 to enable him to travel to Europe. Isabella was a major contributor, so she presumably did not link Bernhard with Joe's suicide.

Before he left, Bernhard gave her a photograph of himself. It shows him with a collar-length set of auburn curls, a classically Grecian profile, and an expression of heart-warming innocence. The pose is as calculatedly sentimental as are the dress and the hairstyle. Both were modelled on an almost identical photograph of Oscar Wilde, whom Bernhard, in his ignorance and probably innocence, imagined to be the embodiment of all that his hero, Walter Pater, meant by an aesthete.

On 17 June 1887, Bernhard sailed from New York for Le Havre.

There were no conditions attached to the money, no thesis to write, just the implicit understanding that he would waste neither his time nor his talents. His last act was to send a brief note of thanks to his major benefactress.

On that first journey to Europe Bernhard travelled light; there were a few clothes, a letter of credit to Baring Brothers, Isabella's London bankers, and a sheaf of letters of introduction, mostly from Logan, to acquaintances who ranged from Oscar Wilde in London to minor officials at continental museums. There was also a handful of books, including, of course, Pater's *Renaissance* and the two volumes of his novel, *Marius the Epicurean*.

Marius is difficult reading because of Pater's discursive style but it was never meant to be swallowed whole, being originally published in sections for subscribers of Mudies' Library. Read slowly in small gobbets, it is easier to digest. The eponymous hero is a young Roman boy, living on the coast of Tuscany in the second century A.D. when the early Christians were trying to reconcile the ideas of Plato with those of the New Testament. Marius trains himself to absorb impressions and then, through rigid mental discipline, relies on his mental and physical sensations to form a judgement. His aim is to become a sounding board or tuning fork which will absorb the words and observe the artifacts of others, distill and evaluate them in one continuous process, and, he hopes, derive physical pleasure from the effect.

The use of the young Roman hero, whose philosophical and aesthetic development is the mainspring of the story, is purely a literary device to give continuity and pace to a series of lectures which are nothing more than Pater's aesthetic and personal credo in easy stages. His literary ability was considerable but his main gift was to understand and inspire the young. He certainly inspired Bernhard. From the moment he climbed aboard the steamer for Europe until he first began to earn an income as an art dealer, Bernhard was more than a disciple of Pater: in thought, word and deed he *was* Marius. It was one of the very few emotional or intellectual debts Bernhard could ever bring himself to acknowledge, for he realised that Pater had not only put into words the feeling of 'It-ness' that he had first experienced long ago on a Lithuanian summer morning, but had showed him how to recapture it.

Bernhard spent the summer and early autumn in Paris, finally settling in comfortable rooms overlooking the Luxembourg Gardens which, despite his rapidly dwindling funds, he furnished with care and taste. By the autumn he was down to his last $100 and wrote to his sister Senda, begging her to borrow money on his behalf. Twice she managed to raise $100, which helped him through November, while fellow Americans passing through Paris also obliged with modest loans. He used the money to see *Faust* at the Opéra, to buy tickets for Sarah Bernhardt, and to enable him to attend shows at the Odéon Theatre and the Comédie-Française. When he was not at the theatre he was looking at pictures, voraciously buying books and taking French lessons. He wrote frequently to Isabella Stewart Gardner, conceding that he was just trying to absorb everything he saw and read.

Despite the constant borrowing he was no scrounger. He was welcome everywhere for his wit, charm and rapidly developing knowledge of painting. He was a favourite with American tourists, anxious to be squired and guided through the Louvre, and willing to give him a luncheon for his time. He was deeply worried about his rapidly increasing debts, which he knew he could not begin to repay until his new-found knowledge and experience distilled into something worth publishing. He poured out freelance articles, posting them home to Senda to try and place with magazines. She sold a few of them but not nearly enough to cover his expenses. He was almost in despair when, shortly before Christmas, his friend and Harvard sponsor, Ned Warren, called to see him in Paris.

Ned had spent the summer exploring the archaeological sites of Greece and Crete. He was laden with photographs and souvenirs which he proposed to catalogue during a leisurely winter in his rooms at Oxford. He quickly saw Bernhard's problems and suggested that he pack his bags and join him at New College for the Lent term where Ned could promise Bernhard not only conversation, company, bed, and board but Walter Pater. Both the invitation and the temptation were irresistible. By the middle of January Bernhard was happily ensconced in Warren's richly furnished rooms at 31 Holywell.

Ned Warren introduced his guest to a way of life far removed from the puritan halls of Harvard. An eccentric, an aesthete and a gourmet, Ned was dedicated to the lifestyle of the previous century: he lived by candlelight, dined off gold plate, and wrote, when he had to, with a goose-quill pen. His wines and his snuff were famous.

His friends, who were equally colourful, accepted Bernhard with delight. He had trimmed off his curls, grown a grave little beard, and been to a respectable tailor. 'He was enigmatic, a bit misanthropic but utterly adorable', wrote the poet Lionel Johnson, newly up from Winchester with his bosom companion, Lord Alfred Douglas. Johnson, who permed his hair and wore silk stockings and face powder, was to die young when, stupefied by a mixture of morphine and claret, he fell off a stool and fractured his skull, thus extinguishing the literary promise with which he had dazzled his contemporaries.

Johnson introduced Bernhard to his friends, three of whom were to play important roles later in his life. Herbert Horne, then editing the *Hobby Horse*, was to share Bernhard's fascination with the Italian Renaissance and follow him to Florence, first as a business partner dealing in pictures and then as a friendly rival arguing with him over Botticelli. Charles Bell, later to become Keeper of the Ashmolean Museum, subsequently introduced Bernhard to his favorite student, Kenneth Clark (later Lord Clark), whom Bell described as 'a remarkably gifted and quite beautiful boy'. The third introduction was to Oscar Wilde. The unfortunate Johnson also introduced Lord Alfred to Wilde with tragic results, but Bernhard's friendly fascination, as opposed to friendship, with Wilde survived the saga of his trial and imprisonment. Bernhard shared Wilde's rooms on occasional visits to London, coolly resisting the older man's advances.

It is a mystery how Berenson managed his finances at this time. Senda continued to raise modest loans on his behalf and remonstrated with him for borrowing from his friends. Bernhard saw nothing wrong with that: he entertained no feelings of false pride.

However, it was probably shortage of funds during 1888 that made him decide to forsake what he later called 'The Brotherhood of Sodomites' and travel to Germany to renew his studies.

From Oxford he wrote despondently to Isabella, worrying that she and his other patrons would be disappointed in his progress. He was disconsolate with himself—though he was enjoying himself, he was not studying. He remembered too well his ambitions when he had left Boston, but was now rejecting what he felt were the affectations and shallowness of the academic world. Yet, though struggling to find something to believe in, he found himself adrift, felt himself changing every day, and did not know what to do with himself.

Isabella sensed the appeal behind the words and, without consulting his professors, sent him a further $750 for another year in which to find himself. Temporarily freed from financial worries he again began to enjoy himself. There were cousins of his mother to entertain him as well as friends from Harvard, including Santayana, Charles Loeser and George Rice Carpenter, who were all at Berlin University on Harvard travelling fellowships. They savoured the delights of opera, theatre and student beer halls together and cheerfully accompanied Bernhard on his now almost addictive rounds of the picture galleries.

On one of these visits he was introduced to Jean Paul Richter, a scholar, peripatetic purchaser and dealer, who did not buy for immediate results but to fill gaps in his collection. When, for example, he acquired a better example of a particular artist's work, he would then sell the lesser. Based in Florence, he was an active member of the art trade caravanserai, attending important exhibitions and sales throughout Europe. Richter had recently written a widely praised book entitled *A Catalogue of the Italian Paintings in the National Gallery* and was one of the numerous people to whom Bernhard had been given a letter of introduction by his Oxford acquaintance, Herbert Horne. Bernhard immediately congratulated Richter on his book.

Richter was flattered by such effusive praise from the young American and soon realized that Bernhard had a genuine interest in Italian painting. Casually, Richter suggested that Bernhard should visit the galleries of Dresden and Munich and study the Italian pictures there, taking with him a book by the Italian connoisseur, Giovanni Morelli, to whom, Richter said, he owed much of his own scholarship.

Morelli's book, *Italian Pictures: Critical Studies of the Works in the Galleries of Munich and Dresden*, changed Bernhard from an enthusiastic amateur into a serious student. It had been published almost a decade previously and had revolutionised European art scholarship with its many challenging re-attributions. When Bernhard read it, he quickly saw that Morelli offered a clear path through the minefield of misinformation that cluttered museum catalogues of the time. The arguments were incisive, exact and authoritative and—which must have appealed to Berenson's young and ever-questioning mind—Morelli had scant respect for such academic elder statesmen as Ruskin, Charles Elliot Norton or the virtual dictator of the museum world, Wilhelm von Bode, Director of the Kaiser Friedrich Museum in Berlin, whom Morelli delighted in describing as 'Der Kunstkorporal' ('The Corporal of Art').

Morelli had trained to be a doctor in Berlin, but gave up his studies to help the emergent Italian nation win its independence. Rich, with no need to earn a living, he soon settled down to study his greatest love, Italian painting. He researched and published for his own pleasure so had been considerably surprised when, in 1861, the newly formed Italian government appointed him to head a commission charged with making an inventory of all the works of art which crowded its churches and palaces: the Italian national patrimony.

Morelli was fortunate that another hero of the struggle for independence, Giovanni Cavalcaselle, a former engineer, was also a passionate amateur connoisseur. Both men had long been disturbed at the confusion which surrounded the work of the old masters. Fakes and replicas abounded and almost any painting of quality was dubbed either a Raphael or a Leonardo. Painters of the stature of Bellini or Botticelli frequently went unrecognized, legends and half-truths were rife.

The situation had been compounded by the centuries-old Italian tradition of selling copies to rich European travelers and by the major painters themselves who frequently employed a battery of assistants. An artist might well have signed a contract to paint a portrait or an altarpiece and the finished product might indeed bear his signature, but most of the work might well have been painted by members of his team.

Independently of each other, Morelli and Cavalcaselle had realised that the only answer was to compare painting with painting and they had visited most of the great galleries of Europe. Neither relied on their memories. Cavalcaselle used a friend, an Englishman called Joseph Archer Crowe, a former reporter on *The Times* and an excellent draughtsman, to make accurate drawings of the paintings he studied. Morelli, too, made use of drawings. He also used his medical training, particularly his knowledge of comparative anatomy, to help him discover and list the many idiosyncratic ways in which the masters handled details. Titian, for example, has a particular way of depicting the ball of the thumb, Botticelli's hands are usually bony with squared nails, while the way Sebastiano del Piombo (Michelangelo's favorite disciple) draws an ear is unmistakeable. These, and dozens of other minutiae, ranging from the setting of haloes to tricks of perspective, reduced the identification of paintings to an exact science—or so Morelli's followers claimed.

This is, of course, an over-simplification of Morelli's technique, for he never meant it to be anything more than an additional tool to be used by a scholar to help resolve a problem of attribution and to distinguish the hand of a master from that of his imitators. Neither did he expect it to be of any use to the sort of person who says 'I don't know anything about art but I know what I like'. In 1884 he wrote to Richter, a close friend, that he never intended his method 'to inject the gift of divination into those who had not been granted it by Nature'.

Today Morelli's ideas are remembered and respected, but in the latter part of the nineteenth century his ideas were new and he had only a small but ardent following, particularly in Germany where it was led by Richter.

Bernhard was determined to follow Richter's advice. He planned to visit Dresden and Munich and test Morelli's scholarship with his own eyes. He managed the trip largely due to the generosity of a former Harvard colleague, George Rice Carpenter, who, as an opera devotee, was planning to attend the Wagner Festival in Bayreuth. He invited Bernhard to join him.

From Dresden they made the diversion to Vienna and then to Munich and Bayreuth, from where they planned, at Bernhard's suggestion and on Richter's recommendation, to travel south and winter in Florence.

Unfortunately for them both, other Bostonians were converging on Bayreuth for the festival. These included Isabella and one of Bernhard's former professors at Harvard, Thomas Sergeant Perry, who had been largely instrumental in persuading Isabella and others to finance Bernhard's original traveling grant. Perry obviously did not approve of either of the young men's plans or of their progress to date. He told Bernhard bluntly that he was a disappointment to him and to his benefactors and Carpenter was told that his Harvard fellowship would not be renewed. Pausing only for a brief and slightly frigid lunch with Isabella and to make polite obeisances to their Boston peers at the performance of *Parsifal*, the two young aesthetes turned their faces toward Paris and the journey home.

Bernhard was heartbroken. Although the ever-obliging Senda scratched up yet another $100, it was not enough to enable him to explore Italy. While he waited for a passage home, he wrote a plaintive and desperate appeal to Ned Warren in England.

His timing was immaculate. Ned's father had just died, leaving him an unencumbered income of $20,000 a year together with the expectation of considerably more when other elderly relations succumbed. Ned determined to spend the money properly, and included Bernhard in his plans.

Ned's idea was to collect the finest works of art and eventually endow the Boston Museum. His taste tended towards the antique but he was prepared to countenance filling the gaps in the museum's own collection. His method was to encourage those travelling graduates whom he considered possessed the required sensibilities to act as scouts on his behalf. Bernhard, of whom he was exceptionally fond, came within his parameters. Ned wrote to him, enclosing a letter of credit for $800 and the promise that he would continue the honourarium for a few years, provided that Bernhard would act as a scout. Ned made one further condition.

Before he 'surrendered himself to his beloved Italians', Bernhard was to use the money to travel first to the Greek archaeological sites, second to southern Italy and Sicily, and only then to Rome and his eventual target, Florence. In this way Ned hoped that Bernhard's eye would become correctly attuned to the sculpture of the classical world before being seduced by the more sensuous delights of the Renaissance. 'Before you begin to see', Ned wrote to Bernhard, 'the veil must be lifted'. Bernhard agreed to Ned's terms. He wrote to Senda telling her that he would not, after all, be coming home. If he could borrow a further few hundred dollars, he told her, he would be able to explore Italy thoroughly. He did not add that he would have to take a long and rambling route to Rome but stressed that travel was all part of his plan to become a truly cultured man of the world. Now twenty-three, he had made a good start.

Again the analogy with Marius is appropriate, for Pater's hero

underwent the same process at Bernhard's age. 'His wistful spec-
ulations as to what the real, the greatest experience might be,
determined in him . . .' wrote Pater, 'a thirst for existence in
exquisite places. The veil that was to be lifted for him lay over the
works of the old masters of art in places where nature had used
her mastery. It was just at this moment that a summons to Rome
reached him'.

Warren's bounty enabled Bernhard to fulfill all his patron's
conditions. He left Paris in early September, arriving in Athens in
early November, having dawdled in Venice and many of the towns
of northern Italy on the way. He spent just over a week in Greece,
dutifully looking at the archaeological sites as Warren had instructed, and then raced on to Rome, arriving shortly before Christmas, with pitifully few dollars left in his pocket. Again friends and
his sister subsidized him through the winter. Warren appears to
have been satisfied with his reports, for towards the end of February 1889 he forwarded him a further $300, though whether this
was a gift, a loan or a commission on some purchase it is impossible
to discover. Nevertheless the money enabled Bernhard to travel to
his own personal Mecca, the ancient city of Florence, which, apart
from occasional absences, was to become his home for the next
sixty years.

In Rome he had managed a brief audience with Giovanni
Cavalcaselle, but did not gain admittance to the one man he wished
to see, the redoubtable Morelli. Happily for Berenson, Jean Paul
Richter was in Florence. He welcomed Bernhard, and from then
on personally supervised his studies. Richter gave him books to
read, mapped out itineraries of what to see and where to find it,
found him small jobs as a guide, and introduced him to a wide
circle of acquaintances.

Again money materialised from somewhere to enable Bernhard
to spend a leisurely month in Spain, again following Richter's
rigorous study programme. By the end of the year Richter judged
that his protégé was ready to meet the Master. Apart from a
flattering letter of introduction, Richter also gave Berenson the
latest edition of a book which he believed would smooth Bernhard's way. Richter inscribed the book 'for the young man from
the East'.

This gift, with its inscription, was in all probability the key that opened the door for Bernhard, launching him on his career as a scholar and eventually as a dealer. The facts are strange.*

The book was *The Italian Masters in the Borghese and Dora-Pamfili Galleries in Rome* by an unknown Russian scholar called Ivan Lermolieff; a note on the title page stated that it had been translated into German from the Russian by Johannes Schwarze and published in 1874. Ivan Lermolieff was a rough anagram of Giovanni Morelli; Morelli had used it as a nom de plume because he had stood for the Italian Senate and was deeply involved in public life. The translator's name, Johannes Schwarze, was also a private joke or weak pun, being a German rendering of Giovanni Morelli.

The title is misleading. The book is far more than a catalogue; it is a collection of essays. Each essay is devoted to a particular artist represented in the galleries and discusses the artist's history and personality in relation to those pictures of his which are genuine. The style is subtly ironic: Morelli does not condemn a painting as a fake but glissades around the point with words like 'uncharacteristic'.

However, the key passage is in the introductory chapter, which is called 'Principles and Methods' and had been written when Bernhard was a nine-year-old child in the east, in Butrymanz. Morelli, following Pater, had adopted a literary device. His Marius was Ivan, a 'young man from the East'.

This introductory chapter is arranged in the form of a series of conversations between Ivan Lermolieff, a young Russian student who is avidly taking notes for a catalogue, and an elderly Italian, an anti-clerical connoisseur with little time for art historians and their fixations with paper pedigrees and bills of sale. The older man offers the younger, whom he sees is on the threshold of a career, all that he has learned in a lifetime's study of his country's art, as long as he will accept his view that the true study of art is the work of art itself, and that the only objective is to try and determine who painted what.

Morelli and Cavalcaselle, until they had grown too old to travel, had scoured every corner of Italy, usually on horseback, identifying

---

* The following account is given by Professor Richard Wollheim, Grote Professor of Mind and Logic, University of London, in his lecture on "Giovanni Morelli and the origins of Scientific Connoisseurship'.

and listing the treasures to be found in remote churches and public galleries. Their lists were government property and, though not for publication, were available for study by serious scholars. One of these scholars was a protégé of Cavalcaselle, Adolfo Venturi, who became a leading Italian art historian. He was present in Morelli's house in Rome when the young Bernhard sent in Richter's introductory letter together with his own visiting card. On the latter was written 'Ivan Lermolieff'.

Morelli warmed immediately to his young visitor 'from the East'. He gave Bernhard letters to almost every sacristan and gallery official in Rome, while Cavalcaselle, in his official capacity, gave him the equivalent of a *'laissez-passer'* which guaranteed him access to whatever he wished to see. Not for Bernhard to have to stand and view paintings hung high above him in the gloom of some lofty building. He was furnished with a lamp and a ladder.

There can be no doubt that Bernhard also had access to Morelli's lists. Throughout 1890, Bernhard travelled Italy from Venice to Sicily, knowing where to go and what to look for. The finances for these trips came from Ned Warren and Charles Loeser, who had settled in Florence in the spring of 1889. Bernhard casually cast off his old friend and sponsor Isabella, almost dismissing her in a cruel letter. Not surprisingly, Isabella was hurt to hear that he had turned to another patron, without so much as a word of thanks. Embittered by such ingratitude so bluntly expressed, Isabella replied coldly, forbidding him to write to her again.

Bernhard was becoming known as an art expert. Both the British and the American embassies recommended him as a reliable person for travellers to consult if they wished to purchase a painting: he would, they said, make sure that they were not cheated. He guided tourists around the galleries of Florence and was fast becoming an active scout for those who wished to purchase or deal.

In May 1889, at Morelli's suggestion, Bernhard was in Bergamo, doubtless playing the role of Ivan rather than of Marius, for, as he was to write in 1947, he was taking coffee in a small café with a friend called Enrico Costa when the idea came to him to out-Morelli Morelli. On impulse he burst out that it was time for people to dedicate their lives to connoisseurship, rather than to make the study of art a dilettanteish affair. He would take up learning with no expectation of reward, so that the great paintings could be correctly attributed and the forgeries cast aside.

It is a significant insight into Bernhard's character that Morelli's life's work, which had been such a help to him, had been downgraded by him to a part-time hobby. Moreover, at the very time that Bernhard was expounding noble sentiments of altruism to Enrico Costa, five Italian paintings which he had purchased on his travels were entered at Christie's in the name of J. P. Richter.

Richter, as we have seen, bought in order to augment his own collection and sold those works he had no further interest in. His closest friend was an auctioneer's son called Otto Gutkunst, who handled many sales and purchases on Richter's behalf and was later to become a director of Colnaghis of London. Both Richter and Gutkunst encouraged Bernhard to act as their scout, briefing him to pick up whatever pictures he could. Richter had the first choice of these finds; if he did not want them, he sold them through either Gutkunst or Christie's, passing a share of the profits to Bernhard. Both Richter and Gutkunst were keenly interested in Berenson's Italian explorations and subsidized him to write detailed letters to them describing what he had found and where. They were probably the first people to realize that Berenson had developed an uncanny eye for a good picture and that this, coupled with his remarkable memory, made him a formidable ally.

Bernhard dabbled in the marketplace out of necessity. Publicly he said that he had no wish to become a dealer and affected to despise most of those he met, but during 1889 and 1890 he had several periods of acute poverty which increased his enthusiasm for dealing. He was now an active scout for Richter and Gutkunst, for Charles Loeser, and for Ned Warren, who had complete confidence in his friend. On 13 July 1890, Warren wrote to the Boston Museum to tell them that Berenson had discovered a fine Madonna and Child by Bronzino at a Venetian dealer's and had bought it for them as Warren's agent.

Later that summer of 1890, Bernhard went to London and renewed a brief acquaintanceship with Logan Pearsall Smith's sister, Mary, now married with two children, aged three and fifteen months. Her husband, Frank Costelloe, was deeply involved in both his law practise and politics, and Bernhard took Mary with him on his visits to public galleries and private collections. From the start she encouraged him, by Christmas they were lovers, and in August the following year she left her husband and children and settled in Florence as his first assistant.

Mary was an apt pupil. Much has been written about her emotional life and countless entanglements, but very little about her capacity to judge a painting or, more importantly, to write about it. She also had the advantage of having a private income of $3,000 a year, which greatly assisted the pair of them as, together, they continued Bernhard's self-appointed task.

They both realised that for either of them to be accepted as authorities they must publish. Minor writers with little knowledge gained an immense following once they had produced their 'art' book. Florence was full of people shouting about art, usually arguing passionately with each other. Bernhard, never one to be silent, aired his own views as vociferously as the others and Mary listened and took notes—mostly of her lover's views but spiced with the observations of Richter and the occasional insights of her brother Logan. 'Tactile', as in Berenson's famous 'tactile values', is a Loganism, but the phrase is a classic Mary/Bernhard compromise. In early drafts it appears as 'Tactile sensations' or 'The tactile ideal/idea/factor/quota/quotient'.

Mary was an able writer. Bernhard was not, as the research for this book made quite clear. His syntax was laboured and he hated the thought of putting pen to paper. His first serious effort, an essay 'on Connoisseurship' started in 1890, was not ready for publication until 1902, and then only after several drastic 'doctorings' by Mary and other literary acquaintances. However, Mary was determined to get into print.

She planned a catalogue of the Italian paintings at Hampton Court, using her literary gifts to demonstrate Bernhard's scholarship. As a sideline she wrote a brief study of the *Venetian Painters of the Renaissance*, which appeared under Bernhard's name in 1894. The evidence that she, Mary Costelloe, is the author is in a letter she wrote to her father, Robert Pearsall Smith, dated 24 November 1893, in which she wrote that she was anxious to get *A Guide to the Italian Pictures at Hampton Court* published, since art people knew of her only as a student of Berenson's. She was somewhat disappointed about *Venetian Painters of the Renaissance* since, although Putnam's had wanted the authors of the book to appear as *both* Mary and Bernhard, Mary's Quaker mother would have feared scandal if her married daughter's name was associated with that of another man. In the end, Mary's name was left out of the book.

Until she married Bernhard in 1900, Mary either wrote in Bernhard's name—as she did the first editions of the sister volumes dealing with the Florentine, Northern, and Central Italian painters of the Renaissance, which appeared between 1896 and 1907—or under the pseudonym of Mary Logan.

That Mary was the author of *Venetian Painters of the Renaissance* is not generally recognized; it is interesting to speculate whether or not Bernhard would have risen to such eminence as an art historian and expert had it been acknowledged that Mary was the author. However, the main reason why *Venetian Painters* caused such a sensation was the lists it contained of all the Venetian painters thought by the author to be genuine, and these lists had been compiled by Bernhard. They decimated the number of allegedly genuine paintings but gave no reason why so many had been excluded nor on what grounds.

Bernhard's opinions were, however, generally accepted, for after the death of Morelli in 1891, followed shortly afterwards by that of Cavalcaselle, few had seen all the pictures in the lists, though many had studied the paintings he (or rather Mary) had written about in detail. No one else felt willing to compete with the formidable authority of the lists and Bernhard's judgement. With the publication of the Venetian lists, and later on of the further lists on the artists of Florence, Northern and Central Italy, Bernhard became the greatest living expert on who had painted what during the Renaissance.

Mary and Bernhard now travelled extensively, widening their expertise still further by visiting almost every noteworthy private and public collection in Europe. They were not always welcome after they had given their opinions, as they remorselessly scaled down many optimistic attributions. Lord Allendale, furious to be told that his Giorgione was a Catena, ordered them out of his house.

Accompanying them that day was a young English collector, Herbert Cook. Angered by Allendale's churlishness, he and Bernhard planned a spectacular revenge. Berenson would write a devastating alternative catalogue for the February 1895 Exhibition of Venetian Paintings. The exhibition was to be held at the New Gallery in Oxford Street. Cook would pay for the catalogue to be printed.

PART THREE

Dalliance

✺ 5 ✺

First Encounter

Fortunately, Bernhard was already familiar with most of the paintings hanging in the New Gallery's 1895 Exhibition of Venetian
Paintings in London, so his catalogue was ready on 4 February,
two days after the opening. Cook kept his role of paymaster secret
but Bernhard revelled in becoming the overnight scourge of the
art trade, the ruthless exposer of artistic falsehood, and the ultimate
arbiter of authenticity.

The alternative catalogue had exactly the result that Berenson
intended. It infuriated and galvanized the collectors and dealers
who had hitherto taken a complacent attitude to both attributions
and authenticity. It is not difficult to understand why.

Berenson's catalogue opened with an attack on thirty-three
'Titians' on display. 'Of these', wrote Berenson, 'one only is by
the master . . . of the thirty-two that remain, a dozen or so have
no connection whatsoever with Titian and are either too remote
from our present subject or too poor to require attention'. He then
detailed nine of these as obvious copies and attributed the rest to
Titian's followers and later imitators. The same operation was
neatly performed on almost every other master on show. Few
survived his onslaught. He passed only three of the nineteen paintings attributed to Giovanni Bellini, and none of the twenty-one
posing as either Bonifazio or Paolo Veronese, and he condemned
seventeen Giorgiones as false. His comments were astringent and
direct. A portrait of 'A Lady Professor of Bologna' by Giorgione,
today in the Ashmolean Museum, Oxford, was, he wrote, 'neither
a lady, nor a professor, not of Bologna and least of all by Giorgione'.

Any fool or self-styled expert can condemn a painting, but

Berenson was neither. Those that he condemned he also found other names for, carefully and for the most part accurately assigning them to the minor hands that had painted them. His logic and evident scholarship made collectors and readers alike reluctantly concede that he knew what he was talking about. What irked them, and particularly infuriated Joseph Duveen, was that he had turned the exhibition into a fiasco, exposing those who saw themselves as the kings of the art world as both foolish and ignorant: they felt that he had embarrassed them all on purpose. Years later, Berenson's wife, Mary, was to admit that that had been their intention.

With rare exceptions, Mary felt, the London art trade had resolved to blackball the Berensons. There were a few exceptions. P. and D. Colnaghis, probably the leading dealers after Thomas Agnew and Sons, played a quiet and cunning game. Publicly they deplored Berenson's action, but secretly they encouraged him. Joseph Duveen kept quiet; he recognised in Berenson and his complicated personality and lifestyle not only his own passionate resolve to succeed and dominate but the same overweening egotism.

Joseph Duveen decided that he wanted to know more. Learning that Berenson was an American citizen from Boston, a Jew who had renounced his faith and allegedly the holder of a degree from Harvard University, he telegraphed Uncle Henry for a full report.

Henry Duveen knew a good deal about Bernhard. They had met by chance the previous November in New York at the house of a Duveen customer, Henry Marquand, who owned a magnificent collection of oriental rugs and porcelain.

Bernhard had been spending a three-month vacation in America, visiting his parents and assiduously enlarging a circle of acquaintances who were, or might become, customers. To these people he had posed as a disinterested scholar, critic and author, a dispassionate surveyor of the marketplace from his Florentine base. In fact, as we know, he was already a scout for Richter, Gutkunst, Loeser and Warren. He was also beginning to deal himself, on a very confidential and private basis.

His major customer at that time was the New England copper magnate Theodore Davis, a prodigious, if none-too-discerning, collector. Bernhard had, on several occasions, stopped Davis from making a fool of himself and had also sold him several Italian pictures. Bernhard was Davis' guest in New York when he met

Henry Duveen, and it was Davis who arranged his visit to the Marquand collection.

When Henry Duveen learned from Marquand that Theodore Davis was to visit his collection, he arranged to be present. Henry's motive was to secure the copper millionaire as a customer. Bernhard's presence was a bonus, and to Henry at least a delight. He immediately recognised Bernhard for what he was: serious, well-informed, in love with his work and, most important, if not yet a fully-fledged dealer, then a potential one. Duveen found Berenson more than familiar with the Yiddish 'argot' of the international art trade, waspish about Duveens' European rivals such as Agnews and Sedelmeyer, and remarkably well-informed on such subjects as Stanford White's Italian foraging expeditions.

Henry was enchanted with Bernhard. He made it clear to him in a word or two that he recognized that Davis was *his* customer and that he did not even pretend to understand paintings. Instead Henry explained the beauties and subtleties of some Persian hangings and oriental porcelains and in the process gave Bernhard an object lesson in how to handle rich and important clients. Finally Henry confirmed Bernhard's public role as an independent critic by inviting him to his gallery to give him the benefit of his opinions on some of the more recherché items of his stock.

Bernhard accepted the invitation. Henry did not record what they talked about, except that Bernhard presented him with an inscribed copy of *Venetian Painters* and a proof of his 360-page monograph on Lorenzo Lotto (which had also been largely re-written by Mary). Henry made a note that he had asked Bernhard to keep his eyes open for fine pieces of Italian majolica ware that might interest Duveens and that he had sent a farewell gift of a package of art books to Bernhard's cabin aboard the steamship *New York* when she sailed for Europe on 21 November 1894. On the same day, Bernhard's name was entered on the Duveen index of 'scouts', which would at a minimum guarantee him an annual letter of goodwill on New Year's Day.

Joseph Duveen's inquiry reached Henry in the spring of 1895, and by then he had learnt a great deal more about Bernhard. One of Henry's sources of information had been the great French collector, Gustave Dreyfus, who shared with Joel Duveen a love of fine bronzes and small bibelots of the finest quality.

In 1870, Dreyfus had purchased the entire collection of another

French collector—and amateur forger—a Monsieur Timbal. He had sought Joel's advice on what to keep and what to weed out and a close friendship had developed.* The Dreyfus children knew the Duveen children and Dreyfus' eldest son, Charles, trained briefly with Joel before joining the Louvre as a junior curator.

In January 1895, Dreyfus had written to Henry and Joel telling them that he 'had met young Mr Berenson who, together with Otto [Gutkunst], has just done an important business with Mrs Gardner. Mr Berenson urged Mrs Gardner to buy my Donatello bust but I had no wish to sell, though he was the most persuasive and well able to appreciate its value'. (Bernhard's 'important business' had been to sell Mrs Gardner Lord Ashburnham's 'Death of Lucretia' by Sandro Botticelli for $15,000. The details of this transaction will be given in the next chapter.)

The Dreyfus report about Berenson's deal, coupled with Joseph's inquiry, caused Uncle Henry to dig deep into Bernhard's background. Henry's second source of information was the banking intelligence network of his friend and customer J. Pierpont Morgan, who lent him the services of his American and European correspondents and agents.

Henry's report on the young Bernhard Berenson is dated August 1895. Morgan's prime source in Italy was none other than Bernhard's Harvard friend Charles Loeser, who at that time was temporarily at loggerheads with Bernhard over money that he had lent to him, and probably over his relationship with Mary. Other contributors were Charles Elliot Norton, his son Richard, a few Harvard contemporaries and Professor George Rice Carpenter, then at Columbia University, New York, who pithily described Berenson as 'a charlatan'.

Most paid tribute to his scholarship, but commented that he was 'difficult', 'opinionated', 'egotistical' and, most common of all, 'fiercely ambitious'. 'It appears', wrote Uncle Henry, 'that he could be most useful to us, but I advise caution as all are agreed that he will never play the second fiddle but must lead the band, if not conduct it. It could be dangerous to be out of step with him'.

Joe greeted Uncle Henry's opinion with relief. He at least knew who was going to conduct the band. From the beginning he saw

* In 1930 Joe Duveen purchased the Dreyfus Collection *en bloc*.

Bernhard as a potential threat and welcomed the family decision to keep an eye on Bernhard's progress and not make an approach to him. He also started what can only be called a 'dossier' on the young critic. For almost ten years he collected every item of gossip on the international dealers' grapevine, listed Bernhard's appearances at major sales and exhibitions, and culled the art journals for his opinions and articles and for any references to him.

In this way Duveens learned just how 'greedy and ambitious' Bernhard could be and probably breathed a sigh of relief when the lesson turned out to be largely at the expense of his former patroness, Isabella Stewart Gardner.

❧ 6 ❧

Isabella Stewart Gardner

Isabella Stewart Gardner had been hurt by Bernhard's casual letter of 1889 telling her that he had found a new patron. She had, as we have seen, told him not to write again. She now proceeded to make her own timid forays into the Italian art market, buying direct from dealers in Florence, Milan, Rome and Venice, usually on the well-meant but ignorant advice of friends, though sometimes she bought exceptionally well.

Her purchase, in 1892, of Jan Vermeer's 'The Concert' at a Paris auction marked her début as a serious collector. The following year, her negotiations for a portrait by Justus Sustermans, a Flemish portrait artist who spent most of his life in Florence and who was Court Painter to three successive Grand Dukes of Tuscany, reawakened Bernhard's interest in her. Isabella bought the picture, against the much-publicized competition of the Empress of Germany, from the Venetian dealer, Vincenzo Favenza.

Bernhard wrote a humble congratulatory note and enclosed an advance copy of *Venetian Painters*. Isabella responded immediately and said that she hoped to meet him in London later that year, when she was visiting Europe.

They arranged to meet in London on 22 July 1894, when Bernhard agreed to show her around the National Gallery. Bernhard himself was adamant that they did meet and that there and then Isabella commissioned him to form a collection of museum quality Italian pictures. But it is most unlikely that the meeting in fact ever took place. Berenson's biographer, Professor Ernest Samuels, is adamant that it did not. Though most of their letters to each other at this time have disappeared, sufficient remain to show that they were in constant touch and that the dominant subject was paintings. She certainly let him know that she was well aware of his activities as a scout for Ned Warren—knowledge probably gained through her husband who was a trustee of the Boston Museum.

A letter dated 23 January 1895 has survived which she wrote to Bernhard from Paris, asking for his opinion on two paintings which had been offered to her. She enclosed photographs and asked for a speedy reply. On his side Bernhard was well aware of her wish to collect and had all the details of her recent purchases at his fingertips, doubtless due to the research of Richter's friend, Otto Gutkunst, who was now deeply involved in the London picture trade with Colnaghis of Bond Street. Bernhard replied by return post, damning both pictures with faint praise, and then cast the bait offering her Botticelli's 'Death of Lucretia', which was owned by Lord Ashburnham, for $15,000 as a way to repay her past kindness to him.

Bernhard had originally told Otto Gutkunst about Lord Ashburnham's Botticelli, and had urged him to buy it. Gutkunst had offered £3,000 ($15,000), which Ashburnham had accepted. Gutkunst then stalled as he was given the opportunity to purchase a substantial shareholding in and a directorship of Colnaghis, who, after Agnews, were the leading picture dealers in England at that time. When Isabella agreed to buy the Botticelli, Bernhard saved his friend Otto considerable embarrassment. Otto handled the negotiations and Isabella acquired a cheap painting as there was no dealer's mark-up. The purchase was finally completed in December that year, by which time several covert arrangements had been made.

Bernhard's position as adviser to Isabella was now formalized: he was to be paid 5 per cent of the purchase price of any picture she bought on his recommendation. Both agreed that this arrangement was to be kept a secret; when Bernhard bought, he was to do so in his own name, drawing cheques on an account at Barings Bank which would be replenished by Isabella as and when funds were needed.

He partially observed Isabella's passion for secrecy in so far as he did not even tell Mary about it until three years later, when Isabella's husband, with good cause, suspected him of double-crossing them. He did, however, tell Otto Gutkunst and Richter.

Bernhard's letters to Gutkunst were destroyed in 1936 at his own request, but the Berenson-Richter letters are still extant, the latter having refused Bernhard's request to burn them. Many of Colnaghis' records were destroyed during the last war, but enough evidence, particularly the carbons of Otto's letters to Bernhard, remains to show that Bernhard had a close commercial relationship with both Richter and Gutkunst.

The Ashburnham Botticelli was the foundation stone of the remarkable collection that Bernhard formed for Isabella. Today it is housed in Fenway Court, Boston, the replica of a Venetian palazzo that Isabella built for herself and her collection after her husband's death. It is open to the public, and the catalogue claims that it is a monument to the princeliness of Isabella's purse and the taste and discrimination of Bernhard Berenson. Bernhard did not confine his advice to paintings alone but chose textiles, books, oriental rugs, ceramic tiles, bibelots, even a set of choir stalls and part of a reredos. The picture collection is in fact a monument to a combination of talents: Gutkunst's and Richter's scholarship, Bernhard's salesmanship and Isabella's good-natured self-indulgence and credulity.

Most of the major pictures in the Gardner Collection were discovered by either Richter or Gutkunst and sold to Isabella through Bernhard. Gutkunst found her four Rembrandts, her Peter Paul Rubens, her genuine Diego Velázquez of Philip IV of Spain and the rather doubtful portrait of Pope Innocent X. It was also Gutkunst who supplied information which led to both her Hans Holbeins, her pair of Francesco Pesellinos, the famous Carlo Crivelli of St. George and the Dragon, her Albrecht Dürer, the Anthony Van Dyck and the most outstanding picture in her collection, Titian's 'Rape of Europa'.

Richter supplied her with the source of her Bonifazio Veronese, her Giotto, her Vincenzo Catena and her Paris Bordone. With the exception of the Velázquez Pope, all these pictures are beyond reproach, but Isabella paid dearly for them. The Giotto, 'The Presentation in the Temple', had fetched £1 at the Mond Park Sale in 1892 when it was acquired by the dealer Henry Willett of Brighton. Two years later he sold it to Richter for £100 ($500) and Isabella, at Bernhard's suggestion, paid $7,500.

Bernhard's tutelage of Isabella was largely by post, and their correspondence is still preserved at Fenway Court. There are certain gaps in Bernhard's letters to her which are the result of severe pruning by Isabella herself shortly before her death, while her letters to him were similarly censored by his secretary-companion, Miss Nicky Mariano. What remains, however, gives a graphic picture of a formidable and at times extreme kind of salesmanship.

In one letter urging the purchase of a picture, he invented a spurious Scots ancestry for himself, claiming descent from Robert the Bruce, and a relationship to Mary Stuart, adding that, as her name was Stewart, they were probably related. He also encouraged her to identify herself with the great Italian patroness of the Renaissance, Isabella d'Este, and sold her a palpable dud of a painting which, he claimed, was a portrait of that lady by Polidoro Lanciani.

This painting was spotted by Berenson in an auction held in Milan on 14 November 1895, when the collection of a fashionable surgeon called Antonio Scarpa was dispersed. It was catalogued as 'after Titian', and was called 'Lady with a Turban'. It was purchased by an agent of Colnaghis for $600. The picture was cleaned, reframed and photographed in Milan. Bernhard then offered it to Isabella for $3,000, saying that it was a portrait of Isabella d'Este. There is not a scrap of evidence as to the identity of the sitter and the authorship is certainly neither Titian, as had been claimed by some, nor Lanciani, as Bernhard had claimed, but possibly one of Titian's more pallid imitators, such as Francesco Torbido.

When Bernhard used sources other than Gutkunst and Richter, the finds were more often than not doubtful as to quality and authenticity. Isabella's Correggio, 'Venus Taking a Thorn from her Foot', for example, is a coarse and feeble Correggesque-style copy of an engraving by Marco Dente da Ravenna; her 'Titian' of the Queen of Austria is by the Portuguese copyist of Titian's works, Alonso Sanchez Coello, while her portrait of the Dauphin François of France, bought as a Clouet, is a copy of a painting by Corneille de Lyon.

Isabella was also used as a depository for embarrassing pictures. In 1896, Bernhard recommended to his friend Herbert Cook that he buy a 'Cima' Madonna and Child, which had already done the rounds of dealers in Milan and Vienna. When the picture arrived in London, Cook refused to accept it. He recognized it as a version of a genuine Cima in the A. T. Loyd Collection at Lockinge House near Wantage in Berkshire. He had already paid for it so Bernhard had to get rid of it in order to reimburse him. Whereupon Berenson wrote to Isabella on April 10, 1897 asking her to take the picture as a genuine Cima, for $2,500.

Bernhard was not alone in suggesting pictures to her. Isabella kept her ears sharply tuned to what the Boston Museum was up to, and had her own network of contacts, mostly social, throughout Europe. Sometimes she bought by herself without consulting him—and occasionally she bought well—but when her target was elusive or involved operations which were not strictly legal, she would co-opt Bernhard to attend to the grislier details. The way she acquired her famous painting of 'Christ Carrying the Cross' is typical.

During September 1895, she learnt that the Boston Museum was negotiating to purchase a Giorgione of 'Christ Carrying the Cross' and had retained Bernhard to act for them. She had already warned him never to act against her interests and wrote promptly to him saying that she wanted it. He replied that Boston had been interested in the picture, and had taken his advice as to its authenticity. He believed it to be genuine but Boston had lost interest when his rival, the expert Venturi, had dismissed it as a copy after a lost original. If she wished, Bernhard said, he would do his best to acquire it.

Venturi was wrong. The composition was devised by Giovanni Bellini, and is known in a number of versions. Modern scholarly opinion is divided as to whether the Gardner picture is by Bellini or the young Giorgione copying one of his inventions, but is agreed that it is not a copy. Indeed, it is a hauntingly beautiful painting and was Isabella's favourite. To this day, under the terms of her will, a single rose is placed below it every morning. It belonged to Count Zileri dal Verme, the head of the family of that name, and hung in the Palazzo Loschi at Vicenza. Negotiations were protracted and it took Bernhard almost eighteen months to prise the picture from the family. They were keen to sell, but there were first certain problems to overcome.

In early May of 1897, Berenson wrote to Isabella to tell her there would be time-consuming delays in getting the picture out of Italy, but that he still hoped to get the picture for $3,000. Two weeks later, he wrote her that two conditions existed for the sale to be made. One, that he provide a copy of the painting and two, that if the authorities found out about the deal, Berenson would assume all responsibility for the sale. Since he was a resident of Italy, their selling to him was perfectly legal.

The copy was for the people of Vicenza, to whom the old Count Zileri had initially willed the painting, and who were determined to fight for their right to have it. In December, Bernhard wrote to Isabella again to say that he was prepared to smuggle the Giorgione out of Italy, only on the condition that if the Italian government brought a claim against Loschi, she would return the picture at the price he had paid for it.

Finally, in early January, Bernhard confirmed to Mrs Gardner that the picture had been smuggled out of Italy and was on its way to London. Zozo Smith, he wrote, would be the best artist to provide a copy.

Zozo Smith was the Boston artist and friend of Isabella's, Joseph Lindon Smith. He was an accomplished painter, famous for his almost photographic realism. He had his own special-ised technique, using dry paint, by which he could represent in-tricate subjects such as wooden carvings and bas reliefs in stone. He is most famous for his numerous copies of Egyptian tomb paintings and studies of archaeological artifacts, but he had a side line to which Isabella had introduced him. During the late 1880s he had been in Venice, perched on a ladder making an oil sketch of Verrocchio's bronze of Bartolomeo Colleoni, when in his own words 'a cultivated woman's voice called up to me and asked what I was doing. "Painting a portrait of a great Venetian general," I replied. "Come down and hold the ladder for me," she commanded'.

Isabella climbed the ladder and as a result not only bought the sketch, but invited him to travel with her party. He painted many copies for her and, as a result of her introductions, supplied nu-merous study copies of notable European paintings to American museums.

Today his Italian pictures are mostly in the Fogg Art Museum but his best original work is in the Boston Museum and the Boston Public Library and Athenaeum. These copies, plus a flair for dealing, financed his real wish, which was to accompany archaeological expeditions, and made him an essential part of Isabella's stable of scouts and others who helped to build her collection. He maintained an arm's length friendship with Bernhard, with whom he never felt at ease. Nevertheless, his copy of the Giorgione earned him $500 and hangs today in Vicenza where the citizens, who own it, may still believe it to be by the master.

❧ 7 ❧

Crisis

Bernhard's dealings did not remain a secret and earned him many enemies. Fellow connoisseurs, who understandably recoiled from his waspish tongue and generally superior scholarship, sought revenge by impugning his ethics. He attributed these insinuations to their jealousy, but the dealers were another matter. Most of the leading galleries in London and Paris were well aware of his connection with Colnaghis and recognized that he was as venal and opportunistic as the worst of them. Agnews, in particular, had little time for him: when asked why they never sold a picture through him or sought his advice, Sir Geoffrey Agnew simply made the comment, 'We never paid him a commission'.

Agnews were particularly well-informed as they had resident agents in Italy who were constantly in competition with Colnaghis, and therefore with Bernhard. Agnews also had numerous American clients of great wealth and others who, though less rich, had considerable influence, such as Charles Elliot Norton and Colonel Lorrimer, the Chairman of the Trustees of the Boston Museum. It was through Bernhard's old enemy Norton that Jack Gardner learned that his wife was being misled.

Gardner's own inquiries were fuelled by the suspicion that his fifty-eight-year-old wife's relationship with her art adviser, who was half her age, had stepped far beyond the proprieties of the time. It was whispered that they had enjoyed rather more than an intellectual holiday together in Venice in the summer of 1897. What and how Jack found out is obscure. Perhaps he had read Bernhard's letters. If so, almost all traces of what happened have disappeared from the correspondence that is preserved at Fenway

Court. The one surviving hint that there was an emotional entanglement did not surface until many years later.

Their letters, in the latter half of 1897, show that they were in Venice together, that Isabella had showered Bernhard with presents, clothes, furniture for his Florence apartment, reference books and photographs for his library. Together they had visited the dealer Vincenzo Favenza, from whom she had earlier purchased her Sustermans portrait, and Bernhard had allowed her to buy two decorative but worthless pictures with ambitious attributions, which the present Fenway Court catalogue dismisses as 'anonymous'. Favenza had not been able to believe his good luck and had later explained the sale to the late Sir Philip Hendy, subsequently Director of the National Gallery who catalogued the Gardner collection in 1928, by saying, 'They must have been in love'.

The letter that would probably have justified Jack Gardner's suspicions did not arrive until 1923. Only Bernhard's posthumous reputation as an insatiable womanizer justifies the suspicion that the relationship was more than that of an emotional older woman doting on a gilded youth. The letter was written to Isabella from Venice on 23 July 1923. Bernhard was staying with the Cole Porters at the Palazzo Barbera, and the familiarity of his surroundings jogged a chord in his memory. He reminded Isabella of two weeks they had spent together in Venice twenty-six years before. He expressed his gratitude for her tenderness and told her that he would always fondly remember that time.

In 1898, Jack Gardner decided to concentrate his suspicions on two of the many pictures that Bernhard was currently persuading Isabella to purchase. He chose the more expensive picture first, Raphael's portrait of Cardinal Tomasso Inghirami of Volterra, a famous early sixteenth-century librarian to the Vatican. Bernhard had written to Isabella saying that it was a bargain at $75,000, and that if a big dealer had it they would ask about $375,000.

Using the facilities of the Boston Museum and taking advice from Charles Elliot Norton, Jack Gardner discovered that the Inghirami family had given an option on the picture to a Florentine dealer called Emilio Constantini, who in turn had offered the picture to Bernhard for $40,000 plus a Zozo Smith copy. Norton wrote to Smith who replied that the painting was certainly in Constantini's gallery, where he was shortly to go and make a copy of it, but that he knew nothing about the price being asked. Norton then wrote to Constantini himself and asked him to write direct to Isabella quoting the price he was asking Bernhard. When the letter arrived, Isabella wrote a series of plaintive notes to Bernhard.

In the first letter, she wrote to Bernhard telling him that her husband forbade her to buy the picture. However, she told him that she was determined to have the Raphael and asked Bernhard again for the smallest sum he would need to acquire it. He replied to her under the assumption that she was short of money—though quite sympathetic, he was blissfully unaware of the storm building up and held firm at his price.

Isabella was stung by his condescension and wrote him stormily that the decision to buy was to be her husband's and that Constantini had offered it to him for £8,000 (Bernhard had asked £15,000). Three days later she cabled Bernhard saying that her husband had told her to check with him before accepting Constantini's offer.

At the last minute Bernhard wrote to her that he had secured the picture for £7,000, offering the lame excuse that the Inghirami family had had a cash crisis and reduced their price in order to cover a loan that was due. He added that Constantini had proved a great help in the final negotiations and, moreover, would assist him in smuggling the picture out of Italy.

It had been a narrow escape, but Bernhard did not realize how narrow. Jack Gardner remained convinced that Bernhard was guilty, but had not the heart to disillusion his wife. Instead he cannily made it exceptionally difficult for her to raise funds to buy the ever-increasing numbers of pictures that Bernhard continued to offer her. During the spring of 1898 he tempted her with a Holbein from the Schonberg Collection for $60,000, which she refused. He still had not learnt his lesson when she declined to pay $2,500 for a pair of decorated cassone chests. She wrote to him to say that Mr Gardner no longer would give her the money to acquire pictures.

The day Bernhard received this stark warning, he replied offering her an Albrecht Dürer portrait from the Czernin Collection in Vienna for $60,000. He added that if she did not want it, then he had another customer in mind who would snap it up. Her reply distressed him. She wrote that she had been offered the Dürer a month ago and at a price far cheaper than the $60,000 he proposed, adding silkily that she would have to deal with the first offerer; she hoped that she and Berenson would not be bidding against each other.

The news that she was prepared to buy without his imprimatur, was in direct touch with his sources of supply, and suspected him of buying for others, came at a bad time for Bernhard. His emotional and social life had reached a low ebb. He had quarrelled bitterly with several of his Florentine friends, and Mary's ever wayward affections had briefly settled on another man for the second time in six months. In desperation he turned to her and confessed that Isabella was not a customer like their many others, but that he was her retained adviser as well.

Mary took the revelation of Bernhard's duplicity philosophically. In a way she was glad of it, for she found herself falling in love with him again. Mary's support was invaluable to Bernhard. Characteristically, now that she realized that her lover was, after all, primarily a dealer, she entered into the game of finding, buying and selling pictures with gusto. Mary never did anything by halves, and her vitality and enthusiasm were largely responsible for a burst of buying for Isabella, who appeared to have regained her confidence in them. However, they were careful to offer only what they knew could not be checked out by Jack Gardner, his colleagues at the Boston Museum, or any of their numerous rivals and enemies.

Mary and Bernhard had attributed the Gardners' tough line during 1898 to someone at Agnews; the Berensons believed that they were the victims of the bitter rivalry which raged between Agnews on one side of Bond Street and Colnaghis on the other. The Berensons therefore decided to pull off a major coup: first they would sell Isabella outstanding pictures which could not be criticized in any way, then—and they hoped that this would be simultaneous—they would discredit Agnews, the firm which they believed to the end of their lives was bent on discrediting them.

Their chance to carry out the first part of their plan occurred when the most famous collection of Dutch paintings in the world came on the market. Begun by a Scotsman called Henry Hope, who had settled in Amsterdam during Rembrandt's lifetime, the Hope Collection had been added to with discretion and sure judgement by his descendants, who had loaned the collection to the South Kensington Museum. But in 1898 Lord Francis Clinton-Hope had succeeded in breaking the entail* and had sold the collection *en bloc* to a syndicate consisting of Otto Gutkunst, representing Colnaghis, and the de Rothschilds' favourite dealer, Wertheimer.

Bernhard argued forcibly and successfully with Gutkunst that it was in their mutual interest to allow Isabella some plums from the collection, and selected for her two undisputed Rembrandts: 'A Lady and Gentleman in Black', which Hope had purchased from the artist himself, and the dramatic 'Storm on the Sea of Galilee'. A third picture, 'A Lesson on the Lute' by Ter Borch, though not of the highest quality (indeed it may well be a duplicate of a similar picture now in the Art Institute of Chicago), was in size, subject and colouring a natural companion to Vermeer's 'The Concert', which Isabella already owned. The price was a not unreasonable $150,000 for the three.

While he was negotiating this deal in London, Bernhard was offered a rare bronze bust of the Florentine banker and patron of the arts, Bindo Altoviti, by the Italian sculptor and goldsmith Benvenuto Cellini. The bust had an impeccable provenance; and furthermore, in his *Autobiography*, Cellini quotes a letter Michelangelo wrote to him praising it to the skies. Bernhard secured this bust for Isabella for $50,000 and sought no commission from the vendor for so doing.

When news of these great acquisitions reached Boston, Isabella had to beg her husband to lend her the money to buy them. He agreed but instructed his wife to write Berenson to say that he was worried at what he had learnt about Bernhard. While she did so, Gardner caused stringent inquiries to be made to check if the prices of the Hope pictures and the Cellini had been inflated.

Bernhard was away when Isabella's letter arrived. Mary opened it and forwarded it to him with a covering note of her own. She stressed the need for total solidarity between them and added that the danger of exposure, while it was very real, had also served to increase her love for him.

* Many valuable properties and heirlooms belonging to aristocratic families were entailed. This meant that the holder of the title held them during his lifetime as a trustee for his heirs.

When they heard about Isabella's letter, both Gutkunst and Wertheimer were persuaded to assist Bernhard. The Hope Collection had been bought *en bloc* with no individual prices put on the pictures; however, it was now discreetly put about that the three paintings bought by Isabella had been sold to her at their cost price, which effectively neutralized Jack Gardner's investigations.

These inquiries were being carried out by Lockett Agnew, one of the two brothers then running the family firm. Lockett now had to concede that the Hope pictures and the Cellini bronze bust were impeccable as to quality and price. At the same time that Jack Gardner was asking him to check up on Bernhard, Isabella—without telling her husband—was asking Bernhard to check up on Lockett. All that Bernhard discovered was that Lockett lacked the scholarship of his famous father and brother, preferring to do business on the racetrack or the grouse moor.

Isabella wanted to check up on Lockett because Agnews had just offered her what they claimed was a genuine Raphael portrait of none other than Bindo Altoviti as a young man, a natural companion to her newly acquired Cellini bronze. They had asked what, by Agnew standards, was a modest price, $150,000. Isabella adored the picture but asked Bernhard to go and see it. He refused, saying that Agnews would never show it to him.

Nevertheless, he persuaded Colnaghis to obtain a photograph and the measurements for him and reported that it had been in Florence with an art dealer named Volpi, and that it had been restored. It was in the style of Raphael, he concluded, but painted by his Florentine imitator, Ridolfo Ghirlandaio. Bernhard added for good measure that he had told a friend of hers, Theodore Davis, the Boston copper millionaire, that this painting was worth no more than $2,500. He could not resist a final swipe telling her not to fear that Agnews would sell it. Their reputation, he wrote, was not impeccable enough for European buyers.

Their Raphael did in fact turn out as Bernhard had foretold; he had a gleeful last word two years later when he wrote to Isabella that they had sold it to a dandy from South Africa for $35,000.*

The threat of exposure, allayed by the purchase of the Hope

* Agnews sold it to a Mr Whitney for $30,000. Today it is in the Getty Collection, Malibu, attributed to Francesco Francia.

pictures, almost disappeared when Jack Gardner died suddenly at Christmas 1898. Bernhard never referred to the death of his persecutor in his letters but continued to offer, and frequently sell, pictures to Isabella. They were a mixed bunch, and almost all from Colnaghis.

In 1899, through the Boston Museum grapevine, Isabella learnt that Sandro Botticelli's 'Madonna of the Eucharist' was on the market. A fine early work of Botticelli's, it was in somewhat bad repair. It hung in the Palazzo Chigi and several experts held it to be a contemporary replica from the artist's studio. Bernhard had championed it as the original and had often said as much to Isabella. On Tuesday 23 May 1899, she cabled him that the Chigi Botticelli was to be sold in Rome that Wednesday. She asked if it was worth $30,000 and he replied that it was not. His reasons were curious, and provide a perfect example of his ambivalent role. Through a Colnaghis partner called Edmond Despretz, Bernhard had already offered $20,000 for the picture and it had been refused. He had then heard that Agnews of London, through their agents, had bid first $35,000 and then $40,000. Prince Chigi, sorely tempted, had circulated leading dealers and museums to say his Botticelli would be offered for private auction on Wednesday 24 May, and Isabella had come to hear of it. When Bernhard cabled his negative response he was already aware that it would never be available for $30,000. The following day he wrote to Isabella that the Prince was not going to auction the picture. He told her that an unnamed dealer had offered the Prince a fantastic sum and that the picture would sell for at least $75,000.

What Bernhard did not tell Isabella—and what he knew at the time—was that Despretz, acting on Colnaghis' and Bernhard's behalf, had purchased the picture for $45,000, plus the promise of an identical copy which Zozo Smith was to paint. Isabella rose to the bait and commissioned Berenson to buy the original for her as cheaply as possible. Eventually she paid $65,000. Then, as now, it was forbidden to export works of art of this calibre from Italy, as has been seen in the case of the Loschi Giorgione. A substitute had to be made and the genuine one smuggled out. Colnaghis and Bernhard had a difficult job getting Prince Chigi's picture out of Italy. They accomplished it with a version of the celebrated three-card trick called 'Find the Lady'.

They had the genuine picture *and* Zozo Smith's replica, but they also knew of an aged copy which was in the Panciatichi Collection. This they now proceeded to acquire through a commission agent called Haskard, funds for this being supplied by Colnaghis. This latter aged copy was in extremely bad condition, so Zozo was asked to improve it at the same time as he worked on the copy for the Prince. Zozo covered up its imperfections by adding numerous decorative details, which, though they tended to spoil Botticelli's design, made it a superficially more commercial proposition. So enthusiastically did Zozo work, that he could not resist painting yet another version, which purported to be a cut-down version of a contemporary studio copy, depicting only the Madonna's head and shoulders.

Haskard then contacted Agnews' agent in Italy, a colourful character called Fairfax Murray, murmuring that the Chigi picture *was* a copy and that the Panciatichi version was the genuine article. Agnews innocently purchased the Panciatichi in May 1900 for around $25,000, believing it to be the original, and sold this version in all good faith six weeks later to the American millionaire P. A. B. Widener for a substantial profit.

The Italian government then stepped in. They, and most of the art dealing fraternity, believed that the picture Agnews had purchased was the Chigi version. When the authorities visited the Palazzo Chigi they found Zozo's copy. The Prince was charged with illegal export and fined $45,000, the amount he had received from Despretz. He appealed, and after he had proved that the picture exported to Agnews was not his but the Panciatichi version, the fine was reduced to a nominal sum of $25.

All this time the genuine picture was sitting in the atelier of the Milan restorer, Cavenaghi. When the uproar died down it was smuggled out to Paris and thence to London, where, to Agnews' chagrin, Colnaghis exhibited it for charity in their gallery, down the road from their distinguished competitor.

The Prince could not be tried twice for the same offence. His replica was accepted with good grace by the Italian authorities and to this day hangs in the Italian Foreign Office as a Botticelli. Zozo's extra version was sold by Bernhard's friend Herbert Horne to the Comtesse de Turenne, and until 1959 was hanging in the Villa Scandicci, Florence, described as 'by a follower of Botticelli', a soubriquet that would have pleased Zozo Smith.

Isabella had her Sandro Botticelli and so she accepted whatever Bernhard gave as his explanations about the cost. However, she seemed to have wished a plague on all Bond Street dealers in general and Colnaghis in particular, for she now wrote to Bernhard to tell him that she did not wish to have any dealings with Colnaghis in future. She instructed Bernhard not to allow them to act for her in any way. Bernhard never alluded to this instruction in his correspondence and seemed blithely to ignore it, except that from now on he did not refer to the firm by name in his letters to her but merely mentioned 'his agent'. This was technically, if not totally, correct as he now confined his dealings with Colnaghis to a private arrangement with their managing director Otto Gutkunst, a subtle distinction which Isabella did not comprehend for some time.

Gutkunst himself found this somewhat disconcerting: he could never understand why Bernhard worried so much about Isabella's probing letters, probably because Otto was unaware of the contents of Bernhard's missives to his client. Nor did Gutkunst care for Bernhard's lordly stance as an academic. He forcefully reminded Bernhard that it had been Colnaghis who had found most of Isabella's better purchases and pointed out that it was hypocritical of Bernhard to pretend to be other than a dealer. 'Business is not always nice', he wrote.

I am the last man to blame you, a literary man, for disliking it. But you want to make money like ourselves so you must do likewise as we do . . . if the pictures you put up to us do not suit Mrs G. it does not matter. We will buy them all the same with you or by giving you an interest in them . . . it is important for both of us to make hay while Mrs G. shines.

And Isabella did indeed continue to buy. Perhaps she felt able, now that Jack was safely buried, to indulge her whim of outdoing the Boston Museum. Whatever the reason, she devoted the rest of her life to enhancing her house, Fenway Court, that idealized replica of a Venetian palazzo. The stone, the woodwork and the craftsmen were imported from Italy and Bernhard and her friends helped her furnish it, not only with pictures but with statuary, antiques, tapestries, miniatures and architectural curiosities, such as a set of Renaissance choir stalls and a reredos.

The main result of the crisis with Isabella was to draw Mary closer into a dealing partnership with Bernhard. From then on until in her old age she became too ill to cope she handled most of his business affairs and his relationships with dealers. Apart from arguing constantly about the division of the profits, she was at least an equal in the seeking out and selling of their discoveries. She gave her own opinions to those who asked for expertise. She employed her own scouts and, with financial help from her brother Logan Pearsall Smith and occasionally from her brother-in-law, Bertrand Russell, she sometimes bought and sold on her own account. Among her many finds, one deserves to be recorded. It is one of the stars of Isabella's collection, though the present catalogue at Fenway Court gives Mary no credit.

On 12 November 1899, Mary had word from an agent that the monks at the chapel of St Francis at Assisi could be persuaded to sell one of their most treasured paintings for $6,000. She rushed to the bank and with help from her family managed to borrow the money. A week later the picture was spirited out of the monastery at midnight, hidden in the back of a cart.

When Bernhard saw it, he attributed the painting to Fiorenzo di Lorenzo. Later authorities suggested Antoniazzo Romano and there has been a suggestion that it may be by Gandolfino di Roreto. But the authorship does not affect the point of the story.

Mary left a vivid series of letters to her mother and her daughter, giving a blow-by-blow account of her smuggling prowess. These letters, together with excerpts from Bernhard's sales letters to Isabella, give a fascinating if somewhat chilling insight into the motives and the methods of Mary and the man she adored.

In late November of 1899, Mary wrote to her family that the painting was hidden, waiting to be restored, and that she hoped to make a lot of money from it. Two days later, she wrote to her daughter rationalizing the smuggling of great art out of Italy, contending that pictures were being ruined through a general lack of care. Mary told her daughter that the Lorenzo Madonna was cracking and the paint was peeling and falling off.

The picture was restored by a new-found acquaintance, Icilio Frederico Joni, probably one of the most successful forgers that Italy had produced in the last hundred years. Bernhard and Mary had discovered him when they realized that several of the pictures they had been buying were outright forgeries. It had been yet another worry during the crisis-ridden summer of 1899. During a trip to Venice in June, they called on Isabella's favourite dealer, Vincenzo Favenza, only to find a great many forgeries. They offered him $500 for the privilege of meeting this great forger.

Favenza then introduced them to Joni, who ran a school of skillful forgers based in Siena. Once created, the forgeries were put on the market through intermediaries; apart from Favenza there were the American collector-dealer Mason Perkins and the Roman aristocrat the Baron Lazzaroni, who was eventually to provide Bernhard and Duveens with a constant supply of 'masterpieces'. Joni rapidly established a humourous rapport with Mary, who commissioned him to search out genuine paintings for her; there is little doubt that he was the agent who found the Gardner Annunciation.

Mary planned to go to London, but smuggling the picture would be difficult. Sometimes dealers substituted pictures at the customs office, other times they used double-bottomed boxes, but quite frequently they simply bribed the officials. By early December of that year, Mary was becoming more cautious, since there had been a strong debate in the Italian parliament concerning their artistic patrimony. A campaign began against the scholar/entrepreneurs they accused of stripping the country of its heritage. Under pressure, Mary's ingenuity was put to the test and came to the rescue. She had a large trunk built with a false bottom into which the picture was packed. She then had a large number of dolls made and placed into the trunk, and had one of Joni's workers pose as a travelling doll salesman. At the border, the trunk was passed through without serious inspection, and the picture was on its way to London.

Trunk and picture arrived at Colnaghis' London gallery on 22 March. There followed a brief exchange between Gutkunst and Bernhard, who then wrote to Isabella. He had already briefed her to expect news of a 'masterpiece'. Bernhard told her that he knew the picture when it had hung in the shrine of St. Francis of Assisi, but that it had disappeared seven years ago only to reappear in London recently. Bernhard had taken an interest in it through a syndicate, he explained, in order to be able to offer the picture to her. The price would be $30,000 and he would charge her no commission.

Isabella was captivated by the picture, but her husband's executors made it increasingly difficult for her to raise the money. Eventually she managed to persuade them to borrow on her behalf against the income her husband had left her. She wrote to Bernhard explaining her problems. He replied saying that $30,000 was at least $15,000 to $20,000 below the market value he anticipated in the coming months.

Her next request must have worried him. She wanted a complete history of the picture, including why it had been allowed to be exported from Italy. He must have suspected that she had learnt of some, or all, of Mary's and his machinations, but this time he also realized that he was writing for the record and for the eyes of her trustees. He had no alternative but to repeat his litany of lies. The picture, he claimed, was the private property of one of the monks, though he had dedicated it to the community of the shrine. When the monks realized the value of the painting, they hid it until it was forgotten, then sold it to Colnaghis, who successfully smuggled it to London. Isabella and her trustees believed him, and this spurious account still appears in the official catalogue of the Isabella Stewart Gardner Collection at Fenway Court.

Neither Bernhard nor Mary could resist the chance to take a profit on many of the more obvious confections of Joni and his confederates. These were mostly sold with the aid of friends who allowed their names to be used in the auction rooms. One such conduit was Herbert Horne, who had now settled in Florence. In 1899 he entered into a formal deed of partnership with Bernhard to sell pictures in London on the understanding that Bernhard's name would not be mentioned in connection with them. It was exceedingly successful until they, inevitably, fell out over the division of the profits.

An even more discreet operation was what Mary called their 'Iniquity Shop', a singularly apt description for a small antique shop in London called Miss Toplady after the elderly sitting tenant who had rooms over the shop and did the cleaning. The shop belonged to Mary's brother Logan and was financed by two of Bernhard's Oxford acquaintances, Percy Fielding and Philip Morell, the extravagant son of a wealthy brewer whose wife, Lady Ottoline, was to become one of Edwardian England's more formidable hostesses. Miss Toplady was nothing more than a tourist trap, the stock being selected by Mary, Logan and occasionally

Bernhard, on their travels round Italy. Their swindles—there is no other appropriate description—were immensely profitable. Mary's and Logan's connection with Miss Toplady merits one brief paragraph in the official Harvard biography of their favourite son, but there is no mention of Bernhard's close and equally profitable connection, though the facts are amply documented. One example will suffice.

In April 1899, Logan bought a picture in Siena for $100. It was an Annunciation of uncertain age which had been transferred from its original panel to canvas and the canvas relaid on to another panel. Mary, whom Joni had taught the basic elements of cleaning and conservation, began to clean it up. She realized that it was almost entirely repainted. It was swiftly touched up and consigned to Miss Toplady, where it remained unsold for two years.

During the summer of 1901 Mary badly needed money for the holidays and the inevitable wardrobes for her two teenaged daughters. Bernhard continually resented having to fund these expenses, but agreed that during a visit to London he would see what he could sell from the Toplady stock. On 25 August 1901, Bernhard wrote to Isabella that, while passing through London, he had seen an important picture and he had attributed it as an autograph Agnolo Gaddi that would provide her collection with an important link between the work of Giotto and Fra Angelico. It was a mere £750 ($3,750).

Isabella eventually gave way, raising the money by cutting down on her carriage horses and letting her stables. In exchange she received more than usually effulgent praise. Isabella was to continue as an occasional milch cow until she died in July 1924, believing to the last that her protégé had always had her best interest at heart. Fortunately she was spared Sir Philip Hendy's withering comments on her Gaddi when her executors invited him to catalogue her collection.

Hendy dismissed the attribution to Gaddi, calling the picture 'Florentine?' After conceding that the Archangel Gabriel's head and hands and the upper part of the Virgin's head and her left hand retained their original shape, he comments:

> The greater part of the picture is a restoration so thorough
> that it is impossible to define exactly even the original com-

position. A network of lines has been painted over the re-stored surfaces in imitation of cracks. The Virgin's robes are painted over, while the crimson, blue and gold damask behind her are mainly, if not entirely modern work. The gold border of the hangings and of Gabriel's tunic and the haloes all modelled in relief may be an invention of the restorer, since such work is not usually found in Florentine pictures of this period. More clumsy restorations on the Virgin's right shoulder and wrist may be more recent or may be intended to assist the disguise . . .

The catalogue rightly concludes that the picture was 'no doubt constructed from the wreck of a Florentine panel'.

Sir Philip had not made these strictures lightly. Before its publication in 1931 he had sent a copy of the Fenway catalogue to Bernhard, who had replied that, after considerable thought, he agreed that the attribution to Gaddi could not be sustained.

℘ 8 ℘

Fortune Hunters

Joseph and Uncle Henry Duveen had been observing Mary's and Bernhard's operations with increasing concern for some time and had gone so far as to have the Berensons' financial standing and business relationships investigated still further. This time they used the Pinkerton Agency in the United States and Joseph's friend the wily banker and diplomat Edgar, Viscount d'Abernon, in England. If the reports proved satisfactory, the Duveens proposed to offer Bernhard a rather better deal than they knew he enjoyed with Colnaghis.

However, apart from the details of his relationships with Gutkunst, Isabella, Herbert Horne, Richter and Theodore Davis, the reports showed both a closer threat to Duveens' American market and a possible connection to a major European scandal. They also disclosed that Bernhard had asked Gutkunst for a partnership and that Gutkunst had delayed his decision until he saw the results of Bernhard's 1903 trip to America: Gutkunst had become increasingly concerned that Bernhard was breaking their agreement and was in active partnership with other dealers.

Gutkunst's suspicions were justified. While in New York in 1903, Bernhard had signed up with the firm of Eugene Glazener and Company of Fifth Avenue and the rue Scribe in Paris. Glazener had also introduced Bernhard to his French bankers and given him authority to negotiate and purchase on his behalf. Whereupon Bernhard had promptly introduced Glazener to El Greco's 'Adoration of the Shepherds', which he knew was for sale in Europe. The painting had been purchased for $7,500 and, on Bernhard's outwardly disinterested recommendation, sold to the

Metropolitan—for $35,000. Bernhard's share of Glazener's profit had been $8,000

Delighted by Bernhard's seemingly benevolent gesture, the Metropolitan had invited him to meet the trustees with a view to becoming their official adviser and with the further possibility of asking him to succeed the then director of the Museum, General di Cesnola, who was due to retire. Eventually both matters were referred to J. Pierpont Morgan, in his capacity as a trustee of the Metropolitan, who consulted Uncle Henry Duveen. On Uncle Henry's advice, a peremptory stop was put to both schemes. For Duveens had not only been monitoring Berenson's activities for almost eight years, they had also been investigating, on behalf of Pierpont Morgan, one of the most unsavory art touts of the era, a self-styled Austrian baron called Godfrey von Kopp, and there seemed to be a possible connection between Kopp and Berenson.

Berenson had met Kopp at St. Moritz in 1898 and had been totally taken in by his appearance and exquisite manners, coupled with a considerable if superficial knowledge of the fine arts. The 'Baron' explained that he had had to leave his native Austria as a result of a matrimonial scandal—he hinted that he had fallen in love with a member of the Austrian royal house—and was now trying to become an 'amateur' scout for collectors of works of art. He promised to keep Berenson informed should he ever run across anything that might interest him. In turn, Bernhard introduced him to the well-known Italian scholar Dr Lionello Venturi, and for almost four years Kopp was a regular correspondent, dealing largely in art market gossip, advising Berenson on whom he had met and what he had seen. Kopp claimed that he maintained homes in both Paris and Rome and now had an entrée into the highest social circles. The facts were somewhat different.

Gottfried von Kopp, the son of a Lucerne pastrycook, had started life as a hotel pageboy. His youthful good looks and undoubted charm led him into a series of adventures with hotel guests of both sexes, which culminated in a strange partnership with a Paris-based Franco-American picture dealer called Charles Wakefield Mori. At the same time Kopp anglicized his Christian name and appointed himself to an Austrian barony.

Mori was a friend of many of the artists of the period and had been particularly close to Toulouse-Lautrec, who included him in his painting 'Le Moulin Rouge' as the man in the exaggerated top hat.

Mori's contacts and Kopp's charm were a formidable combination. They took a small shop in the rue Grenouille and inserted an advertisement in the Paris edition of the *New York Herald*, saying that 'Fine Pictures by the Great Masters' were available to be purchased. Prospective customers would be told that the pictures were from a private collection, and usually the two managed to elicit which artist the customer desired. A further appointment would then be made in a few days' time to view the painting, when it 'came up from the country'. During the few days, an appropriate work would be manufactured by one of Mori's contacts.

In the period 1899–1902, the main source of these fakes was a young man called Gaston Duchamp-Villon, a former student of Toulouse-Lautrec, who at that time eked out a modest living as a newspaper cartoonist and free-lance engraver. He was also a high-speed producer of Constables, and several of his works found their way into reputable collections. Gaston eventually made his own name as an abstract painter under the name of Jacques Villon and became an acknowledged and well-regarded artist.

One of Mori's relatives worked in the American Embassy in Paris and would advise him when rich American tourists needed a guide. Mori was only too happy to show them Paris and its environs, taking a modest commission from the shops and restaurants to whom he introduced his clients. Occasionally they would also buy one of Gaston's 'Constables' from the distinguished Baron.

Unhappily, Kopp grew too ambitious. On Mori's introduction he sold a version of 'Flatford Mill' to John R. Thompson, who owned a chain of restaurants in Chicago. Thompson explained that he planned to make an eighteenth century-style 'Grand Tour' of Italy, visiting Venice, Rome and Naples. He also made the mistake of confiding his intention of forming a major art collection. Kopp offered to accompany him and his offer was gratefully accepted.

Venice and Naples bored Thompson but he was captivated by the crumbling grandeur of Rome, in particular by the monumental Arch of Constantine. In his dreams he saw it outside his most exclusive restaurant.

The following day Kopp came to Thompson with important news. Kopp had learnt that the Italian government was desperately short of foreign exchange. In these exceptional circumstances the government was prepared to allow Thompson to purchase the Arch for the merest bagatelle of $500,000. The matter, of course, would have to be handled with the utmost secrecy. An excited Thompson agreed. The following day Kopp produced an impressive sheaf of documents which he said was the sale contract. He explained that the government required a deposit of one-fifth of the purchase price, namely $100,000, and that the balance would be payable on delivery of the dismantled monument to Chicago. Mr Thompson happily wrote his cheque and sailed to New York from Genoa with a light heart.

Not surprisingly, the arch never arrived, and when Thompson discovered he had been swindled there was very little he could do about it. The ease of the transaction made Kopp realize that not only Rome but all Italy was his for the selling. His next victim was Charles T. Yerkes, an American railway magnate who had helped finance the underground railway system which had just been installed in London. Yerkes agreed to purchase Trajan's Column for $250,000.

Kopp was then joined by two further partners, both genuine counts, an Austrian called Baltazzi and an Italian, the Count Enrico Bosdari. Between them they gulled J. Pierpont Morgan into paying a substantial deposit on 'the bronze doors of Bologna Cathedral'.*

Both Morgan and Yerkes were customers of Duveens. Rather than seek redress at law, they asked Joe Duveen to make inquiries on their behalf. He, in turn, delegated the job to Edward Fowles, then a young gallery assistant in London, who spoke fluent French. Fowles went to see Charles Wakefield Mori to inquire as to the present whereabouts of his partner, Kopp. Mori, in exchange for a promise of anonymity, told Fowles the complete story and added the latest installment of Kopp's activities.

Berenson had apparently mentioned to Kopp that a small and somewhat pernickety collector called John T. Walters of Baltimore had written to him asking him to buy suitable pictures on his

* This anecdote comes from Edward Fowles' diaries; Bologna Cathedral does not have bronze doors. Perhaps Fowles confused them with the bronze doors and marble surrounds of the Florence Baptistry.

behalf. Walters had laid down such stringent financial limits and was so indecisive that, at the time, Berenson had not thought him worth the trouble.

Kopp had thought otherwise. He had pulled off a remarkable coup and sold Walters the complete collection of a Roman dignitary called Dom Marcello Mazzarenti for a modest $1 million. Allegedly the collection contained eight Raphaels and six Titians plus choice works by Giorgione, the Bellinis and Botticelli and a large assortment of classical statues and marble sarcophagi. Every item had been certified as genuine by Dr Lionello Venturi who, in his capacity as the Italian government's adviser on the export of works of art, had arranged that, in lieu of the export duty demanded, which totalled a further $200,000, the Italian government should accept three of the 'better' pictures. These were a 'St. George' by Giorgione, a portrait of the artist, Bernini, by Philippe de Champaigne, and a self-portrait by Raphael.

If a tenth of the paintings were genuine, then Mr Walters had made a substantial coup. Duveens investigated further. Joe discovered that his father had visited the Mazzarenti Collection in 1889 and had dismissed it as rubbish. His notes, written at the time, said that most of it was *'ghadish'* (Hebrew for new, but in art dealers' vernacular, imitation). Digging a little deeper it was discovered that Dom Marcello was a leading member of Rome's thriving 'gay' community, with an unsavory reputation as a blackmailer and dealer in forged works of art. Finally, Joe cornered Kopp, who conceded that almost half of Mr Walters' $1 million had been split between himself and his associates, including Venturi—and, by implication, Berenson.

The evidence against Berenson was purely Kopp's word, plus an ambiguous confirmation from Venturi that Berenson had 'passed the collection verbally'. In fact, Bernhard had never seen any of the actual pictures, but had examined photographs, shown to him by one of Walters' many 'advisers', and observed that they 'were remarkable'.

Joe Duveen was in a quandary. In his hands he held evidence that would expose the chicanery of the Italian art market and remove many of his rivals from the scene. He relished the idea of a major scandal with himself cast in the role of the arbiter of what was genuine and what was not. Uncle Henry urged a wiser and quieter course of action. He suggested that they privately brief the art critic Robert Langton Douglas, who was an adviser to Pierpont Morgan. Douglas should check their own inquiries and report to Morgan who, in his turn, would tip the word to Walters.

Douglas accepted the assignment. He not only exonerated Berenson in his report but privately warned him of the expected dénouement. In his turn, Berenson wrote to Walters saying that he had heard a rumour that he was considering the Mazzarenti purchase and urging him to take a second opinion. He had seen photographs of the pictures and told Walters his agents were being duped.

A dismayed Walters took Berenson's advice, but, as he had already purchased the collection and had it hanging in Baltimore, he tried, unsuccessfully, to hush the matter up by closing the gallery, ostensibly for redecoration, while the impostors were weeded out. However, he had not reckoned with the newspapers.

Today, no one knows who was responsible for the leak, but the first story was published by A. R. Carter, who later became the influential art critic of the London *Daily Telegraph* and who enjoyed a close relationship with Joe Duveen. (He was given the Duveen cigar collection when Joe gave up smoking and for many years the London branch of Duveens paid his tailor's bills.)

Carter's article sparked a frenzy of what today is called investigative journalism. The luckless Venturi was pilloried mercilessly. It transpired that the Italian government's three masterpieces, taken in lieu of export duty, were worthless, the Bernini portrait being a recent copy of the original in the Louvre.

The only person against whom criminal proceedings were taken was Kopp's partner, the wretched Count Enrico Bosdari, who was fined 100,000 lire. He emigrated to Paris, changed his name to Henri Brémont, and, in due course, became an expert on eighteenth-century drawings and prints. In 1947, financed by Agnews of London, he formed the collection of Irwin Laughlin, then the U.S. Ambassador to Spain. Agnews have always been credited with the outstanding quality of the Laughlin drawings, but the credit is Bosdari's, who bitterly regretted that his earlier Kopp escapade denied him his memorial.

Neither Mori, Kopp nor Berenson was mentioned in Carter's article, which they suspected was probably due to the kindly intervention of Joe Duveen. Over the next three years he gained his reward.

The first to pay was Mori. He called on Joe to say that he had been tipped off that, while in Rome, the American Senator 'Champ' Clark had become enamoured of Antonio Canova's famous marble statue of Pauline, Napoleon's sister, in the Borghese Gallery. He felt that if Duveens could locate a good Canova marble, then Clark would be an easy customer.

Edward Fowles was asked to do the research. He discovered that some time previously the Duke of Marlborough had asked Duveens to sell just such a piece for him and that Joe Duveen had suggested an asking price of £5,000. Fowles told Joe and Mori the result of his researches and later recalled what happened:

> Joe promptly received a lesson from Mori which he never forgot. Mori told him that any alleged masterpiece at £5,000 was not a masterpiece—at least, not in the eyes of an American millionaire. He told Joe to ask at least £20,000 plus a 10% commission for himself [Mori] in exchange for teaching him how to deal with people like Senator Clark. Joe swallowed hard and did as he was told. Clark paid £22,000 on the spot.

The next to pay his debt was Godfrey von Kopp. After the Walters affair he had thought it prudent to avoid Italy for a time; he had spent a year in Germany, visiting the various health spas and wintering in Berlin. In the course of his travels he had met Frau Hainauer, the widow of Germany's legendary collector, Oscar Hainauer.

Hainauer had been one of the most important private bankers in Berlin and the representative of the Paris Rothschilds. He was an astute collector, blessed with an excellent eye for quality. He began to collect seriously in the mid-1870s and bought nothing but the best. His taste ranged over a broad spectrum: tapestries; the finest oriental rugs; sculptures in bronze, marble, and terracotta by the greatest masters of the early Renaissance such as Rosellino and Donatello; the finest early Italian and Flemish paintings, and breath-taking examples of the work of leading medieval and Renaissance jewellers and goldsmiths. He retired in 1892, intending to devote himself to fufilling his dream of owning a perfectly balanced museum of outstanding quality. The Kaiser, anxious that the collection should stay in Germany, authorized Dr Wilhelm von Bode, Director of the Berlin Museum, to prepare a detailed catalogue, in the hope that it would eventually be acquired by the nation. But Hainauer developed cancer of the throat and died in June 1894. On his deathbed he told his wife that if times ever became hard the collection was worth at least $750,000.

The Kaiser now issued an edict that no dealer was to offer for the Hainauer Collection: von Bode then put in a bid of $375,000 on behalf of the Berlin Museum. The price explosion of the early 1900s made the collection infinitely more valuable than even the deathbed sum the owner had named but now his wife was only being offered half. Frau Hainauer stalled. If she did not accept, von Bode warned her, she would incur the imperial displeasure. While she was wondering what to do, Godfrey von Kopp offered her $750,000 and promised to spirit the collection out of Germany and to protect her from the Kaiser's wrath.

She was incredulous, but the increasing anti-Semitism of the Berlin aristocracy and the unsettled political situation of 1905 made her an easy prey. She agreed to give Kopp a chance to prove his worth. He promptly travelled to London and told Joe and Henry Duveen. One look at von Bode's catalogue and the Duveens valued the collection at not less than $5 million. The same day Joe and Kopp set off for Berlin. Happily for them von Bode was abroad.

Frau Hainauer took considerable persuasion. Eventually she agreed to sell for $1 million, payable to an account in Lausanne where she intended to settle. She insisted the collection had to be out of Germany before von Bode returned from his summer vacation. It was crated up and in Paris within three days.

Neither Henry nor Joe had bothered to tell Joel Duveen about the purchase. He was away in Egypt and Henry had other ideas for financing the deal. He told J. Pierpont Morgan that he planned to pay $5 million for the collection and asked to borrow $1 million (the actual purchase price) against a promise of first choice. Morgan agreed. When Joel was eventually told, the collection was in Paris and Pierpont Morgan, P. A. B. Widener and Benjamin Altman had already spent more than $5 million on their selection from the sculptures alone.

Joel could not argue with a clear profit of $4 million plus dozens of fine paintings and several hundred bronzes, gold snuff boxes and pieces of early jewellery. Some idea of the scope of the collection is given by the fact that when Norton Simon purchased the remaining stock of Duveens in 1964 there were over a hundred Hainauer items still unsold. It was an inspired deal, though the ethics of it horrified Joel. It is every art dealer's dream to buy for little and sell for as high a price as possible, but the collection was so well-known that Joel was terrified that the truth would emerge. He eased his conscience by offering to pay for a new wing for the Tate Gallery to house the Turner Collection.

Henry soothed von Bode's discomfort by presenting half a dozen items to the Berlin Museum, but this did not save the unfortunate museum director from an unpleasant interview with the Kaiser, who forbade him to have any dealings with Duveens in future and ordered his Chancellor, von Bülow, to draw up a decree forbidding the export of any works of art from German collections.

A few days later the Kaiser relented, having realized that Germany was a net importer of fine art and that the risk of reciprocal action from other countries would leave Germany's already comparatively sparse museums far behind their international rivals. So complete was his change of heart that he presented Henry Duveen with one of his personal orders of chivalry, which Henry took great pleasure in returning in 1914.

Godfrey von Kopp received a commission of $80,000 for telling Duveen about the Hainauer Collection, which he promptly spent on women and cards. He then went to seek a further fortune in Vienna, where he was quickly exposed and sentenced to seven years' penal servitude. On his release, Joe gave him a further $5,000 and he settled down in Monte Carlo as a concierge. There he died in relative obscurity in 1929, remembered only by his erstwhile partner Mori, who was by now the curator of the Monaco Museum. Mori died in 1954 at the age of ninety, bequeathing his private, if occasionally somewhat doubtful, art collection to the Principality.

Bernhard received a double benefit from the Kopp affair. First, a grateful John T. Walters of Baltimore asked him to become his paid adviser on a retainer of $7,500 a year and, second, Uncle Henry now thought that Duveens should approach Berenson to

ask him to recatalogue the Hainauer Collection: Langton-Douglas'
exoneration of Bernhard had convinced Henry that he was the
best man for the job. Living in New York, Henry was far more
aware than either Joe or Joel of Bernhard's burgeoning reputation
as a scholar. His own clients, particularly Morgan, Altman and
Widener, kept referring to Berenson as the ultimate arbiter as to
who painted what, and there were doubts about certain pictures
in the Hainauer Collection.

Several art connoisseurs, including Berenson, had recently chal-
lenged the great Dr Wilhelm von Bode's scholarship. Von Bode
could not very well be asked to re-appraise them himself since
Duveens had just spirited the whole collection from under his nose
and gained him a wigging from the Kaiser as a result. Moreover,
having catalogued the pictures once himself, he was understandably not keen to revise his own attributions.

Joel and Joseph disagreed, however, with Henry's choice of
Berenson to do the job. In rare harmony, father and son wrote to
Henry saying that 'Berenson is not accepted in the best circles, and
according to Dowdswell, he is apt to be greedy'. They suggested
Dowdswell for the task.

Walter Dowdswell was a tall Bohemian figure who, until recently, had been a partner in the old-established London firm of
Dowdswell and Dowdswell. But he had had a financial disagree-
ment with his partner—a cousin—and an unfortunate brush with
the Jockey Club over the matter of his racing debts. At the time
that Joel and Joseph wrote he was acting as a scout and adviser
to the London branch of Duveens and frequently represented them
at provincial auctions. He was also a considerable authority on
both Dutch and Italian pictures and had on several occasions worked
in partnership with Bernhard. Together they had sold Isabella
Gardner her stupendous portrait of Queen Mary of England, by
Mor, which Dowdswell had discovered at Costessy Hall in Norfolk, the seat of Lord Stafford-Jerningham.

Dowdswell did not feel that his scholarship was up to the task
of re-cataloguing the Hainauer Collection, so he suggested to Duveen that he should write to von Bode and ask him if he had any
suggestions to make as to whom, among the numerous scholars
of his acquaintance, he would recommend for the job.

Von Bode replied saying that in his opinion the best scholar in

Europe was probably Robert Langton Douglas, closely followed by the German art historians Gronau and Friedländer. Charitably, he gave Bernhard a mention:

> His eye is unsurpassed when it comes to line. Drawings are his metier, and he should stick to them, as he has neither a sensibility for colour nor an understanding of paint. However, his fingers are daily on the pulse of modern scholarship, but I fear he would not be a natural collaborator.

Von Bode further justified his choice of Langton Douglas by pointing out that he had recently been retained by J. Pierpont Morgan to form a collection of the finest Sienese paintings and that he had also convincingly bested Bernhard in a dramatic academic argument as to which of them had discovered the painter Stefeno di Giovanni, called Sassetta.

At that time—1906—Bernhard was adamant that it had been he and no one else who had identified Sassetta as one of the earliest and most important of the Renaissance Sienese masters. He based his claim on an article he had written for the *Burlington* magazine in September 1903, called 'A Sienese painter of the Franciscan Legend'. Douglas had had an article in the May issue of the same magazine called 'A Forgotten Painter', but Bernhard had both publicly and privately put it about that Douglas was nothing more than an artistic gadfly whom he had been foolish enough to befriend. In return, Douglas had betrayed Bernhard's trust and taken his scholarship for his own.

The controversy had raged in the learned periodicals for almost two years when Douglas, stung into a public reply, pointed out that he had first mentioned Sassetta in his book *Fra Angelico* in 1900 (George Bell, London), and again in considerable detail in his book *A History of Siena* published by John Murray in 1902. Both books had been researched and written in the late 1890s, long before he had ever met Berenson. Finally, Douglas nailed his opponent to the floor by proving that Bernhard had not seen fit to include Sassetta in his first lists of Central Italian painters, and had later dismissed him as a second-rate mannerist.

When Douglas volunteered for the army in 1914, he wrote a private letter to his children which was only to be opened in the event of his death. The views expressed in this letter make clear the deep differences in opinion and attitude between Douglas and Berenson. In the letter, Douglas first explained his background and education—he had read theology at Oxford and been ordained in 1892—and then wrote that he had decided that the pastoral life was not for him. He had resigned his living and for eight years tramped Italy, earning his keep as an independent art historian and critic. Though his monograph *Fra Angelico* and his *History of Siena* had been best-sellers, he had found that he could not make ends meet: his only recourse had been to become a dealer:

> It had been suggested to me [by Otto Gutkunst] that I might add to my income, privately, by dealing in pictures, as well as by helping other tradesmen to sell their wares, or that I might take a permanent post as the privy adviser to some firm of art dealers [Agnews]. But this furtive kind of picture jobbing did not seem to me to be an honest occupation for an art historian. I thought then, and I still think, that it is quite legitimate for a student engaged in dealing to write on his own special subject, or to give lectures on it, if by doing so, he can add something to the sum of human knowledge, provided that all the world knows that he is a dealer. But I held then, and I still hold, that for an art critic or historian to pose as an impartial judge, when he is, in reality, a paid advocate, is a thoroughly dishonest practice. I decided that, if I had to engage in trade, I would openly declare myself to be a tradesman.
>
> I announced this fact in the *Morning Post* and numerous art periodicals, and in order to learn my job, I was for a short time a salesman in New Bond Street [with Colnaghis]. In the spring of 1904 I started business on my own account.

In terms of experience and closeness to Italian art, Douglas was an almost exact contemporary of Bernhard. As a dealer, however, he was primarily interested in pictures of museum quality and his first independent assignment had been to become the British buying agent for von Bode and the Kaiser Friedrich Museum in Berlin. His next triumph had been to be asked to catalogue the exhibition of Sienese art at the Burlington Fine Arts Club in 1904. J. Pierpont Morgan had been impressed and retained him to form a small collection of Sienese pictures; it proved outstanding.

Douglas was travelling in Italy when Dowdswell approached him on Duveens' behalf about recataloguing the Hainauer Collection. Douglas refused the offer, explaining that there were certain items in the Hainauer Collection in which he believed Morgan to be interested, and he felt that there might well be a conflict of interest. Neither he nor Dowdswell knew at the time that Morgan had financed the Hainauer deal for Duveens.

However, to Dowdswell's astonishment, Douglas remarked, 'Why don't you ask Berenson. I know he needs the money'. There was a brief interchange of cables between Siena, London and New York; then, at Henry's insistence, Dowdswell was authorized to travel to Berenson's house, I Tatti, and 'take soundings'.

Dowdswell chose an oblique approach. He said that he had been asked to suggest an expert because of the embarrassment of using von Bode; that he had discussed the matter with J. Pierpont Morgan in London and that the idea of using Berenson came from Morgan. This appealed to Bernhard immensely. The thought of the one customer who could possibly replace Isabella Gardner asking him to take up the cultural cudgel against von Bode was irresistible. He agreed to come to London and give a verbal opinion on the paintings. When a picture was sold to a private collector, he would send the purchaser a written certificate. He asked for a fee of 5 per cent on the sale prices of the paintings concerned, but settled—on Dowdswell's advice—for an outright payment of $10,000 plus his expenses.

And so, at long last, Bernhard Berenson had come, by the long and circuitous route of Kopp, Walters, J. Pierpont Morgan, Dowdswell, Langton Douglas and the Hainauer Collection, to suggest attributions for the House of Duveen.

✧ 9 ✧

The Kann Collections

Bernhard spent three afternoons in London examining the Hainauer Collection for the House of Duveen. On the whole he could not fault von Bode's scholarship but Edward Fowles, who was present at the time, was convinced that consciously he was trying to do just that. 'Jealousy motivated him', wrote Fowles. In several cases he re-attributed pictures to minor artists and they were sold for a fraction of their true value. Twenty years later he was to admit his mistakes, but by then it was too late for the firm.

Fowles particularly recalled Francesco Pesellino's haunting 'Madonna and Child with a Goldfinch', which Bernhard assigned to a minor follower, Pseudo Pier Francesco Fiorentino. It was sold for a pittance to a collector called Robert Hoe, and after his death it was acquired by Harold Pratt. In 1932, when Bernhard reluctantly conceded that he had been wrong, Pratt sold it for a substantial profit to the Museum of Art at Toledo, Ohio, where it hangs today.

At the time Duveens were blithely ignorant of the difference between one Italian painter and another. They knew that the pecking order of prices started with Leonardo and Michelangelo and descended through Giorgione, Titian and Bellini to Raphael and Botticelli. Anyone after that was, as far as they were concerned, a nonentity, but pictures had to have a name put to them and the better the name the higher the price they could sell it for, so long as they could pronounce it.

Fowles recorded a splendid example of this trait. Bernhard had announced that the finest picture in the collection was 'Profile of a Lady' by Antonio Pollaiuolo (currently attributed by the Gardner Museum to Antonio's younger brother, Piero). On hearing of its importance, Joseph suggested that Henry sell it to Benjamin Alt-man, but Henry demurred. Fowles recorded Henry's explanation: 'I realize it is a rare, and great picture, but I cannot pronounce the name. In the presence of a client I would stutter and look foolish. Don't insist. Let B.B. sell it to Mrs Jack Gardner'.

Bernhard had requested that his visits to the Hainauer Collection remain a secret, but Joseph discreetly let most of fashionable London know. In this he was assisted by several friends, particularly Aline Sassoon, the daughter of Baron Gustave de Rothschild, with whom Bernhard quickly became infatuated. By degrees, Aline Sassoon persuaded Bernhard to throw in his lot with the Duveens, and by degrees he accepted her idea. She was rarely far from him. Mary spent the spring of 1906 in London, while Bernhard and Aline toured northern Italy together. Afterwards she persuaded him to attend a meeting with Henry and Joseph Duveen in London. The others present were Nathan Wildenstein, Edward Fowles, and Henry's son, Godfrey.

The profit from buying the Hainauer Collection had made Henry and Joe believe that they were financially independent of Joel, who at that time was in Monte Carlo. They had pressed him to retire—he was sixty-three—but he had refused. They planned, therefore, to break the partnership. Henry and Joe would form a new company. Henry would operate from New York and Joe would leave London and open a gallery in Paris. He had already purchased a lease on a site in the Place Vendôme and building work had started. It was to open in the spring of the following year. The new firm would deal only in the finest antiques and works of art. In the initial stages, as far as works of art were concerned, they would be advised by Nathan Wildenstein.

These facts were briefly summarized at the meeting with Bern-hard, though Fowles remembers that Bernhard asked pointedly what would happen if Joel refused to dissolve the partnership, for Joel, who was about to be knighted for his gifts to the Tate Gallery, was the lynchpin on which the firm depended—at least in Europe. Henry, who had never lost his Dutch accent, replied, 'Joel hasn't got de goods. De customers go ver de best goods are'. Nathan Wildenstein had got the goods.

Two of the finest collections in France belonged to the Kann brothers, Rodolphe and Maurice. Rodolphe owned no fewer than eleven Rembrandts, over a hundred Dutch and Flemish minor masters, and a small but breath-taking group of Italian pictures and sculptures. His bronzes, tapestries and old master drawings were all of museum quality, while his bibelots—small ivories and jewelled boxes—were famed for their excellence. The brothers owned adjoining mansions in the Avenue d'Iena and had knocked down the dividing wall between two of the upper storeys to form one enormous gallery. They had originally planned to have a combined museum, but since they were both avid collectors, they had fallen out over who should own some of the finest pictures and had become bitter rivals in the salerooms. In their old age they were no longer on speaking terms; when Rodolphe died in 1905 without making a will there was considerable dispute over the ownership of certain of the finer pieces.

Under French law, Rodolphe's son Edouard was the natural heir, but the estate could not be settled to the satisfaction of the French courts until an accommodation had been reached between Rodolphe's executors and the increasingly infirm Maurice. Into this vacuum stepped the enterprising Nathan Wildenstein.

Nathan shared a love of horseracing with young Edouard Kann, who respected his judgement on the merits of a promising two-year-old filly as unreservedly as he did his judgement of his father's and uncle's collections. Nathan proposed the following compromise.

Professor Wilhelm von Bode should be commissioned to catalogue both collections. He should have access to both men's archives and examine each work of art. In this way he would settle not only any questions of authenticity, but also the matter of ownership. Von Bode's catalogue would then be published as a fitting memorial to the two brothers.

Nathan's idea was accepted. But who was to pay von Bode and pay for the publication of the catalogue? Eventually it was agreed that Nathan would 'underwrite' these costs in exchange for an exclusive option to purchase any item from the Kann Collections should they one day be offered for sale.

Nathan used the word 'underwrite' deliberately for it meant that he would be responsible for seeing that the costs were met, not that he himself had to foot the bill. He now approached Henry Duveen and persuaded him to pay both von Bode's fees and the publication costs in exchange for a share in his, Wildenstein's, option to purchase.

Von Bode produced an erudite catalogue in four volumes. While he was doing this, Maurice Kann died and Edouard was named as his uncle's heir. Nathan Wildenstein then persuaded Edouard to break up both Maurice's and Rodolphe's collections.

The plan was that Henry and Joseph Duveen, in partnership with Nathan Wildenstein, would secretly purchase both the collections from Edouard; J. Pierpont Morgan would produce the initial down payment in return for first pick of the collections. Bernhard would vet the Italian items for the Duveen-Wildenstein partnership and weed out any misattributions. This was to be paid for on a fee basis, but Bernhard was also invited to write to his own modest circle of collectors and museum officials and hint that he could perhaps get them a private view or even an opportunity to purchase before the collections came on to the open market. Any sales that materialized from his own customers would earn Berenson a commission of 5 per cent.

Fowles says that Bernhard was extremely surprised at how much Henry Duveen knew about his dealing activities and his relationships with other dealers. Bernhard was also startled to discover how few Italian items were there in the Kann Collections, though these few were of outstanding quality. It was also Fowles' opinion that what prompted Bernhard to agree to the proposal was the chance of meeting new customers. 'It was like letting a child loose in a sweetshop', recalled Fowles. 'The temptation to him was irresistible'.

Bernhard had not been told how much the Kann Collections had cost nor how the purchase was to be financed. He learned these details from an 'enemy friend', the scholar Roger Fry, who had just returned from an Italian trip with J. Pierpont Morgan and Langton Douglas. To Bernhard's amazement, Fry knew that Joseph and Henry Duveen were planning a coup against Joel and volunteered the information that Morgan had told him that he had promised to lend $2 million (half the Kann purchase price) to the Wildenstein syndicate. Fry added, doubtless with some pleasure, that he and Langton Douglas were to have first pick of the collection on Morgan's behalf.

Roger Fry, unaware of Bernhard's new standing with the Duveens, also let slip that Nathan Wildenstein had secretly kept old Joel Duveen fully informed of all the secret plans because he, Nathan, hoped eventually to complete the deal with Joel instead of Henry and Joseph. Nathan's motives were simple. Joel was becoming increasingly infirm and Nathan wished to have control. Nathan did not relish the idea of Joseph opening a gallery in Paris.

Bernhard saw his chance of a slice of the action evaporating, and endeavoured to preserve his position. He wrote privately to Joel, giving him an accurate account of what he had been told at the meeting with Henry, Joseph and Nathan, and declaring that he would be delighted to assist 'Duveen Brothers' along the lines suggested, and stating that certain of his own clients would be interested in several of the pictures. In particular he mentioned Isabella Gardner, the Metropolitan Museum and the American millionairess Arabella Huntington and her son, Archer, whom he had met only very briefly a dozen years previously and so hardly knew; he did not know that Henry and Joseph were already angling for their patronage.

Bernhard's letter provided Joel with just the spur he needed. He called a family meeting at the Hermitage Hotel in Monte Carlo. He threatened to preempt his brother's and his son's secret plans to outflank him and said that there was no question of the partnership being dissolved. If they attempted to do this, he was prepared to vote his eldest son Joseph out of any executive role in the company and replace him with his younger sons, Charles and Ernest, who would then join the board as managing directors. Joel then made it quite clear to Henry that when he, Joel, retired or died, his two younger sons would have voting control.

The alternative, he said, was for him to place the firm into voluntary liquidation. Neither he nor Rosetta, his wife, had drawn their full entitlement to salary or dividends for some years. If they called them in, many of the firm's most valuable assets would have to be sold. He made it plain that they would be purchased by a new company he had already formed with his second son, called Charles Duveen Ltd.

Finally, he played his master stroke. He announced that he had changed his name by deed poll from Joel Joseph Duveen to Joseph Joel, and henceforth he would be known by and would trade in that name. He also ordered that if, or while, his son Joe remained in, or associated with, the firm, he would be known as Joe Duveen and would have to trade as Duveen Brothers.

He now informed his family that he had been confidentially advised that he was shortly to receive the honour of a knighthood and that the King had graciously agreed to invest him as Sir *Joseph* Duveen.

In the face of such implacable opposition, Henry and Joe capitulated. They agreed that Joel should remain the head of the firm, and for the time being dropped all plans to set up on their own. They knew something which Joel did not—that he was terminally ill with Bright's Disease. They therefore meekly initialled the draft plan that Joel put before them and agreed to certain stipulations he said he would write into his will.

Briefly, Joel was to remain as the head of the firm until he either retired of his own accord or died. On his death he was to leave his shareholding to Rosetta, his wife, and she in turn would leave it to be split equally amongst all the children. The value of his shareholding was to be agreed as of 30 December 1907, and 10 per cent interest was to be paid on it, before any profit was calculated, to himself and in due course to his widow.

In exchange, the children were to agree never to sell their shares to anyone outside the family; if they did wish to sell, they had to offer every member of the family an equal chance to buy. He wished each of the sons to be appointed a director of the company and after his death he trusted that it would still operate as Duveen Brothers. Joe was to be the director in charge of the Paris operation, with Ernest, then aged eighteen, as his deputy. Louis, Charles and John would manage the London house while Benjamin, Edward and 20-year-old Henry would operate as attachés, taking it in turn to help Uncle Henry and his son, Godfrey, in America.

Charles and John demurred. They said they wanted a quiet life, and asked for their inheritance in advance to set up on their own. With his father's permission, Joe purchased their interest from them in return for an annual income for life. Charles then infuriated his elder brother by announcing he was going to trade in London as an art dealer, using the new company Charles Duveen Ltd. This was resolved by Joe agreeing to pay him $7,500 a year never to use the name Duveen and allowing him to choose $120,000 worth of stock, which was to be debited to Joe's account. Charles traded for some years as Charles of Bond Street.

Edward and the young Henry also opted out of any executive role. They preferred to draw their honorarium but confine themselves to assisting their father with his extensive property interests.

Once these matters had been agreed, Joel or Joseph, as he now called himself, announced that he would travel to Paris to inspect the Kann Collections personally. He declined to let anyone accompany him except John, his third son, who had opted out of the firm, and his favourite nephew, James Hangjas Duveen (his sister Betsy's son).

Joel was despondent about the future, remarking that his eldest son, Joe, would sooner or later drive all the other members of the family out of the firm as he could not bear to play second fiddle to anyone, hated having his taste questioned, his actions impugned, or his finances supervised.

The quite extraordinary attempts made by young Joe and Uncle Henry to outwit Joel were noted in an account written by James Hangjas Duveen of their visit to Paris to inspect the Kann Collections.* On one occasion, a maid was discovered sifting through the wastepaper baskets at the hotel for their notes, and she admitted that Joe had paid her to advise him of everything she could find or overhear.

They need not have worried for Joel was immensely impressed with what he saw in the Kann mansion. He calculated that the furniture and the Rembrandts alone would more than cover the purchase price, leaving several hundred other paintings and works of art as profit. He promptly renegotiated the deal.

The final purchase price was $4.2 million, which included the legal expenses of all the parties involved and the numerous commissions promised by Nathan Wildenstein to the various intermediaries who had persuaded Edouard Kann to sell—and advised him that the price was a fair one. This time there was no fear that the details of the transaction would leak out. The Kann Collections had never been open to the public, there was no vengeful von Bode or Kaiser to cry 'swindle' and, most important of all, the Kann family shared the French penchant for obsessive secrecy where their personal finances and tax obligations were concerned.

* J. Hangjas Duveen, unpublished manuscript in Edward Fowles archives.

The $4.2 million was payable in two installments: a down payment of $2 million was to be made on 1 August 1907 (this was to come from J. Pierpont Morgan), and the balance was to be paid within two years. During this time nothing could be removed from the house until it had been paid for. Duveens would have the right to have their sales staff living on the premises, and had to assume responsibility for the maintenance and insurance of the collections. Effectively this gave them a palatial and rent-free Paris showroom, with two years to sell those items that Morgan did not want. In addition, Nathan Wildenstein was bought out of the deal. He was paid $400,000 plus the promise of 5 per cent commission on items sold to customers he introduced.

Morgan spent his advance on Domenico Ghirlandaio's portrait of Giovanna Tornabuoni, two fine wings of a triptych by Hans Memling and a couple of dozen Dutch and Flemish pictures. A series of purchases by leading collectors and impetuous millionaires covered the balance of the purchase price within six weeks. Benjamin Altman took four Rembrandts, including the portrait of the artist's son Titus, for $500,000, while similar sums were spent by Philip Lehman, Calouste Gulbenkian, the Baroness James de Rothschild and a syndicate of dealers led by Kleinberger of New York. Wildenstein took his $400,000 in paintings and bronzes at mutually agreed prices.

For an old and—though Joel was still unaware of the fact—mortally sick man, it was a superb achievement. It brought a temporary respite to the bitter family squabbles and laid the foundation for the firm to become internationally famous as purveyors of the finest works of art. In October 1907, Joel retired to Hyères in the south of France where shortly afterwards, probably worn out by his exertions in Paris, he suffered a severe relapse. He lingered on for a year, just managing to make the trip to Buckingham Palace in June 1908 to receive his knighthood.

King Edward VII, seeing him supported by his nurses, excused him from having to kneel, and dubbed him, according to his wish, Sir *Joseph* Duveen. He died at Hyères on 9 November 1908.

It is unlikely that Henry Duveen ever learned that Bernhard had written to his brother, for he continued to press him to write to his private customers and persuade them to buy from either the Hainauer or the Kann collections. Isabella received a characteristically effusive invitation from Berenson to buy the Pollaiuolo, which Henry could not pronounce, and a couple of others which Bernhard had selected for her, a Castagno and a Benozzo Gozzoli. He added that Duveens were willing to give her indefinite credit. Isabella bought the Pollaiuolo for $60,000, delivered to Boston.

Berenson's salesmanship impressed Henry, who remarked to Joe in Fowles' presence, 'One BB letter is worth a month's pandering to a client. It is a wonderful gift'.

To which Joe replied rather sourly, 'He could write the book of Genesis if he tried, but that doesn't mean he believes a word of it'.

Joe, unlike Henry, knew perfectly well that Bernhard had written to his father, but allowed his uncle to believe that it was only Nathan Wildenstein who had betrayed their plans. Joe's suspicions about the source of his father's information were confirmed when, after the satisfactory conclusion of the Kann purchase, his father suggested that a likely client could well be Mrs Arabella Huntington, adding that Bernhard had advised him that he knew her well. This was good news to Joe, for Uncle Henry had been fishing for that lady's custom for several years, ever since her first husband, Henry's first customer, Collis Huntington, had died. During June 1907 Arabella was staying in Paris, largely at Henry's suggestion, but to his chagrin she had decided to patronize Duveens' greatest rival, the dealer Jacques Seligman. Bernhard was given the job of bringing the errant lady into the fold. It was a formidable assignment, for she was a formidable personage.

≫ 10 ≪

Arabella Huntington

Arabella Duvan Yarrington was probably born about 1848, but neither the date nor the place can be confirmed for she took considerable trouble to hide her antecedents. In her early life, before the Civil War, she claimed to come from Alabama, but when, in September 1868, she married a septuagenarian New York banker called John A. Wortham, she announced herself as a resident of Virginia, and gave her age as seventeen. This was a relatively minor deception, however, for she also forbore to mention to her husband, who was to die three months later, the fact that she was pregnant.

The father was an eighteen-stone tycoon called Collis P. Huntington, one of the more notorious American railroad entrepreneurs, who has justifiably been described as 'scrupulously dishonest'. He was married, but met Arabella in Washington shortly after the end of the Civil War; within days of the meeting she became his mistress. He found her somewhere to live and paid her to act as an attractive and, as it turned out, extremely efficient lobbyist for his railroad interests. Arabella's parties were equally popular with the East Coast financiers and the senators and congressmen from the extreme west, who, far from home, were only too ready to listen to all the reasons why the railroad and tramcar companies of Collis and his three partners, Charles Crocker, Mark Hopkins and Leland Stanford, should be given government permission to drive their railroads where they wished. The fact that her guests were also given the opportunity to subscribe for shares in Collis' numerous joint stock companies may have had something to do with her popularity.

Three months after her husband's death, Arabella gave birth to a son, whom she christened Archer, and promptly moved to New York where Collis leased her a house on Lexington Avenue. From this headquarters she began to deal in land and property, almost certainly on Collis' behalf. Some idea of her success, and of the people with whom she dealt, may be gauged from a deal she made in 1877. She purchased a large and ugly house at No. 4 West 54th Street, New York, plus the vacant plots of land on either side, for a total of $331,500. She refurnished the house, which she then used for her lobbying activities, until she sold the entire property, lock, stock and barrel, to J. D. Rockefeller and William Vanderbilt for a net profit over the whole transaction of $311,000.

Arabella was a striking woman. She was remarkably tall, long-legged, wasp-waisted and full-breasted, with an abundance of dark auburn hair, parted in the middle, swept back and pinned by day, but dramatically piled high for the evening. As a result of an accident while cycling, she was also so short-sighted as to be almost blind unless she was wearing spectacles. With her glasses on she seemed the ambitious and hard-headed financier she really was. Without her glasses, her eyes appeared as totally trusting and devoted as a spaniel's; many men were to be taken in by this look.

In 1883 Collis Huntington's wife died, and he lost little time in marrying Arabella, shortly afterwards formally adopting the boy Archer. By now Collis was one of the richest and most powerful men in the United States and Arabella began to enjoy herself. Within two years she had tired of two New York mansions and persuaded Collis to build her a third, a vast Romanesque pile on the corner of Fifth Avenue and 57th Street, on the site now oc-cupied by Tiffany. It was Romanesque inside as well as outside, floored in coloured marbles, with pillars and porticos capped by gilded entablatures. There were three extravagantly painted ceil-ings and thirty-one vast murals which, to Uncle Henry Duveen's chagrin, left him little room to supply any pictures.

Arabella chose the furniture, which Uncle Henry provided; it was almost entirely reproduction French in the styles of Louis XV and XVI, made by Carlhian and Beaumetz in Paris and shipped across to New York. Collis had the final say as regards the murals and the few pictures he did buy.

Bernhard had been introduced to Collis and Arabella by Stan-ford White. In 1894 Bernhard had sold Collis a large Italian narrative painting of a group of cardinals for $25,000. Collis did not buy it for aesthetic reasons but because the cardinals reminded him of his partners—Crocker, Stanford and Hopkins—whom he believed left most of the work to him. He described the picture to a friend:

> There are seven figures in it—three cardinals of the different orders of their religion. There is an old missionary that has just returned [Collis identified himself with the missionary]; he is showing his scars, where his hands are cut all over; he is telling a story to these cardinals who are dressed in luxury. One of them is playing with a dog [an allusion to Stanford]; one is asleep [Charles Crocker]; there is only one [Mark Hopkins] looking at him—looking at him with that kind of expression saying what a fool you are, that you should go out and suffer for the human race when we have such a good time at home.

Collis Huntington died in August 1900. Arabella—though she wore black for the rest of her life as became a respectable widow—suddenly discovered the truth of Mark Antony's words on the death of Caesar: 'The evil that men do lives after them . . '. Collis had been so feared, so hated and despised, among the social class with whom Arabella felt her wealth entitled her to mingle, that she found herself one of the wealthiest women in the country, if not the world, and yet a social outcast. In 1907, after several expensive and disastrous attempts to break into society in New York and San Francisco, she sailed to Europe with her son and began the first of a series of long summers in Paris.

On this first trip she stayed, at Henry Duveen's suggestion, at the Hotel Bristol, reserving the suite that had been specially furnished for King Edward VII when he was Prince of Wales.

The Duveens were among the few people who did not ostracize Arabella: they quite understood that she wished to acquire social cachet, hitherto denied her, by outdoing the Morgans, the Altmans and the Wideners. The Duveens' attentions were not altruistic, but nevertheless she was grateful for their courtesy. Though she did not become a major customer at that time, she relied upon them for guidance in matters of taste: the provision of the right kind of table silver or dinner service, or even such minor matters as obtaining tickets for the opera or theatre. One reason why she did not become a major customer was that her late husband had very carefully tied up her money. Although she was unbelievably wealthy, she only held a life interest in the capital, which was administered by her trustee, her husband's nephew Henry E. Huntington, who was two years older than she. Henry Huntington had known and admired Arabella since she had first fascinated his uncle. In 1906 he divorced his wife and began an extraordinary collecting saga with his aunt by marriage, whom he was to marry in 1913. Henry's archives are preserved at the Huntington Art Collection at Pasadena, California. From late in 1906 there are sheafs of letters and telegrams from Arabella telling what she had purchased, what she thought he should purchase, and what she had chosen and wished him to pay for.

Arabella was the inspiration behind what is today called the Huntington Collection, which, with the exception of the English drawings and watercolours and the world-famous library, was eventually to be supplied almost entirely by Duveens. But not at first. In the early stages Arabella avoided Duveens because she believed that they would give their established clients first refusal of the finest things they had for sale. During that first Parisian summer of 1907, she therefore confined her custom to the dealer Jacques Seligman.

The rivalry between Duveens and Seligman stretched back to 1901 when Seligman had planned to buy a magnificent Gothic gold thread tapestry called 'The Adoration of God the Father'. Formerly part of a series belonging to the Dukes of Burgundy, the tapestry had descended through Charles the Bold and Mary of Burgundy to the Spanish royal house of Hapsburg. Looted by a French officer during the Peninsular War, it had ended up hanging in the Château Agglades near Marseilles, owned by the Marquis d'Esternoulles, who now wished to sell.

Seligman learned that Duveens were interested and wrote to Joel offering to buy it in partnership as he had an entrée to the Marquis' household. Seligman thought $50,000 would be a fair price, but was not aware that Joel Duveen was away on his cure and that Lord Esher had written to Duveens on behalf of Edward VII, who had just succeeded to the throne, saying that the King had expressed a wish that the tapestry should be borrowed from the Marquis for his Coronation, which was to be held in a few weeks' time. When Henry Duveen learned of Esher's letter, he conceived the brilliant idea of buying the tapestry and then selling it to J. Pierpont Morgan, who would then have the privilege of lending it to the King. Morgan agreed that if the tapestry could be bought, he would pay $500,000 for it. During the negotiations with the Marquis, which were conducted by Joe and his brother Louis, Duveens telegraphed Seligman that the final cost would be $78,000. Was he prepared to continue with the partnership? Seligman, unaware of the arrangement with Morgan, replied that if this sum excluded 'commissions' to be paid to the intermediaries, then 'the purchase would be folly'. Duveens then went ahead and bought it on their own account.

The tapestry arrived in London on 27 February 1902, and Seligman met Joe on 4 March. Joe informed him that there were three further commissions to be paid, each of them of 10 per cent, which brought the total purchase price up to $105,000. Seligman dropped out, writing the same day to Joe, 'I am in business for profit, not for fun'.

The tapestry was promptly sold to Morgan for $500,000, but the Coronation was postponed as King Edward developed appendicitis. The deal remained a secret. Some months later, when the Coronation did take place, Morgan's purchase and loan were widely publicized, as was the price he paid.

In the meantime, Seligmans had made their own inquiries. They found that Duveens had paid the Marquis $60,000, that travelling expenses, insurance and shipping costs had amounted to $1,800, and that there had been only one commission, of $4,000, to a lady friend of the Marquis' eldest son; the total was thus $65,000, as opposed to the $105,000 Joe had told them. They launched an action in the High Court claiming fraud, deception and damages. In the preliminary proceedings they demanded that the tapestry be handed over to the court as an exhibit. This would have been a grave embarrassment as it was already in Westminster Abbey. Joel Duveen, fearful of losing Morgan as a client and incurring the royal displeasure, promptly settled out of court for $210,000 plus Seligman's costs. This settlement remained a secret, but the two firms never did business together again.*

* Duveens remained on excellent terms with Jacques Seligman's brother, who traded as Armand Seligman.

Arabella Huntington knew nothing of the tapestry saga and so did not know of the bad blood between Seligman and Duveens. She now rubbed salt into Joe's wounds by buying from Seligman a suite of tapestry chairs that Collis had sent back to Uncle Henry and which Henry had then sold at a knock-down trade price to his rival Seligman before the tapestry case. Joe knew that if he tried to poach Arabella, Seligman could respond by publishing the terms of the tapestry settlement, which would probably alienate Pierpont Morgan as well as many of his other customers. Joe needed a different stratagem to infiltrate the enemy camp. By a fortunate coincidence, Arabella provided her own Trojan horse.

Edward Fowles noticed that her frequent escort at the opera and other social functions was none other than the swindler Godfrey von Kopp's erstwhile partner, the Count Baltazzi. The Count, who was a genuine aristocrat, had been banished from the Austro-Hungarian empire because of his involvement in the sensational suicide of the Austrian Crown Prince Rudolf, son of the Emperor Franz Joseph. Baltazzi was the uncle of the Baroness Mary de Vetsera, the Crown Prince's eighteen-year-old mistress, whom he had shot before killing himself at a hunting lodge at Mayerling in 1888.

The 'Mayerling Tragedy' had been a sensation at the time, and though it had occurred twenty years earlier it remained a favourite topic of conversation with those old enough to remember. The circumstances of the tragedy, which were still a mystery, had provided Baltazzi with a ready meal ticket ever since.

It will be remembered that it was Baltazzi who had lent credibility to von Kopp's aristocratic posings, but hardly anyone knew of his connection with the swindling of Morgan and J. T. Walters of Baltimore. Joe Duveen decided to refresh the Count's memory. Joe was himself unacquainted with the Count, but happily he was well-known to Bernhard, who made it a point of honour to know as many titled people as possible. On Joe's instructions, Fowles briefed Bernhard about Baltazzi's guilty secret during the morning of 30 June 1908.

Bernhard was to invite Baltazzi to bring a small party of his friends to a private view of the Kann mansions. Baltazzi, if he wished to avoid exposure, was to stress to his guests that such invitations were at a premium, and that it was only due to his friendship with the great connoisseur that he had been able to procure such a favour. His party was to include Mrs Huntington and, should she be tempted to purchase, then both of them could be assured that Duveens would be more than generous.

Joe had decided that Arabella, still in her widow's weeds, would probably settle for some of the duller religious paintings that remained in the house. He was delighted when she chose Rembrandt's 'Aristotle Contemplating the Bust of Homer', together with furniture and other items totalling $2.5 million. Baltazzi received $50,000 for his trouble and Arabella deserted Seligman in favour of Duveens for the remainder of her collecting life. During the period 1908–27 Henry and Arabella Huntington individually and jointly spent over $21 million with Duveen Brothers.

Bernhard's reward was the offer of a contract. Duveens promised never to touch an Italian picture without his advice and offered to give him 10 per cent of the profit on any Italian items they sold. Mary noted in her diary that they would have a most prosperous future.

❧ 11 ❧

Affluence

The offer of the Duveen contract was extremely welcome to Bernhard. Mary's two daughters by her first marriage had left school and she planned to send them to university in the United States. Apart from their education, they were increasingly expensive to maintain as they were as cheerfully extravagant as their mother. Bernhard grudged Mary's open-handedness, for he had his own plans for the future. His first priority was to regularize their housing problems.

Since their marriage in 1900 they had rented a comfortable villa near Florence called I Tatti; the original owner was Lord Temple Leader, who owned the estate in which the house was situated. His Lordship had died in 1905, and his heir, Lord Westbury, had indicated that he would not renew the lease when it expired at Christmas 1907. Bernhard believed Westbury was short of money, as he had recently had some disastrous losses at Monte Carlo, so he offered him £5,000 for the entire estate, including the I Tatti villa. Westbury accepted.

In addition to their villa, they then found themselves the owners of two small farms with their attendant cottages and buildings, a smaller villa, a private chapel, and some fifty acres of olives, vineyards and cypress groves. They had financed the purchase from their dealing profits and by borrowing from their neighbour, the retired American banker, Henry W. Cannon. Duveens' fee for vetting the Kann Collections almost paid this off, but Bernhard and Mary had grandiose plans and Duveens' offer of a contract would now make these possible.

It is very probable that if the Duveen connection had not materialized during 1907 the Berensons would have returned to America for good. Bernhard was forty-one, Mary a year older, and after seven years of marriage they still had no settled home or regular income. During the negotiations for I Tatti, they had more than once considered this option, and they had definitely planned to put their possessions into store and spend at least six months in New York and Boston if the purchase fell through. Now that they were landowners on a not inconsiderable scale, they resolved to stay. However, they planned to improve both the villa and their standard of living.

Architects, builders and landscape gardeners were called in. A new library extension, guest wings and bathrooms were designed, and a sixteen-acre formal Italian garden was planned with its attendant avenues of cypresses interspersed with statuary, and a succession of bosky dells and pleasant groves. A new car was ordered and, as Roger Fry mischievously remarked, 'that essential adjunct to the academic life', a butler, was engaged.

Mary spent the summer in England, then sailed for America with her daughters to enter them at Bryn Mawr. Bernhard amused himself at St Moritz, not this time with Aline Sassoon, but with his latest conquest, a young woman called Gladys Deacon.

Gladys had a rather more raffish background than most of Bernhard's friends. She was the youngest daughter of an unhappy woman who had married a man almost thirty years older than herself. After fathering three daughters in twenty-eight months, Mr Deacon had tired of his wife, bought her an apartment in Paris, and told her to find herself a lover. She had obeyed. Unfortunately, she had soon tired of him and of his successors, one of whom was Gladys' father. Mr Deacon, irritated by his wife's by now well-known open-handedness, had burst in one morning and shot the current favourite as he hid behind a sofa. Pausing only to throw Gladys and her mother into the street, he had sold the house and fled with the three eldest children who he presumed were his. An understanding French judiciary had treated him gently, only locking him up when he announced that he was a nephew of Moses.

Gladys was just seventeen and acknowledged as an outstanding beauty when she met Bernhard at St Moritz. She and her mother were being maintained there in great style by the Duke of Marlborough. The pressing need to bolster the ducal finances had led in 1895 to his marriage with Consuelo Vanderbilt, but Gladys was his heart's desire! He kept her and her mother but preserved appearances by officially inviting Mrs Deacon to be the travelling companion of his sister, Lady Norah Churchill. Lady Norah needed one. One of her foibles was to carry live frogs in her handbag, which she had trained to jump from her bag into her mouth and back again.*

When he learned of the Gladys-Bernhard liaison, Joe Duveen did not approve, for the Marlboroughs were good customers. He therefore encouraged Berenson to join Mary in New York. Once Bernhard had arrived, Joe not only orchestrated the Berensons' performance and encouraged them to travel everywhere, but he paid the bills. There was breakfast with J. Pierpont Morgan, dinners with Altman and the Wideners, and even a five-minute audience with President Theodore Roosevelt, who, greeting Bernhard, murmured, 'Mr Berrington, of course, who hasn't heard of Mr Berrington?', and proceeded to tell him three 'smoking room' stories in as many minutes.

Joe Duveen and his wife gave several dinners for them, one of which Mary described in detail in a letter to her mother, omitting to mention that Duveen was now their employer.

It was a dinner with a red theme—all the food and decorations were dyed red. About twenty extremely and gaudily wealthy people attended—the women were dripping jewellery, sometimes having to remove some pieces because of the weight. Joe sat on Mary's right and a portly gentleman on her left. This gentleman was quite taken by Mary and clung to her for the rest of the evening. In the days to come, Mary received invitations from him and his wife for dinner and other occasions. It turned out that Mary and Bernhard had been wanting to meet this couple, as they believed he was worth $100 million and stood to inherit another $80 million. The man was Arabella Huntington's son, Archer.

The Berensons were not above doing a bit of dealing on their own account as well: they sold Perugino's 'Madonna and Child with Bird in Hand' to John G. Johnson of Philadelphia, for $10,000. They had bought this painting from a Florentine dealer six years earlier for $300 but, after Isabella had turned it down at $22,500, had taken it into their own collection.

---

* The Duke divorced Consuelo in 1921 and married Gladys.

Isabella also featured on the agenda. She had a problem. United States customs had discovered a considerable number of works of art concealed among some crates shipped to her from London, marked 'Household Effects'. They were threatening to charge her with smuggling, but she managed to settle the matter by paying a fine of $152,000. Her defence was that a friend had shipped the crates to her in error, but neither Bernhard nor Mary believed her for they had been actively smuggling on Isabella's behalf for a decade.

At first, avoiding paying duty had been easy. There had only been the compliant and venal Italian authorities to bribe or outwit. Then, in 1897, a new American import duty was levied under the Dingley Tariff Act; this reimposed a 20 per cent duty on works of art that a previous Act of 1890 had abolished. The duty had been widely attacked in the press as evil and stupid, but in the meantime dealers and their customers frequently took a chance and either smuggled or, more often in Isabella's case, had the items described on the shipping invoices as something of less value than they really were. In 1900, for example, Isabella, on Bernhard's recommendation, had purchased a small Raphael Pietà through Colnaghis for $25,000. The American duty would have added a further $5,000; Isabella had asked for it to be smuggled. Otto Gutkunst had drawn the line at that; instead he had shipped it to a third party in New York, describing it on the invoice as 'School of Perugino' and valuing it at $3,000. Isabella had collected it from Colnaghis' agent and saved herself $4,000.

The customs agents were elated at the publicity generated by Isabella's misfortune and began to focus increased attention on the activities of other notable dealers and collectors, going so far as to offer, as a reward to anyone who helped them, a percentage of any duty or fines levied on those they trapped. This could not have come at a worse time for Duveens, and was to delay Bernhard's promised contract for two years.

Joel's death at the end of 1908 gave Uncle Henry and Joe the opportunity to reconstitute the company. Joe was then forty. They had two motives. First they wished to freeze out the other members of the family and, second, they wished to avoid British taxation. Early in 1909, the law relating to company taxation was changed, making it obligatory for a UK-registered company to pay tax on the profits of its overseas subsidiaries and associated companies.

A new American company called Duveen Brothers was formed. Henry owned 50 per cent, Joe 35 per cent, with the balance divided amongst Joe's brothers Ernest and Ben and Henry's son, Geoffrey. This company then registered a wholly owned subsidiary of the same name in Paris. The old companies were quietly dissolved and the main London company sold its stock at Joe's and Henry's valuation to the new concern. Full advantage was taken of such accountancy devices as depreciation, and the stock, on its circuitous route to New York via Paris, depreciated even more. The old London company received $625,000 for stock worth $20 million.

The $625,000 was used to establish a new London company, also called Duveen Brothers Ltd. Its sole asset, apart from the stock money, was the freehold of the Bond Street gallery, which was closed and then leased to Gieves the outfitters. A suite of offices was taken close to Christie's in King Street, St. James's; here Louis was installed to run the day-to-day business, which mainly consisted of acting as a post-box and paying the honorariums due to members of the family under Joel's will. When the family protested, Joe told them to go ahead and sue him, pointing out that any compensation they might be awarded would have to come out of any assets remaining in England, as the Paris and New York companies were outside the jurisdiction of the English courts.

The reconstruction was immensely profitable. The Duveen ledgers show that the sales from the Paris gallery in 1909 amounted to more than $13 million, with over 2,500 items still in stock, while the New York stock had a value of many millions more than the figure at which it had been imported.

In May 1910, on the strength of this tax-free windfall, Henry and Joe bought a forty-year lease of a site on the corner of Fifth Avenue and 56th Street and commissioned the French architect, René Sergent, to design a scaled-down replica of Joe's favourite building in Paris to be erected on the site. This was the Ministry of Marine, which overlooks the Place de la Concorde. The stone, woodwork, carpets, fittings and furnishings were shipped from France, and the American architect Horace Trumbauer of Philadelphia was engaged to supervise its construction.

The foundations were dug during August that year and two

freighters loaded with the building materials docked in New York the same month. Henry and Joe had left young Ben to mind the New York shop while they spent the summer in Europe selling off the Kann Collections.

A brilliant season was had by all. Bernhard, who happily authenticated the Italian items and gained a 5 per cent fee on any sales which he made to his own customers, reported to Mary that he had earned enough to pay for all the alterations to I Tatti and that the surplus would run to a new car. Joe and Henry not only sold four Rembrandts to Altman and many paintings to other rich collectors, as already mentioned, but persuaded Henry Clay Frick to purchase François Boucher's suite of eight painted panels known as 'The Arts and Sciences'. Early in October Henry sailed home to New York with his baggage containing works of art of outstanding quality to stock the new building which he believed would make Duveen Brothers a household word across America.

Unhappily, the name Duveen was to achieve fame of an entirely different kind. When Henry and Joe had sailed for Europe that summer, anxious to choose the stone and fittings for the new gallery, they had foolishly left their master ledgers behind. These showed the true financial affairs of the enterprise as opposed to those shown to the Revenue or other members of the family. A junior ledger clerk, angered by what he considered an unfair reprimand from Ben Duveen, made copies of some of the more incriminating material and posted them, together with precise details of where the master ledgers were kept, to President Roosevelt's newly appointed Collector of Customs, Henry Loeb. It was Loeb who had prosecuted Isabella, and the reward he had offered was doubtless an added incentive to the vengeful clerk. After a secret investigation, which convinced Loeb that the copied documents were genuine, he decided to act. The date was Thursday, 13 October 1910, Yom Kippur, the Jewish Day of Atonement.

At 4 P.M. a seven-man raiding party dashed into the gallery. The staff, believing it was a hold-up, panicked. Ben was arrested and taken to the police station. A reporter from the *New York Times* wrote that Mr Duveen showed great nervousness when charged, saying, 'Yes, yes, I know nothing whatever about it'—which was taken to be a plea of not guilty. His lawyers then personally put up security for the $50,000 bail demanded.

While the unfortunate Ben was raising his bail money, U.S. Marshal Henkel learned that Uncle Henry was aboard the *Lusitania*, which was anchored in the Hudson River, going through the quarantine procedures which were then standard. Once these were finished, the liner would be shepherded by tugs to her berth. Henkel enjoyed his moment of glory. He immediately secured an arrest warrant, and without waiting for the liner to dock sent a team of four agents out to her in the customs cutter *Calumet*.

Henry Duveen had no inkling of the charges against him and was stunned to be suddenly arrested by special agents of the Department of Justice and hauled unceremoniously off by cutter to the Federal Building, where his bail was fixed at $75,000.

The following day further warrants were issued against Joe and his brother Louis, who managed to obtain bail *in absentia* for the same sum as Henry. The firm trumpeted that the charges were political and that the customs service, which was notoriously corrupt, had brought the case to divert attention from their own shortcomings. This argument, though partially true, failed to impress. The *New York Times* revealed, with some delight, that the New York Customs official adviser and valuer of imported works of art was Uncle Henry, and that there had in the past been numerous protests that he had consistently overvalued his rivals' imports and undervalued his own.

The most serious result of the charges was that until the case was disposed of neither the firm nor any member of it could do business in the United States. Work on the new building was halted, and their enormous stocks were placed in bond. The following March, all four Duveens pleaded guilty to three specific charges: Joe and Louis, who were abroad, were fined $10,000 each, while Henry and Ben were each obliged to pay $15,000. Public interest in the case subsided as quickly as it had arisen, the small scale of the fines convincing the public of the truth of the firm's defence that at worst they were only guilty of a misdemeanour, and that only as a result of a clerical error by a shipping clerk.

The truth was remarkably and expensively different. The Customs commissioned an independent valuation of the items which they alleged had been undervalued. This was carried out by the respected New York firms Knoedlers and French and Co., who calculated that the firm had evaded duty of $5 million between

November 1908 and December 1909. This sum only related to goods still in the showrooms or customs sheds, not those which had been sent direct to their purchasers. The Customs claimed the usual penalty of twice the amount due, $10 million.

Henry was crushed by the publicity and the demand for duty but Joe decided to fight the assessment. On Bernhard's advice he engaged a young lawyer called Louis Levy, the junior partner of the firm of Stanchfield and Levy, who had a reputation as a 'fixer'. It was Levy who had acted for Isabella, and he had an excellent relationship with the authorities. His brief was to get the assessment reduced. Joe asked what the fee would be. 'Ten thousand', murmured Levy, thinking in dollars. 'Pounds or dollars?' asked Joe. 'Pounds', said the delighted Levy.

Levy asked for a list of all the customers to whom Duveens had shipped goods from Europe. It had been the firm's practice to quote prices delivered and usually installed in a client's house. The list was formidable, including President Taft himself, numerous senators and, of course, financiers such as Morgan, Widener and Altman, none of whom was without political influence. Levy diplomatically pointed out to the Collector of Customs that technically these clients were also parties to the offences. If the Collector insisted on the 'ridiculous' assessment then Duveens would challenge it in court and ask for all their clients to be joined in their defence.

The post of Collector of Customs for New York is a political one, and at that time technically in the gift of the Secretary of the Navy. The Collector quickly realized the political implications and magnanimously reduced the assessment to $1,400,000, payable immediately.

Uncle Henry raised the money from the First National Bank of New York, by borrowing against monies owed to the firm by Benjamin Altman. It was paid over on 8 February 1912, and the firm was then free to trade again in the United States.

PART FOUR

Partnership

❧ 12 ❧

Doris

The Duveens were running a highly complex organization with master ledgers, official Revenue accounts, figures for the family, and much subtle bookkeeping. Not surprisingly, they found it easier to use code names. Objects or people—whether artists, dealers, customers, prospective customers, or members of their staff—were allotted names which were used religiously in all correspondence, cables and telegrams and even in letters between members of the family.

The practice had been started by Uncle Henry who, until his death, took a personal delight in choosing appropriate names. He was Zeus, Joel had been Jove, Joe was Alexander. When Joel died, Joe was promoted to Jove. When Uncle Henry died, Joe became Dynam—short for dynamic. Henry had evidently considered Bernhard to be rather less than Olympian and had christened him 'Doris' after a dyspeptic character in a Broadway revue.*

In 1909 Uncle Henry had asked Doris to take Benjamin Altman in hand. Altman was an old customer of Duveens as well as a personal friend and with Henry's help he had built up a magnificent porcelain collection. Gradually, Henry had persuaded him to broaden his tastes to include sculpture, fine oriental rugs, and paintings. However, he preferred Dutch paintings, particularly the finest Rembrandts, to Italian artists. Doris was told to widen Altman's horizons in the direction of Italy.

Bernhard had his work cut out. He wrote about his frustration to his friend, customer and occasional legal adviser, John Graves Johnson of Philadelphia, saying that Altman was only interested

---

* Bernhard suffered from dyspepsia all his life.

133

in pictures that were not for sale and that his taste was a slavish imitation of Henry Duveen's. It was no good Bernhard trying to interest Altman in Italian items for he would only buy if Henry told him that they were worthwhile. This is an important letter, for Johnson was one of the very few people to whom Bernhard was prepared to admit that he had a business relationship with Duveen, though he never spelled out the details. Johnson believed that Duveen, like himself and other collectors, paid Bernhard a 'finder's fee' and was always cautioning him to stick to serious collectors and not become involved with the dealers.

Bernhard ignored Johnson's advice and wrote to Henry saying that if he, Henry, would drive into Altman's head that Italians were worth collecting then he, Doris, could do the job; otherwise it was a waste of time. It would also, he wrote, cost Duveens more than a flat fee. He also wanted either 10 per cent of the selling price or one-third of the net profit. Henry winced but finally agreed to Doris receiving a quarter of the net profit. Bernhard promptly persuaded Altman to buy two sculptures from the Kann Collections attributed to Donatello.*

Henry was not impressed. He pointed out that he wanted Doris to find and sell *paintings*. Berenson had already received his fee for authenticating the Kann Collections and Altman already collected sculpture. The argument began the dialogue that led to the first formal contract between Doris and Duveen Brothers.

The negotiations were interrupted by the customs raid. Bernhard believed at first that the firm was finished, writing to Mrs Gardner that they were 'clabbustered'. He discreetly distanced himself from Duveens and attempted to arrange a similar contract with Arthur J. Sulley of London. Sulley, known as 'Silent Sulley', from his reputation for only speaking twice when he had a painting for sale, first to name the artist and second to state the price, was cautious. He welcomed Bernhard's knowledge and his access to the Italian market, but fought shy of any contractual arrangement, simply agreeing to pay introductory commissions and, on occasion, to buy and sell in partnership with him.

Early in 1911, Joe Duveen's lawyer, Louis Levy, wrote to Bern-

---

* Life-size terra-cotta relief, 'The Virgin and Child'. Metropolitan Museum, Altman Collection No. 55; stucco relief, 'The Young St John'. Metropolitan Museum, Altman Collection No. 58.

hard from New York that he was confident that an agreement could be reached with the customs authorities and that the firm would be trading again by Christmas. Emboldened, Bernhard asked Levy to negotiate the much-delayed contract on his behalf with Uncle Henry. While Levy negotiated, Bernhard returned to his assault on Altman. As he did so, he obviously had a twinge of conscience. He wrote two curious letters to clients of his, asking their opinion of his becoming the retained adviser to Duveens. The first letter, to Henry Walters of Baltimore, brought a swift reply advising him to have nothing to do with the company as they were 'dishonest'.

The second letter was to John Graves Johnson. Bernhard explained that he felt that by advising dealers he could ensure that their customers did not get fleeced. He wrote that Sulley and Duveens were the only dealers who he was sure would never mislead a customer; as he wanted pictures to come to America, he preferred Duveens. Altman, he said, was paying absurd prices. If he was involved, then at least Altman would get something worthwhile—though it was not his business to prevent Altman squandering his fortune. Johnson advised Bernhard to be careful and not to trust Duveens. Altman, he said, was well able to take care of himself.

Bernhard's Altman siege in the latter half of 1911 and throughout 1912 is instructive. As a foundation for an Italian collection Bernhard selected five pictures for the aging millionaire, who he knew liked madonnas as long as they were pretty. The quality of these five pictures (all now in the Metropolitan Museum, New York), and Berenson's observations about them, tell their own story.

The first was a Madonna and Child endorsed by Bernhard as a genuine Verrocchio.* This was a dramatic change of heart from the opinion he had written about the picture in 1903 when he had claimed it was entirely the work of workshop assistants. Its history is somewhat mysterious.

It turned up at a Christmas sale in May 1911. Bernhard advised Otto Gutkunst of Colnaghis to buy it, which he did for £650 ($3,150) in the name of Harvey. Bernhard then told Dowdswell

* Metropolitan Museum No. 14, 40, 647.

about it, saying that Dowdswell should suggest it to Duveens and that he, Bernhard, would then authenticate it. Dowdswell did tell Duveens about the painting, whereupon Duveens bought it for $6,250, which gave Bernhard a commission from Colnaghis as well as his 25 per cent of Duveens' profit. Altman paid $125,000.

The second Madonna* was sold as a Sebastiano Mainardi, and is indeed a larger version of a painting now in the Cini Collection in Venice. Whereas the Cini picture is in almost perfect condition, however, the Altman Mainardi had been heavily repainted and prettified by Bernhard's close friend, the Baron Michele Lazzaroni, the year before Altman purchased it.

A third Madonna is the prettiest of the lot. Bernhard said it was by Filippo Lippi†; it is now tentatively attributed to Raffaelino del Garbo, an attractive but minor follower of Lippi. Here, too, there is evidence of extensive repainting, which may well have been the work of Federico Joni or the Baron Lazzaroni.

The fourth painting‡ is undoubtedly genuine. It was Sandro Botticelli's 'Last Communion of St. Jerome', a private devotional picture painted for Francesco del Pugliese, as was subsequently established in a scholarly article by Herbert Horne published in 1915. The picture in question, which had hung in the Palazzo Capponi in Florence since at least the middle of the last century, is one of a number of surviving versions of the composition. It was regarded by some art historians as a work from the School of Botticelli, but Berenson had accepted it as autograph in print as early as 1903. Bernhard negotiated the purchase from the Marchese Farinola early in 1912, and managed to export it from under the noses of the Italian authorities.

The history of the fifth picture sold to Altman could and should have been traced and exposed at the time. It was a portrait of a young man which Altman was led to believe had been painted by Giorgione.∫ Bernhard had known it ever since it had arrived in Florence, for it belonged to neighbours of his, the family of the late Walter Savage Landor. It had been exhibited at the New Gallery exhibition in 1895 as a Giorgione and had featured in Bernhard's

* Metropolitan Museum No. 14, 40, 635.
† Metropolitan Museum No. 14, 40, 641.
‡ Metropolitan Museum No. 14, 40, 642.
∫ Metropolitan Museum No. 14, 40, 640.

controversial catalogue where he had noted that it was in a deplorable state of preservation and had dismissed it as possibly a very early Titian but 'probably only a copy'.

The Landor family had promptly sold it to Bernhard's neighbour, the Countess Turenne, who dabbled in the market in an ignorant way. (She was the owner of the Botticelli fragment, painted by Zozo Smith, based on the Chigi picture Bernhard had sold to Isabella.) In 1912 the Countess sold it to the dealer-cum-restorer Luigi Grassi of Florence, who converted it, according to Berenson in a letter to Duveens, into a portrait of Ludovicio Ariosto in wonderful condition, by Giorgione.

The most damning piece of evidence in the whole affair is that Bernhard wrote this letter to Duveens suggesting its purchase and describing it in such glowing terms *before* Grassi carried out the conversion. The implication is that Grassi and Bernhard were working together. The Metropolitan Museum has recently cleaned the picture and now concedes it to be 'a sad wreck—a ghost'. It is no longer attributed to Giorgione.

Duveens were delighted with the five Altman purchases. Joe wrote to Doris telling him that he planned to 'make a market in Italian pictures . . . and build a good business with your help'. Bernhard replied he would be glad to help, for the right price.

They evidently did so, for on 18 August 1912 Joe and Doris initialed a 'Heads of Agreement' drafted by Louis Levy which Joe then sent to one of his London solicitors, Florence Guedella, to incorporate into a legal contract. This was signed on 25 September 1912. For copyright reasons the contract cannot be reproduced, but the 'Heads of Agreement' document is reproduced in Appendix 1 at the end of this book.

Briefly Bernhard—Doris—was to receive 25 per cent of the profit on all items of Italian origin whether they were paintings, drawings, sculpture, manuscripts, jewellery, curios, or bric-a-brac. Louis Levy had certainly done his best for his client.

Both sides were bound to secrecy. Clause 7 states that 'neither party shall divulge the fact, or leave anybody to infer, that "Doris" is paid by Duveen Brothers on a percentage basis'. The secrecy was taken to quite extraordinary lengths. All transactions on which a percentage might be due were to be recorded in a secret ledger kept by 'X'. This was to be known as the 'X' ledger. Both sides agreed that the decision of 'X' as to what was owed to whom, would be final. Duveens were to keep 'X' informed of all purchases and sales as they occurred and 'X' would issue a half-yearly statement. Doris would have the right to inspect the 'X' ledger at any time.

'X' was the London firm of chartered accountants, Messrs Westcott Maskall and Co. of 29 Broad Street, EC2. Until 1927, they were unaware of the identity of Doris, sending their statements to him through Guedella and Co.

Neither Duveens nor Berenson was allowed to keep a copy of the agreement, or even to make a note as to its contents. Their individual copies were to be sealed and handed over to Westcott Maskall, only to be opened with their joint permission, or in the event of Doris' death.

That eventuality is covered as follows:

Doris to leave with his wife or lawyer, or some other trusted person, whose name from time to time he shall give to Duveen Brothers, a memorandum concerning the agreement, to be opened in the event of death. Such memorandum will state there are or may be monies due to Doris from Duveen brothers and the holder of the memorandum is to communicate with 'X'.

13

The Four Kings

Although the 'Doris' agreement specified that Bernhard should
advise on the purchase and authenticity of Italian marble and
bronze sculpture, he was constantly irritated to discover that his
opinion was rarely sought on these matters. Moreover, when he
suggested to Duveen that he knew of the existence of some superb
sculptures which were for sale, Joe would never listen. Berenson's
anger almost reached the breaking point in 1917 when he discovered, quite by accident, that he had not been paid his percentage
on certain Italian items which Joe had sold and omitted to tell him
about. He also learned that Joe's statuary exports from France
alone had averaged $2 million a year since 1908. Surely some of
these must have needed his authentication, Bernhard thought. He
therefore wrote a bitter letter of complaint to Joe's Paris office on
14 September 1917. In return he received an invitation to come
to Paris as soon as possible to discuss the matter.

Joe had several reasons for wishing to see Berenson. Since the
initial arrangement with Doris, Joe had been worried, not only by
his new partner's lack of knowledge of the plastic arts but by his
close association with some of Florence's more unscrupulous dealers. Berenson also seemed to be dabbling in murky waters with a
French sculpture restorer called Demotte. Alarming rumours had
been reaching Joe from New York which disturbed him greatly:
it sounded as if Bernhard might be involved with several notorious
knaves.

Joe knew that the Italian tradition for forgery was an ancient
one and was well aware that it had reached its peak during the
latter half of the nineteenth century with the exposure of the sculpture of Giovanni Bastianini (1830-68). In a brief life the talented

Giovanni had produced an incredible crop of marbles and terra-cottas in the Renaissance style. These had been eagerly snapped up by such august institutions as the Louvre and the Victoria and Albert Museum, whose basements still hold what are probably the largest collections of Bastianinis in the world outside the stock of some present-day Florentine dealers. Giovanni was a peasant craftsman from Fiesole, who had been fascinated by the sculpture on display at the nearby Villa Medici. He had begun to copy his favourite pieces when he met a local dealer called Giovanni Freppa, who encouraged him to do his own thing—albeit in the Renaissance style.

Freppa bought whatever his protégé produced, placing these pieces amongst his other stock, cheaply priced and with no attribution. His customers, who were largely Paris dealers, were only too happy to make use of their superior knowledge to spot what they decided was the genuine handiwork of Ghiberti or Rossellino. Freppa, doubtless with tongue in cheek, assured them that their purchases were merely commonplace items, but they knew better. Freppa continued this operation for nearly twenty years.

At first most of his stock ended up in leading museums, which rarely announced what they paid for their acquisitions. In 1866, however, the Louvre announced that they had purchased a magnificent plaster bust of the fifteenth-century Florentine philosopher-poet Girolamo Benivieni (1453-1539) for the then remarkable sum of 13,250 gold francs. As Freppa and his protégé had only shared a beggarly 500 francs for the bust a few months before, they decided that the time had come to blow the whistle. Freppa published a detailed account of his Bastianini sales to the Paris trade in the 15 December 1867 issue of the magazine *Chronique des Arts*. Amidst considerable embarrassment dozens of so-called Renaissance masterpieces were consigned to obscurity.

As several hundred found their way back to Italy, antique sculptures from Florence were soon regarded with extreme caution by most reputable dealers. When in 1913 the American millionaire, P. A. B. Widener, paid $3 million to Elia Volpi of Florence for Donatello's statue of the boy David, Henry Duveen and other leading dealers of London, Paris, and New York stood aside, because they were too frightened to trust their own judgement and terrified of Bastianini's posthumous reputation.

Joe had taken elaborate precautions to see that he was never misled by a Bastianini forgery, even paying Wilhelm von Bode an annual retainer to authenticate all pieces offered to the House of Duveen. Much to Berenson's joy, however, his arch-rival von Bode had apparently proved to be by no means perfect.

In 1909 Dr von Bode had acquired, for $40,000, a wax bust of 'Flora', which he exhibited as an original work by Leonardo da Vinci. A whispering campaign began and was apparently justified when a letter appeared in *The Times* which stated that 'Flora' had been made by a London sculptor called Richard Lucas. This was followed by a claim from Lucas' son Albert that he knew his father had made the bust and that the matter could be confirmed if the base was examined. Inside, claimed Lucas, would be found a fragment of *The Times*, dated 1872. With von Bode's consent, the bust was examined in London and fragments of *The Times* were discovered. Von Bode was discredited.

Berenson had revelled in *The Times* revelations. He had good reason to do so, for three years earlier another arch-enemy, Robert Langton Douglas, had offered the very same bust to Isabella Stewart Gardner. Berenson's advice had been sought and, after canvasing his London contacts, he had dismissed it as a forgery. (In 1957 the German scholar, H. H. Pars, proved that Richard Lucas had only done restoration work on the bust after it had been damaged. Pars quoted Sir Kenneth Clark as saying that Lucas would have been incapable of making such a bust: it was a clear example of Leonardo's later sculpture.)

If even von Bode could be so easily discredited, then Joe Duveen felt that Italian Renaissance sculpture was best ignored, unless provenance and expertise were beyond reproach. Instead he turned his attention to Romanesque and Gothic sculpture from France, which had a ready market amongst architects and decorators in New York. A fortunate accident had moreover provided Joe with a seemingly inexhaustible supply of such artifacts.

In 1906 the anti-clerical French government of the time had passed a statute authorizing the state to catalogue, and then take over, the property of the churches. This statute was violently opposed in many country districts. In many areas the local squire or count, who had the gift of the living, acting in concert with his curé, began to dispose of the more valuable objects in exchange for cash and a copy of the original. One of the most enthusiastic buyers was a daredevil former cavalry officer, complete with saber-slashed cheeks, called Gilbert Romeuf. He scoured the provinces of France in an elaborate touring coach, drawn by a matched pair of splendid horses, staying with his friends among the minor nobility. If they had something to sell, Romeuf said he could be relied upon to find a discreet customer.

In fact he was one of Joe Duveen's agents.

When Joe was in Paris negotiating for the Kann Collections, Romeuf came to him with the news that a strange American dealer appeared to be working the same profitable seam of churches and monasteries that he was. He showed Joe a printed leaflet which the American was leaving with country people and their priests. The leaflet assuaged Joe's worries about a competitor, for the American was not after altar pieces, tapestries, silver candlesticks, or communion plates. He was buying pieces of stone—in particular stone feet. The leaflet offered one franc for feet with pointed toes (Gothic) and half a franc for more conventional, and therefore more modern, extremities. It gave the name of Barnard and an address in the village of Moret-sur-Loing, which is on the outskirts of Fontaine-bleau, near Paris. Joe called on him and found a cheerful extrovert called George Grey Barnard, revered by some authorities today as possibly America's greatest sculptor.

George had started life as a taxidermist in Iowa. From his earliest youth he longed to sculpt. In 1883, after working his way through the Art Institute of Chicago, he had sold a portrait bust for $300 and promptly sailed for Paris, where he had spent ten years of bitter poverty learning his craft. He had made his public début at the Salon du Champ de Mars in 1894, when his work created a sensation. His largest exhibit, an eight-foot-high duo of male nudes, had been purchased by Alfred Clark of the Singer Sewing Machine Company fame. Clark had presented the figures to the Metropolitan, thereby establishing George as Iowa's answer to Michelangelo.

George had returned in triumph to New York, where he had begun to teach and to sculpt portrait busts. He had not prospered and had been on the point of returning to taxidermy when a friend at the Metropolitan had persuaded him to tender for the supply of thirty-three twelve-foot-high figures, intended to decorate the state capitol buildings of Harrisburg, Pennsylvania. He won the tender and decided to settle in France, where he planned to execute the commission. Unhappily, he had not done his sums correctly. In 1905, with only eleven of the figures completed, he had exhausted the money advanced to him to buy the materials to complete the set of thirty-three.

To support his family, and meet his obligations, George began dealing in stone, selling to two cronies from his student days called Demotte and Boutron, who rented a group of studios in Paris at 36 rue Dutot. 'The money I earn', George wrote to his parents, 'comes a 1000 times easier than my own sculpture'. Demotte and Boutron were primarily restorers, but George had an eye for quality and a deepening love for Gothic and Romanesque art. Amongst the three of them a new business developed. George would scour the countryside for fragments of antique stone carving and would then sketch a possible sculpture that the pieces could be made into: his two friends would do the rest. This is how one of the cheekiest art frauds in history began, though at the time neither Barnard nor Boutron had any criminal intentions.

George was not a modest man. His stories about the provenance of his reconstituted figures became increasingly dramatic. He claimed that he had found the Metropolitan limestone relief of 'The Miracle of St Hubert and the Stag' in a pigsty and that their thirteenth-century tomb figure of Jean d'Allue had been used face downwards as a bridge over a country stream. The truth was usually somewhat different. The origins of St Hubert and Jean d'Allue are unclear but it is known that the Metropolitan's seated King of Avignon was entirely made by Henri Boutron to a sketch by George, while the model for their statue of St Paul was Demotte himself.

Between 1907 and 1917 George designed and Henri Boutron made several hundred medieval masterpieces; Demotte did the selling and Duveens handled the shipments. The Metropolitan purchased some 3 million francs' worth, though it is clear from the Paris police file on the operation that a percentage of this was recycled to the Metropolitan's Curator of Decorative Art, Joseph Breck.

George and Demotte had other useful contacts at the Metropolitan besides Breck. They were, for instance, on intimate terms with Robert de Forest, one of the younger but more prestigious trustees. The friend and admirer who had persuaded George to tender for the monumental Harrisburg commission was William Clifford, the librarian, but most important of all was William W. Kent, probably the most influential museum official in the United States. A professional museum consultant, Kent had become a guru to the growing profession of interior decorators. He was also in receipt of an annual retainer from Duveen Brothers.

When George Barnard first met Joe in the summer of 1906, he, Henri Boutron and Demotte had just purchased for 500 francs the remains of a crumbled wall at the Abbey de Parthenay. The abbey wall had been a classified monument and the Louvre had recently inspected it. Their report stated that the wall contained three badly eroded torsos, and that some stones nearby showed traces of carving on them. There were no legs, arms or heads. The Louvre report recommended that the wall and stones be declassified as the figures were beyond repair. Happily for scholarship, and unhappily for the partnership, the Louvre report contained an engraving dated 1830, showing one of the figures to be a seated man wearing a crown or halo, with bare feet and pointed toes, of which more will be heard later.

From this and other iconographical details the figures were identified as the Magi, the Three Wise Men. George had not decided what he was going to do with the Parthenay material, as he called it, when Joe called upon him at Moret-sur-Loing. For the moment they were just a jumbled heap of stones in his garden. George had other priorities. He was still troubled by the unfinished Harrisburg commission, and he had had a vision, the sweep and breadth of which captivated Joe. Both men liked to 'think big', and George thought bigger than most.

'Why bother with single statues?' said George. 'Why not buy complete monastic cloisters, ship them to the States and reassemble them?' Once erected they would be the perfect backdrop to a 'collection of statues'. Taking Joe into his confidence, he showed him that he had already started on his ambitious project. Stacked in his orchard were substantial portions of no less than three Gothic and Romanesque monasteries, Saint Guilhem-le-Desert, Trie, and Bonnefort-en-Comminges. In a neighbor's barn sat the gem of his monastery collection, which was a large part of the masonry from the most important Benedictine building in southern France, the Abbey of Saint Michel-de-Cuxa.

The abbey had been founded in 878 A.D. Nine hundred years later it had been abandoned and local farmers had begun to use the reddish brown stone for field walls and farm buildings. They had ignored the central courtyard, which had been surrounded by a cloister of graceful columns, topped by Romanesque arches. This had been taken by the inhabitants of a nearby village called Prades. Most of the columns, with their bases and arches, lay in local gardens but twelve of the finest arches had been used to embellish the local public bathhouse.

The bathhouse owner had refused to sell, but George had managed to acquire forty-eight columns and fifty-six arches from local gardens. He explained to Joe that, using his bits of masonry from the other monasteries, he would be able to duplicate the seventy odd Cuxa columns that he needed. Once he had done that, he boasted, he planned to sell the lot as a Romanesque monastery for $100,000 to J. Pierpont Morgan and the Metropolitan Museum. In fact, he was expecting Sir Caspar Purdon Clarke, the then Director of the Metropolitan, to arrive and complete the purchase any day. Once he had the money, he would have sufficient funds to complete his Harrisburg commission.

Joe was fascinated by the scheme, but as far as he was concerned it had one serious flaw. Morgan was *his* customer. He did not mind semi-antique sculptures being sold to American tourists as though they were the genuine article, but to sew up Morgan and the Met with a hybrid monastery was pushing it. However, he assured George that he would see what he could do.

Joe could do quite a lot—and he did. First Morgan and Sir Caspar Clarke suddenly went cold on the idea. In a letter to Sir Caspar, George had claimed that his reassembled Cuxa would be 'a poem to Americans who never can or will see Europe'. But it did not take Joe long to convince Morgan and Clarke that, to any American who had seen or could visit Europe, the poem might rather be a bad ballad.

George was bitterly disappointed by Morgan's loss of interest. Desperately he reduced the price of his masonry collection to $50,000 but no one showed the slightest interest. He never suspected that Joe had spoiled the sale. In fact, George was extremely grateful, for Joe organized a group of New York businessmen to unscramble George's problems. The Harrisburg project was refinanced and George was given a monthly cheque to cover his housekeeping expenses. Three years later his thirty-three twelve-foot-high figures were completed and exhibited at the 1910 Paris Salon, where they were much praised. Other commissions followed, including a monumental figure of Lincoln for the city of Cincinnati. Despite his personal success, however, George remained committed to his vision of the reassembled Cuxa cloisters and his determination to acquire the twelve Romanesque arches which were now part of the Prades bathhouse.

The bathhouse owner was a widow called Madame Baladud de Saint-Jean. In 1913 she eventually agreed to sell. George numbered, dismantled and crated every stone and was about to ship his entire collection to New York when the French government began to take an unhealthy interest in his affairs. They promptly classified the bathhouse material as of national interest and forbade its export from France. Fortunately for George they were unaware of the three collections of monastic masonry in his orchard. George made a brave show of challenging the Prades classification. This delayed matters sufficiently for some dextrous substitutions. The dross from the orchard went into a set of crates identical to those that contained the bathhouse. Eventually George publicly acknowledged the justice of the French claim and grandiloquently presented one of his two sets of crated stones to the People of France.

The gift was publicly applauded. On 31 December 1913 the French Senate, encouraged by George's apparent surrender, passed a new decree that totally forbade the export of historic statues or architectural artifacts. What the Senate did not know was that, on 29 December, George, with Joe's help, had shipped his entire collection to New York.

George's masonry was reassembled and the Cloisters Museum opened to the public on a site off Fort Washington Avenue, Washington Heights, New York, shortly before Christmas 1914. William Kent and an architect friend of Joe's called Welles Bosworth praised it to the skies. Welles took his favourite client along for a private view. The client was John D. Rockefeller.

Rockefeller was fascinated and became permanently hooked on medieval art. Joe eagerly fanned this enthusiasm and a steady stream of medieval carvings and choir stalls and other bits and pieces began the trek from Europe to the United States. Ten years later Rockefeller gave the Metropolitan $1 million to purchase all of George's masonry.

The opening of George's cloisters encouraged American interest in the medieval. Throughout the First World War museum curators and rich collectors regarded Washington Heights as a place of pilgrimage. The partnership between Joe and George was a harmonious one. Each stuck to his last, Joe to works of art and George to masonry. Joe calculated that if the rich cared to build themselves Gothic mansions, with the fireplaces, fountains and stained glass windows supplied by George, they would come to him for the rugs, pictures, tapestries and furniture they needed to complete the illusion.

George Barnard's former partner, the restorer Demotte, had no intention of letting George and Joe Duveen make all the profits. He had been angered by Barnard's obsession with reassembling cloisters in America. He wished to press ahead with his own plans, which envisaged 'creative restoration' on an even grander scale. George had left behind in his garden the jumbled heap of stones from Parthenay, which the Louvre had identified as the three Magi, and which he and Demotte had just purchased that summer of 1906 when Barnard first encountered Joe Duveen. Demotte now decided to make use of these Parthenay stones. He metamorphosed them into two pairs of seated kings and a pair of stone archways. When the four kings were finished he very cleverly showed photographs of them to Bernhard Berenson, whom he had learned from the dealer René Gimpel was dissatisfied with his lack of commissions on sculpture from Joe.

Bernhard was entranced. Demotte told him in confidence that the Louvre had an option on one of the pairs of kings and one doorway. He was prepared to allow Bernhard to sell the remaining figures and archway to Isabella, provided she would pay the same price as the Louvre.

Demotte then spun the same story to the Louvre, citing Isabella's interest. Both fish bit. Isabella was unaware that Demotte had designed the figures to fit her plans for Fenway Court.

Bernhard wrote to Isabella on 12 July 1914, praising the sculptures and enclosing detailed elevations (supplied by Demotte showing how her architect could fit them into the corridor at Fenway Court), and adding, almost as an afterthought, that the cost would be $150,000 for the Kings and $80,000 for the doorway. It was, he claimed, the same price the Louvre paid for similar pieces, and that he did not have any financial stake in the deal. This was a lie. Demotte paid his commission to him through Gimpel.

Demotte collected a net profit of some $400,000 out of Isabella and the Louvre, and invested his money in opening palatial showrooms in New York, offering a direct challenge to Joe Duveen where medieval antiquities were concerned and, of course, benefiting from the publicity generated by Barnard's cloisters. However, as he no longer had Barnard as a source of ideas, he had to look elsewhere. He turned to two Italian dealers, Elia Volpi of Florence and Romano Palesi of Rome, a notorious forger of antique furniture known to the international art trade as the Woodworm King.

These rogues had recently discovered a master forger of sculpture who was even better than Bastianini. His name was Alceo Dossena and he was able to turn out both Renaissance and Gothic pieces to order. Volpi and Palesi paid him a regular salary and set him up in a studio in the Via del Vantazzo in Rome. With Demotte's assistance they devised the following cover story to explain the flood of masterpieces which they planned to launch on to the market.

Somewhere on Mount Amiata, they said, there was an abbey that had been buried in an earthquake in the late seventeenth century. A priest, a Dom Mario, had discovered the location but, because of certain unexplained indiscretions, he had been exiled to a small chapel in the hills above Bernhard's villa, I Tatti. The dealers had been able to obtain a map from the obliging cleric which showed the location of the buried sculptures. Because of the stringent laws about exporting works of art, they said, the items had to be purchased by overseas customers on the strength of photographs and written certificates of authenticity, supplied by the now aging and gullible von Bode, the young and gullible W. R. Valentiner, Director of the Detroit Institute of Arts, Demotte, and the self-styled Professor Volpi of Florence.

Demotte and Volpi gave Bernhard photographs of many of their pieces and he, too, believed their story. There is no doubt that if the same cock-and-bull kind of provenance had been offered to him about pictures he would have thrown the dealers out of his house. Sculpture was a different matter and the endorsement of Demotte, whom he had no reason to suspect, seemed ample reassurance.

Edward Fowles visited Bernhard in Florence from 4 to 7 September 1917, and was horrified to be shown photographs of what he believed to be forgeries of a Donatello relief of the Madonna with St Anne, a carved Gothic wooden figure of a Madonna attributed to Simone Martini, and a similar version in marble by the same artist.* All had been sold to the Frick Museum for a total of $475,000. Bernhard fervently believed in their authenticity. He proudly told Fowles that the gem of the collection was also under consideration by Miss Helen Frick. This was a complete Renaissance sarcophagus, attributed to Mino da Fiesole.

While he was showing Fowles the photographs, Bernhard complained bitterly that Joe would not listen when he told him about these marvellous sculptures. Fowles held his tongue, suggesting that Bernhard write to Joe setting out his case. This was the genesis of Bernhard's letter to Joe, dated 14 September 1917, which led to his being invited to Paris to discuss the matter, as we saw at the beginning of this chapter.

Back in Paris, Joe listened to Edward's report on the photographs of the sculpture he had seen at I Tatti with growing concern. He was aware that Demotte had recently been increasingly active in the American market, but the news that he was dealing with such customers as the Frick Collection, the Metropolitan Museum and the Boston Museum worried him deeply, and confirmed some disturbing rumours that had already reached him from New York. A series of coded cables was sent immediately. Was this to be a repeat of the J. P. Walters Dom Mazzarenti scandal? Then Bernhard had been exonerated by Langton Douglas. The evidence had been slight and circumstantial and from tainted sources. Now replies from New York pointed to a far graver state of affairs.

Answering cables confirmed that the Frick had indeed purchased the items Bernhard claimed and that they were seriously considering the Mino da Fiesole sarcophagus. If Frick turned it down, Boston Museum were the next in line to purchase it. Further in-

---

* The marble is currently owned by the University of Pittsburgh. The wooden version was purchased by Lord Clark and is at Saltwood Castle in Kent. It appears on the dust-jacket of Lord Clark's autobiography, *Another Part of the Wood*.

quiries showed that Boston had learned about it from Berenson's old Harvard and Oxford friend Ned Warren, who in turn had been tipped off by Bernhard. In Joe's suspicious mind that confirmed to him that Bernhard was making sure that, as usual, he had two bites at the cherry. If Demotte did not pay him a commission for the Frick sale he would get one from Warren if Boston bought.

At the same time Duveens' New York inquiries disclosed that the Metropolitan had just spent almost $600,000 on a series of major Etruscan terra-cotta figures and were contemplating the purchase of several more. The negotiator was the Metropolitan's assistant keeper of Classical Art, a Miss Gisela Richter, the daughter of J. P. Richter, Bernhard's silent partner in many an old master deal.

Joe's information came from sources within the Metropolitan who were jealous that Miss Richter had been allocated purchasing funds denied to their departments. They told him that the most important item purchased by her was a seven-foot-high Etruscan figure of the warrior god Mars, which had recently arrived in separate fragments.

In fact, the Metropolitan's Etruscan purchases were a separate hoax. Demotte was peripherally connected, but the main beneficiaries of the swindle were Pietro Stenniner, then a senior official in the Rome post office, a Rome-based dealer called Domenico Fuschini, and a family of forgers from Assisi called Fioravanti. Between them, over a period of nine years, they swindled the Metropolitan Museum out of almost $2 million.

Joe, unaware that the only connection between the two operations was Demotte, leapt to the conclusion that Bernhard was up to his ears in both plots. The misconception was based on Miss Richter's and Warren's involvement, Bernhard's connection with Demotte, and his possession of the photographs that Fowles had seen. Joe's letter cordially inviting Bernhard to Paris was the first stage of a defensive plan to isolate himself, Duveen Brothers and, because he had to, Bernhard from the inevitable denouement. The second stage was secretly to advise the Frick, and Miss Richter's rival curators, that their recent purchases were doubtful to say the least.

The Frick took him at his word, and courteously allowed the

BB (*counter-clockwise*):
In 1887 (*BBC Hulton Picture Library*)

In the green garden at I Tatti, 1938
(*Photograph from* Berenson *by Sylvia Sprigge,
Allen & Unwin*)

With Mary Costelloe, 1895 (*Photograph from* Berenson *by Sylvia Sprigge, Allen & Unwin*)

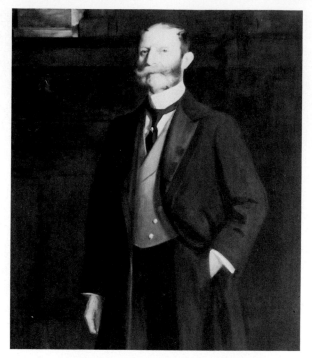

Sir Joseph Joel Duveen (*Tate Gallery*)

Lord Duveen (*BBC Hulton Picture Library*)

Isabella Stewart Gardner in Venice, 1894—painting by Anders Zorn
(*Isabella Stewart Gardner Museum, Boston*)

Arabella Huntington—painting by Oswald Birley
(*Henry E. Huntington Library and Art Gallery*)

The "scrupulously dishonest"
Collis P. Huntington, Arabella's first husband
(*Bettmann Archive*)

Henry E. Huntington, Collis's nephew,
who became Arabella's second husband
(*Bettmann Archive*)

J. Pierpont Morgan (*Bettmann Archive*)   Benjamin J. Altman (*Bettmann Archive*)

Andrew Mellon (*BBC Hulton Picture Library*)   John D. Rockefeller (*Bettmann Archive*)

Julian S. Bache
(*BBC Hulton Picture Library*)

Mrs Horace E. Dodge
(*UPI/Bettmann Newsphotos*)

Samuel H. Kress
(*UPI/Bettmann Newsphotos*)

Henry Clay Frick
(*Bettmann Archive*)

Duveens, New York—corner of East 57th Street and 5th Avenue

Duveens, London—21 Old Bond Street (*Architectural Review*)

The "X" ledger

The entry for one of the
controversial Salomon pictures

The entry for the Northbrook Crivelli—note the
heavy expenditure on restoration

Lord Lee of Fareham

Lord Farquhar

Lord Esher

Lord d'Abernon

(All pictures on this page: BBC Hulton Picture Library)

Left: Kenneth Clark
The carved wooden figure of a Madonna, attributed by Duveen to Simone Martini, was in fact a modern copy made by Alceo Dossena
(*Photograph from* The Other Part of the Wood *by Kenneth Clark — John Murray*)

Right: John Walker, Director of the National Gallery, Washington
(*UPI/Bettmann Newsphotos*)

"The Annunciation", by the Master of the Gardner Annunciation (Piermatteo d'Amelia?)
(*Isabella Stewart Gardner Museum, Boston*)

"Christ Bearing the Cross", now attributed to Giovanni Bellini
(*Isabella Stewart Gardner Museum, Boston*)

"The Madonna of the Eucharist", by Botticelli
(*Isabella Stewart Gardner Museum, Boston*)

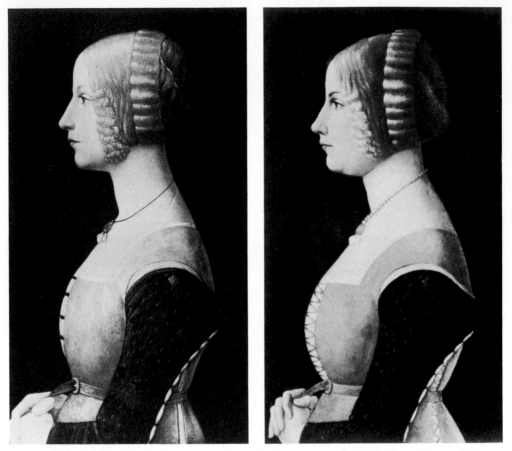

"Portrait of a Lady", by Sebastiano Mainardi: (*left*) as "restored" and sold by Duveen to Andrew Mellon; (*right*) the original as revealed after cleaning. In the process of restoration a middle-aged lady in mourning was "prettified" into a fashionable young woman. (Present whereabouts unknown)

"Madonna and Child", by Crivelli. This is the Northbrook Crivelli referred to in one of the pages reproduced from the "X" Ledger.

The Allendale Nativity, sometimes known as "The Adoration of the Shepherds", by Giorgione

Boston Museum to acquire the Renaissance sarcophagus, where it is today. The Metropolitan took no action for years. Eventually, in 1933, they publicly announced their acquisition of the figure of Mars and in 1936 they published a scholarly dissertation about it by Miss Richter. It was not conceded to be a forgery until 1961.

The meeting between Joe and Bernhard was arranged for eleven o'clock on the morning of 20 October 1917. It was to be held at the Paris Ritz, where both were staying, and Joe, according to Fowles, took extreme precautions. He reserved the rooms on either side of his suite and had them stuffed with mattresses to muffle the noise of what he expected to be an acrimonious and noisy discussion, but Bernhard outwitted him, turning up at the Place Vendôme Gallery instead, pretending that he had misunderstood the arrangements. By the time Joe joined him there his temper had cooled slightly. Fowles heard their arguments and noted that it was a deeply humiliating experience for Bernhard. One by one Bernhard produced photographs of the sculptural masterpieces he had wished the firm to buy and each time Joe snapped, 'No, a forgery, what's next?'

Bernhard defended Demotte, citing the pairs of kings purchased by the Louvre and Isabella, but did not dare tell Joe that he had been Demotte's intermediary. He was horrified to discover that Joe knew all about the transaction and had an affidavit from George Barnard giving their true history. Joe then administered the *coup de grâce*. Professor Elia Volpi, he revealed, was about to stand trial in New York for fraud.* If the Doris-Duveen contract was to continue, Bernhard had to wash his hands of Volpi, Demotte and their associates; and if the contract was to be renewed, sculpture had to be excluded.

Bernhard had no alternative but to agree, but he pointed out that Joe himself had also been involved with Barnard and his cloister and could also be peripherally connected with Demotte. To add weight to his arguments, he protested that he had not been paid his percentage on certain Italian items which Joe had sold and omitted to tell him about. A compromise was arranged.

Joe asked Berenson to stay in Paris, or at least away from Italy,

---

* Spence *v.* Elia Volpi, Supreme Court of the State of New York (1917).

until the inevitable scandal broke over the sculptures. He pointed out that Bernhard could be useful to the firm in Paris as he, Joe, had to return to New York and Edward Fowles was about to be conscripted into the army. Fortunes were being made and lost in Europe as a result of the war, and Paris, not Bernhard's Florentine backwater, was the vantage point from which to take advantage of this situation. Joe also needed Bernhard's opinion on the Schickler Collection, which was about to come on the market. If Bernhard agreed to stay, he would find that the fees to be earned on the Schickler purchase would certainly make it worth his while. Bernhard agreed.

It was discreetly put about that Bernhard had decided to take an extended holiday from Florence as his markedly pro-ally sentiments had made him temporarily unpopular in northern Italy, where there was a strong pro-German body of opinion. Also, as the United States had now entered the war, he was resolved to do his duty to his country. Equally discreet lobbying by Edith Wharton found him a sinecure at the U.S. Army headquarters in Paris where he was asked to advise on matters of liaison between the Intelligence services of the U.S. Army and the British Expeditionary Force. A sinecure is the correct description, as the British Intelligence headquarters was located in the offices and library of the Duveen building in the Place Vendôme. His first duty was to inspect the Schickler Collection.

Baron Arthur de Schickler had been a prominent Viennese financier. With the advice of Dr von Bode he had formed a superb collection of Italian Renaissance painting and sculpture, all of which was fully authenticated and, of course, known to collectors and dealers all over the world. There were no disputes about the attribution of any item so Bernhard's imprimatur would be as easy to give as it was profitable.

When the Baron died, the collection descended to his daughter, who was married to an eccentric Frenchman, Count Hubert de Pourtalès, who lived in a damp and draughty château at Martinvast near Cherbourg. It was so draughty that he had cut up several enormous tapestries and used them as curtains. It was not a suitable setting for his father-in-law's *objets d'art*. For that matter it was not a suitable setting for his wife either, a fact that Joe had realized when she came into her inheritance. She needed little persuasion from Joe to take a lease on the same Paris mansion on the corner of the Avenue Gabriel that he had earlier decorated for Arabella Huntington.

The finer objects were moved from Martinvast to Paris and the de Pourtalès began to live a somewhat fuller life. As Joe had cannily foreseen, their money began to run out and the Count became anxious to sell. He had already approached several dealers in order to find out what the collection was worth but had had little luck. What he did not know was that Joe had organized a syndicate with Nathan Wildenstein and Arnold Seligman: whoever bought from the collection would share the profit with the others. Stage two of the plan was to invite the eminent Berenson to visit and pass an ostensibly disinterested opinion.

Bernhard received an invitation from the Count to call on 28 October 1917, when he duly pronounced on such diverse and genuine gilt-edged objects as the Mino da Fiesole bust of Astorgia Manfredi II of Faenza,* Sandro Botticelli's 'Portrait of a Youth in a Red Cap',† and a complete fifteenth-century black and gilt lacquer room.‡ His ecstatic comments delighted his hosts, as did his opinion that the collection deserved to be kept as a whole.

Shortly afterwards Joe's syndicate offered the de Portalès $2 million for the collection, provided it included the tapestry curtains. The Count demurred. They would not sell the curtains at any price. He wished to leave them to his eldest son. The final deal was for $2,285,000 payable in three six-monthly installments. Bernhard's share of the profit was $200,000.

The collection was sold very quickly but the tapestry curtains stayed at Martinvast until the château was used as a bivouac by British troops in 1939, when they disappeared. After a respectable period they turned up in New York in the hands of a dealer named Brummer, whose story was that they came from an impoverished English ducal seat. James J. Rorimer of the Metropolitan swallowed the story and bought them. Between Martinvast and the Metropolitan a metamorphosis had taken place. They had become perfect tapestries again. They are now known as 'The Heroes' and are on display at the Cloisters Museum.

* National Gallery, Washington (Widener Collection).
† National Gallery, Washington (Mellon Collection No 19).
‡ Stavros Niarchos Collection, Rue Chanaleilles, Paris.

Bernhard enjoyed himself in war-torn Paris. Almost his first action was to change the spelling of his name to Bernard, dropping the Germanic 'h', and to actively encourage his friends and associates to call him by his initials, BB. He rapidly formed a wide circle of acquaintances: his face was seen as often in the fashionable 'salons' by night as it was glimpsed in the libraries and cabinets of the Louvre by day. He had an international reputation as an 'expert', a wit and a 'ladies' man', spiced with the mystery of his job as 'something in Intelligence'.

BB was delighted to be away from the pressures and intrigues of Florence and from Mary who, in his eyes, was becoming increasingly tiresome. Her demands for money for her family irritated him, as did her love affairs, and the series of probably self-induced illnesses which necessitated frequent visits to nursing homes, health cures and clinics. Mary alternated between her family home in Surrey, brief visits to I Tatti, and one disastrous visit to Paris where she surprised her husband with his latest lady friend, the Baroness Gabrielle La Caze. In a fit of hysteria she tried to throw herself out of a window, but BB prevented her and packed her off to England.

Joe did not want to renew the Doris contract that autumn, but Uncle Henry overruled him. Although the elder man still dominated the firm, his age and increasing infirmity made it clear to Joe that it would not be long before he himself was in full control. When that happened BB would not have a contract with Duveens for Joe had calculated, not without reason, that BB was bound to him already: there was no need for expensive commissions and retainers.

Joe replaced BB in Florence with the loyal Walter Dowdswell, whose primary brief was to keep his eyes and ears open and report. Dowdswell spent his time in a café in the centre of Florence, sipping coffee and strega with the dealing fraternity and lapping up the gossip of BB's denigrators, all of which he reported in mischievous detail to Joe in New York.

BB quickly discovered Dowdswell's attempt to infiltrate and undermine his position in Florence and, sensing Joe's hostility, he attempted to organize alternative sources of income. In particular he endeavoured to strengthen his relationship with a number of leading dealers, especially Nathan Wildenstein. Joe's criticism of his 'eye' for sculpture rankled deeply; it made him disenchanted with his role as an expert, even on pictures. He therefore spent less of his time dealing and more making scholarly inquiries into what happened to the arts between the glories of Greece, the wonders of Rome and the Renaissance.

If both Joe and Edward Fowles were out of Paris for any length of time, it was Berenson's duty to make occasional supervisory visits to those restorers who were working for Duveens. This was Demotte country, the unseen underworld of studios occupied by artists, sculptors, marblers and gilders, bronze and lead casters, carvers, tapestry restorers, picture reliners and plain forgers in the St Ouen district—an area much frequented by the fashionable dealers from the rue de Rivoli and the Place Vendôme.

One complex of studios was particularly significant. Here worked Henri Boutron, who created Demotte's and Barnard's antique sculptures. Next door was the studio of the late Rodo de Neiderhaisern; the German sculptor had died in 1913, but the studio still housed over a hundred unfinished commissions. Then came Edward Bouet and Jean André, Joe's marble restorers, who specialized in reproducing the portrait busts of Jean-Antoine Houdon. A short distance away was the foundry of Rudier and the warehouse of Henri Visseaux, who concentrated on garden statuary.

At that time Rudier, Bouet and Visseaux were working full-time for Joe, creating the fine statues that today grace the gardens of the Huntington Museum at Pasadena, California, and the 'Versailles fountains' at Whitemarsh, the Philadelphia home of the millionaire E. H. Stotesbury. On one of his supervisory visits, in March 1918, BB purchased half a dozen of Visseaux's Italianate figures for his own garden at I Tatti. They still masquerade there today.

Henri Visseaux was a remarkable man. Edward Fowles described him as

. . . in his early seventies, with a long white beard, flowing hair—a 19th-century Leonardo. His studio and his business dated from the reign of Henri IV of France. His storerooms were filled with hundreds of moulds and models from which he could produce or duplicate pieces in stone, marble, terracotta and bronze which were indistinguishable from the antique. The finest pieces were kept at his home, a converted watermill on the Pont aux Dames on the River Morin.

Fowles records that Visseaux had his own personal method of putting the patina of centuries onto his marbles, though the process took a year:

> First they would be submerged in the mill pond for a summer when the water was slack and the algae and pond weed could dye them through. Then during the winter they were buried in a hot bed of manure and turf cut from the water meadow nearby. He used the bed to overwinter his seedling peaches. When the spring floods came they were suspended in the mill race itself to finish them off.

Also to be found wandering around the maze of studios in the St Ouen suburb of Paris at this time was the American academic Arthur Kingsley Porter, a Yale professor with a substantial private income. Porter had somehow arranged to attach himself to a French commission charged with reporting on the war damage done to notable monuments. This enabled him to have the rare wartime privileges of a chauffeur-driven car, ample gasoline and freedom to move around the countryside. His main interest was collecting material for his *magnum opus*, a ten-volume study of the Romanesque sculpture to be found along the pilgrim roads through France to Rome. He and Bernard soon got to know each other and BB frequently accompanied him, not only on his countrywide explorations but also to Henri Visseaux's country house.

Porter was fascinated by the old man's reference library, for over the years successive generations of the Visseaux family had made accurate drawings and measurements of any statue or monument which they had been asked to create, repair or copy. During these visits BB would theorize on how great art had slumbered from the collapse of the Roman Empire until the Renaissance. On one occasion Visseaux made a number of sketches showing how sculptors through the ages had depicted the horse. His final sketch showed how much an imaginary French 'impressionist' would owe to the sculptors of ancient Greece. He gave the drawings to his guests, whether to BB or to Porter, Fowles does not record.

Shortly afterwards, Henri Boutron had Visseaux's 'impressionist' drawing in his studio and suggested to one of his students that he try his hand at making a maquette, a small clay model, from it. The student was a young Italian called Marino Marini, a painter with an ambition to sculpt in the manner of the ancient Greeks. 'The maquette', recalled Fowles in 1969, 'was about the size of a chihuahua'.

The Marini clay maquette came into Fowles' hands in 1921. He had purchased it from Prince Antoine de Bourbon, whom he described as 'a shady aristocrat closely associated with Demotte'. The Prince claimed that the horse had been given to him by BB in exchange for arranging an audience with the Queen of Spain in 1918. When asked, BB confirmed that he had given the maquette to Prince Antoine. It was only of academic interest and had been too delicate for him to take with him on his travels; he said that he had originally been given it by Demotte.

Early in 1924 the Metropolitan announced the acquisition of a fifth-century bronze horse, celebrating the occasion with an illustrated brochure. Fowles noticed its startling likeness to his clay maquette and sought advice from Carl Dreyfuss, head of the Sculpture Department at the Louvre, and Leon Nicolle, a senior member of Dreyfuss' staff. Both men noticed the uncanny resemblance. Both the clay model and the Metropolitan's bronze had 'doe-like eyes—like a Chinese advertisement for Babycham'.

Fowles remembered another and rather more telling similarity. Both the clay and the bronze had a hole pierced in the lower neck, which Marini had placed there to support a martingale. The hole was far too low for a fifth-century horse's harness but just about in the right place to support a martingale, which was part of the standard harness of a modern French cavalry horse.

Fowles gave his model to Leon Nicolle of the Louvre. He felt sure that his Marini maquette was the progenitor of the Metropolitan's archaic bronze horse but he knew that in the museum world dog rarely eats dog. He knew too, from bitter experience, that if Joe learned about it, he would not be able to resist denouncing it as a fake—without thought for the consequences.

❧ 14 ❧

Sir Joseph

Joe had not, as has just been seen, wanted to renew Berenson's contract, but he had been overruled by Uncle Henry. By now these three powerful individualists were locked in a complex relationship with each other whether they liked it or not. Sometimes feelings between them were amicable, at other times irritation set in; there was a ceaseless jockeying for power. As the First World War dragged on, Uncle Henry's energy waned and his influence decreased, while Joe quietly gained the initiative; Berenson, having blotted his copybook, had to sit quietly in a back seat for a while.

Until 1914, nobody in the firm had dared to doubt Uncle Henry's authority, as his twice-weekly letters which supplemented his daily cables made clear. Each letter was a *'tour d'horizon'* of the firm's interests and activities. A typical letter to Joe is quoted in full as Appendix II. It was written on 3 April 1913, from Paris, and is exactly as he sent it, with the gaps, the words left out, and no signature. He had arrived in Europe a fortnight earlier and had already visited clients in Monte Carlo, BB in Florence, and dealers in Rome, Milan and Paris; he had also found the time to discuss the European situation with a variety of contacts ranging from the British Ambassador in Paris to King George V's private secretary, Lord Stamfordham. By the same post he wrote to his accountant in New York saying that he smelled 'war in the air', urging strict financial retrenchment, and instructing him to sell out his British stocks and buy into U.S. securities, particularly the steel combines. Then he turned to his twice-weekly homily to Joe, whom he had left in New York minding the store.

First he castigates him for losing a sale to Altman, then he teaches him how to sell to Henry Frick, warning him not to overcharge him to begin with. He summarizes the firm's future relations with customers such as the Lehmans, Mr and Mrs J. B. Duke, and the Blumenthals, and gives strict instructions on how to handle the interior decorators hired by the firm to do up their clients' houses. Finally, he reprimands him for failing to send over copies of important letters and for associating with the banker Leopold Hirsch, of whom he disapproved.

Henry spent much of the following two years in Europe, masterminding numerous major deals, but always taking care that he had the item concerned well sold before he purchased. It was Henry who persuaded Lord Cowper to part with Raphael's famous 'Small Cowper Madonna' for $300,000. The Wideners then paid $565,000 for the picture, which included a commission of $50,000 for Lady Desborough, who had arranged the sale. It was Henry again who managed to extract the Huntingtons from France after the outbreak of war in 1914 and to ship them and their collections home to Pasadena. It was Henry who took an option on Leonardo da Vinci's Benois Madonna for $5 million, again on behalf of the Wideners. Unhappily, the Benois family of St Petersburg insisted that the Tsar should have first refusal at that price, and to the dismay of both Henry and the Widener family the Tsar exercised the option and the picture went to the Hermitage, where it is to this day. Finally, it was Henry who took the decision on 14 July 1914 to ship most of Duveens' European stock to New York, where until early in 1917 he and Joe concentrated on furnishing Henry Frick's New York house and building up the Frick Collection.

It was at this time that Henry and Joe decided to oust Louis and the remaining brothers from the firm. The initiative for this came largely from Joe. By May 1917, Henry and Joe were the sole partners, but the effort of the last few years had exhausted Henry. Early in June he suffered a severe stroke and rapidly became little more than a cypher in the company he had created. He sat gloomily in his office watching Joe dramatically reorganize the company, and since he found it difficult to either talk or write coherently there was little he could do.

Joe lost no time in putting his personal stamp on Duveens. Most of his uncle's staff were replaced by people who were totally subservient to him and who did not share Henry's caution or, as

Edward Fowles recalled, Henry's opinion of his brash nephew. According to Fowles, 'Henry could deflate Joe's ego with a look'— and Joe did not want anyone around who could recall the fact. Many of the older men made the mistake of assuming that Henry would recover and Joe would get his come-uppance. They were quickly given their marching orders.

Amongst the replacements was a most unusual Englishman who came to have a far greater influence in the firm than has been realized. He was to end his days as a vice-president of the company and, but for an ill-judged conspiracy with Berenson and the lawyer Louis Levy, could well have been Joe's successor.

He was a former merchant seaman called Bertram Boggis—at least that is what he called himself when he deserted from an English cargo ship in New York in January 1915 rather than face the ordeal of another U-boat-threatened convoy to England. He was eking out a precarious living on the New York waterfront when he presented himself at Duveens in answer to an advertisement for a warehouse porter. There was a line of applicants. Twice he was turned away and each time he rejoined the end of the line and told a different story at his interview. Joe, fascinated by his impudence, hired him not as a porter but as the commissionaire in charge of the entrance hall.

Fowles always believed that Boggis had heard on the waterfront about the Duveen smuggling case and only applied because he wanted to 'get a slice of the action from the inside'. He was a squat, broad-shouldered man with a face like a bullfrog, taciturn and streetwise. Few visitors to Duveens realized that the resplendently uniformed commissionaire had a pistol and a marlin spike concealed in his coat-tails.

He rapidly became Joe's closest confidant in New York. Their relationship is not hard to understand. In England Joe was regarded as a coarse and vulgar man, tolerated only because of his outwardly inexplicable relationship with the royal household and the depth of his pocket. He was well aware that this was how he was regarded, and he played up to this image. There is a well-documented account of his calling on the Duke of Westminster to purchase some paintings. Amidst the dulcet tones of the ducal advisers, Joe stood before a painting and said, 'This is Joe Duveen talking. I'll give fifty thousand smackeroos for these little trifles, any other bids? Right, sold to honest Joe'. The Duke roared with laughter and parted with a pair of Gainsboroughs. In New York Joe was a caricature of an Englishman, immaculately dressed, ostentatious and imperious, speaking in the clipped, fashionable tones of an Edwardian country gentleman. Kenneth Clark gave a telling example when he described a party at Joe's New York residence:

> Duveen gave us a grand dinner in his house. It was large and pretentious, and on the walls were copies of English eighteenth-century full-length portraits of the kind that had made his fortune, men in red coats, ladies in large hats. All his richest clients were present, the men with white ties and creaking shirts, the ladies so weighed down with jewellery that a few of them (no one will believe this, but it is true) brought pieces of jewellery in their hands and laid them down on the dinner table. This could have happened in the Middle Ages. We dined on a blue and gold Sèvres service made for the Empress Catherine of Russia. Since my boyhood I have had a mania for ceramics and I expressed my delight to Lady Duveen. She replied, 'Yes; it is nice. And we don't get it out every day, I can tell you. The last time we used it was for Mr Ramsay MacDonald'. After dinner I said to my host (whom one had to address in his own language): 'Marvellous that Sèvres service. Privilege to eat off it'. 'Sèvres service', said Lord Duveen, 'Sèvres service? Nothing. Eat off it every day'. That was the real Duveen. After dinner we adjourned to the drawing room, also hung with copies of English portraits. A huge soprano from the Metropolitan Opera, swathed in pistachio-coloured satin, accompanied by a small orchestra, sang pieces of Puccini at the top of her voice. Nobody paid the slightest attention. Duveen was regal. In London he might be a clown; in New York he was a king.

Clown or king? That was Joe's problem, for in truth he was neither. With Bert Boggis he could relax, for each recognized the other for the adventurous hustler he was.* Bert rapidly became Joe's body-

---

* Boggis' influence burgeoned when prohibition was introduced in 1920. With Joe's blessing he became a bootlegger extraordinary to the firm's major clients, using a fashionable delicatessen on the corner of Madison and 78th Street as his base. His contacts on the waterfront and in the customs department insured that his imports escaped scrutiny.

guard and confidant and, most importantly, established his unique intelligence network.

Bert adapted quickly to that esoteric world peopled by head porters, bell captains, butlers and the valets of important clients. If a rich mid-westerner booked into the Plaza or the Biltmore, Bert knew within the hour. When Mrs Abby Rockefeller accidentally broke one of her husband's Sèvres vases her maid had called Bert to have it replaced by a duplicate before the master of the house returned.

In time Bert's network of contacts and informants became immense. His regular payroll included the key domestic staff of Bache, Huntington, Kress, Rockefeller, Clarence McKay and Mellon. The telegraph clerks at the cable offices, telephone operators, Pullman car attendants and, down in the docks, clerks in the steamship offices and customs officers all offered information as it came their way.

Each post brought summaries of the contents of confidential letters written by the curators of leading museums or the executives of rival dealers such as Knoedlers.* It was Boggis' boast that when Andrew Mellon was Secretary of the Treasury, the contents of his wastepaper basket were on the train from Washington to New York within an hour of his leaving his office in the evening.

When Joe, now aged forty-eight, left New York for Paris in the summer of 1917 to sort out the various problems with Berenson, Uncle Henry, sixty-four and not at all a well man, knew that he did not have long to live. He seemed to be barely aware of what was going on, for Joe took care to conceal much from him— although Edward Fowles always believed that the older man knew more than Joe thought he did. He certainly knew enough to wish to redraft his will in the last few weeks of his life.

The several company reconstructions and liquidations, and the arrangements between himself and Joel's children, together with the differences in English, French and American company law, had overtaken and nullified Joel's stipulations. Henry was advised that as an American resident and chief shareholder of Duveen Brothers his controlling interest was his to dispose of as he liked.

---

* This behavior was not unique to Duveens; Wildenstein's New York branch was convicted of tapping Knoedlers' telephone.

'He had become thoroughly disillusioned by Joe's behaviour', wrote Fowles, . . . he had realized that he was unable to control him, so, apart from his stamp collection,* he left everything he had to his only son, Geoffrey, reasoning that Joe would either have to buy him out, which he believed he could not afford to do, or wind up the company and split the proceeds with Geoffrey and incidentally pay his brothers and sisters what he owed them.

The new will was signed on 23 December 1918. A week later Henry suffered a further stroke and lapsed into a coma. He never recovered consciousness, and died on the morning of 12 January 1919, leaving his son, Geoffrey, as the new head of the firm.

Geoffrey Duveen was then a lieutenant-commander in the Royal Navy awaiting demobilization. He had been the only member of the Duveen clan to play an active role in the First World War and it had cost him a pair of shattered eardrums during the bombardment at Gallipoli. This destroyed the career he had planned for himself—he had qualified as a barrister shortly before the outbreak of war. He was a quiet, erudite man who shared his father's love of stamp collecting and was none too keen to enter the hurly-burly of the art dealer's world, always assuming that Joe would have been able to stomach working as a junior partner to his young cousin.

When Geoffrey examined his inheritance he was presented with what appeared to be a sorry state of affairs. The firm owed its bankers almost $20 million, partially offset by debtors such as Henry and Arabella Huntington, Lady Michelham, Clarence Mackay and Rockefeller, who owed $11 million, while Henry Frick had almost another $5 million worth of goods on approval at his home. The balance of the bankers' advances were secured against the values of the leasehold premises in New York, Paris and London and the partners'—Joe's and Henry's—joint and several guarantees. Geoffrey, of course, inherited his father's obligation jointly to guarantee the bank overdraft.

The assets which provided the real indication of the firm's worth were the remarkable inventory stored in the cellars in New York. However, it had suited Joe and his uncle to show these at their

---

* The stamps went into a trust for Geoffrey's children.

original cost less depreciation. Since they were largely the remains of the Kann and Hainauer collections, which had been bought *en bloc*, they were valued in the books at less than $500,000, though their true worth was many times that. On paper at least the firm was only solvent while the banks remained content with their security.

Geoffrey's problem was that, though he had a controlling share in the supposed $500,000 worth of stock, he also had a liability of several times that to the banks. Should Frick not purchase the goods which he had on approval, he would have further liabilities of almost another $5 million. He was therefore delighted when Joe generously agreed to purchase his shareholding in exchange for assuming his guarantee to the banks and promising to pay him 60 per cent of the stock's book value in installments of $25,000 a year. Geoffrey signed over his inheritance and left Joe the sole owner of the company.

Joe had now, at the age of fifty, achieved his greatest ambition. He owned Duveens. In August 1919, as a further indirect result of Uncle Henry's death, King George V created him Sir Joseph. Ostensibly, this was in recognition of his services to his country, but apart from lending his Paris offices to Lord Esher during the war and promising $100,000 to a convalescent home for officers run by Lady Esher, which incidentally was never paid, he had done little to deserve such an honour. The real reason for his elevation is a charming one and does posthumous credit to his father.

His father, Joel, had rendered sterling service to King Edward VII, including the redecoration of Buckingham Palace and the embellishment of Westminster Abbey for his Coronation. He had also been more than generous to the King's banker, Lord Farquhar, and the Lords Esher, Knollys, and Stamfordham, buying works of art from each of them at inflated prices. Finally, and without prompting, in 1907 Joel had donated the new Turner Wing to the Tate Gallery at a personal cost of some $175,000. In May 1908, King Edward VII offered him the hereditary title of baronet, which would not only be his but which he would also be able to pass on to his son. Joel refused this honour, although he did accept a non-hereditary knighthood. Joel explained that if he accepted a baronetcy, then on his death, which he knew to be imminent, his son would make life practically impossible for his brother Henry. His son, Joel explained in a memorandum to Farquhar, was not yet ready for the obligations the honour would impose, but he would nevertheless be grateful if the matter could be reconsidered after Henry's death.

Farquhar was as good as his word. Three days after Uncle Henry's obituary appeared in *The Times* the Prime Minister, Lloyd George, was tactfully informed that the Royal Household expected to see Joe's name in his next honours list. It was one of the few personal debts that Farquhar ever paid.

Farquhar, who died in 1923, was probably the greatest scallywag of the many who surrounded Edward VII. He peddled honours, influence and worthless shares with impunity, yet managed to retain the confidence of two monarchs and to remain relatively untouched by public scandal until his death, when the true extent of his machinations was discovered but quickly hushed up. Jacob Astor paid him $1 million for a viscountcy. He was told that $200,000 was to go to a private charity in which the King was personally interested and that the balance was to be divided between the Conservative Party and Lloyd George. Neither received a penny. On his death it was found that Farquhar had misappropriated a further $200,000 while Treasurer of the Conservative Party and embezzled $40,000 from the estate of the late Lord Fife, whose executor he was.

In 1907 he had pushed shares for a company floated by Horatio Bottomley and Lord Michelham. Lord Lincolnshire noted in his diary in February 1907:

> A Siberian gold mining company has been formed by some Jew speculators. Francis Knollys, Lord Stanley, Lord Howe and others accepted directorships, and the shares were rushed up to £16. They have gone down with a rattle and Horace Farquhar is said to have netted £70,000 . . . it is deplorable that the King's private Secretary and the Queen's Lord Chamberlain have been 'let in' and mixed up in an affair like this.

Farquhar lived in great style at No. 7 Grosvenor Square and rented two country properties, White Lodge in Richmond Park from the King and Castle Rising in Norfolk from the Howard family. All three properties were furnished by Duveens and were little more than extensions of their galleries. When Farquhar died in 1923 his possessions were provisionally valued at $2 million. His will was as grandiose as his lifestyle. King George V was left two Louis XIV wine coasters together with his choice of the contents of Castle Rising. Queen Mary was left a Louis XVI commode she had often admired together with the contents of White Lodge. The remainder of the furnishings, including the contents of the Grosvenor Square mansion, were divided amongst Princess Victoria, Princess Maud and Prince Arthur of Connaught.

In the end, no one received anything. By the time Duveens had removed those items which were not paid for, and which had helped secure their indebtedness to Farquhar's bank, and his other creditors had taken their due, nothing remained except a mystery or two. One of the most intriguing is what happened to the pictures that the Howard family left at Castle Rising during Farquhar's tenancy. When they repossessed the property they noticed that they had been rehung, somewhat higher than before. It was not until several years later, when they were taken down for cleaning, that they were found to be modern copies. The clues are tantalizing. So far only one of them can be located. 'The Edge of the Common' by John Crome the Elder now hangs in the Huntington Museum at Pasadena, purchased from Sir Joseph Duveen and allegedly from the collection of P. M. Turner Esq.

Farquhar left Joe two minor legacies. He introduced him to Lord d'Abernon, another banker with a somewhat dubious reputation whom Lloyd George had seen fit to appoint as British Ambassador to Germany in 1918, from which position he more than earned his keep as scout for Duveen Brothers. In fact he displayed such an interest in the arts that, in due course, the Prime Minister appointed him a Trustee of the National Gallery. A second introduction was to Arthur, Lord Lee of Fareham, who took over the lease of White Lodge. Lee, an amateur collector, was rapidly introduced by Joe to the delights of commerce and White Lodge continued to be a Duveen sales annex. In due course Lord Lee became Chairman of the Trustees of the National Gallery and, in Kenneth Clark's words, 'the most hated man in the Museum world'.

It is easy to see how the likes of Farquhar, Lee and d'Abernon flourished in the somewhat shady circles frequented by King Edward VII but it is more difficult to understand how they survived the rectitude of King George V. One explanation is that they amused the King, who was himself not above taking advantage of the newly appointed Sir Joseph's ambition. One example amongst many must suffice.

Shortly after Joe received his knightly accolade he was invited by Lord Esher to luncheon at Windsor. Esher, who was responsible for the contents of the castle, said that he required advice on rearranging some of the royal works of art. Joe was so excited that he wrote to Andrew Mellon telling him of the honour and travelled to Windsor expecting to be appointed Keeper of the Royal Collections at the very least.

King George V and Horace Farquhar joined Esher and Joe for a leisurely tour. In one of the passages stood an ugly and undistinguished bronze of a river god, representing the Nile. 'Look, Sir Joseph', said the King, 'Leonardo da Vinci I am told'.

Obediently, Joe enthused over the bronze, knowing full well that it was not a Leonardo; nor, since it was part of the royal collection, could it be for sale. 'It is magnificent, Sire. You are remarkably fortunate. What wouldn't I give to have such a specimen in my own collection'.

Lord Esher pressed him as to its value. 'At least £10,000', replied Joe.

'As a matter of fact', replied the King, 'it's my own property. Take it—I'm tired of it, send the cheque to Farquhar when it's convenient'.

The bronze is now in the Norton Simon Collection, Los Angeles, with the provenance 'ex coll: King George V, the Right Hon. the Earl Farquhar'.

With the House of Duveen firmly under his personal control and a handle to his name, Joe was ebullient, but some formidable problems lay ahead. There was the lurking danger posed by De-motte: Joe felt that if he could control the timing of the exposure of his frauds, the skirmish would be of manageable proportions, but others in the firm thought the whole matter was best left alone. Then there were the anxieties caused by the ailing health of Henry Frick, who had a million pounds' worth of Duveen goods on approval, as yet unpaid for. Lord Michelham was another worry. One of the firm's largest debtors, he had died in 1919, the week before Uncle Henry.

❧ 15 ❧

Cupid

The House of Duveen first became involved with the Michelham family back in 1898 when Joe's brother Ernest took Octavius Bradshaw of Powderham Castle in Devonshire and his pretty young daughter, Aimée Geraldine, to see the Oaks run at Epsom. Ernest was after the Powderham Castle tapestries and had already entered Aimée, then just eighteen, into the Duveen code-book as 'Cupid'. Ernest's other two guests that day were the financier (and eventually convicted swindler) Horatio Bottomley and Bottomley's adviser on racing matters, a ubiquitous lounge lizard called Jefferson Davis Cohn.

In the next box at Epsom were Sir Blundell Maple, the founder of the famous furniture firm, and his guest Herbert de Stern. The favourite for the Oaks was Blundell Maple's filly Nun Nicer, which Aimée Bradshaw backed. When the Duke of Portland's horse, Airs and Graces, won, Aimée commiserated with her next-door neighbour. Whereupon Blundell Maple asked her to join him and introduced her to his guest. Three months later Herbert and Aimée were married, and because of Herbert's exceptionally handsome marriage settlement her father no longer had to sell the Powderham tapestries to Duveens.

However, Ernest was undeterred by the loss of the tapestries because he knew he had gained the de Sterns' goodwill and he realized that soon they would have a house, or houses, to furnish. He therefore set about educating Aimée in matters of taste, for he had discovered that Herbert was the son of the late Baron de Stern—the title was a Portuguese creation—who had a substantial private banking business with branches in London, Paris and Ostend. Herbert had inherited $50 million from his father and a further $40 million from his brother who had died in a lunatic asylum, so he could afford to be lavish in his expenditure. Ernest sent Aimée books on decoration and French fashion illustrations and gradually began to interest her in the finer, possibly artistic and certainly more expensive, things in life. She proved an apt pupil.

Herbert allowed himself only one diversion from his business, and that was horse-racing. He adored his young wife and somewhat illogically reasoned that, as he had met her on a racecourse, that was where they should spend their leisure hours. Undaunted, Ernest arranged Herbert's initiation into the arcane world of buying, breeding, and training racehorses and suggested his friend Jefferson Davis Cohn as tutor.

Cohn was a mysterious figure. In England he was regarded as an American millionaire, while he managed to pass as an English gentleman among Americans who were not too worldly-wise. In France he was assumed to be either a Belgian or an Austrian who had recently acquired both American nationality and an American fortune. In fact his main source of income between 1896 and 1931 came from a standing arrangement he had made with the Duveen family, who paid him 15 per cent commission on any goods they sold to customers he introduced. He had similar understandings with insurance brokers, house agents, auctioneers and solicitors; otherwise his so-called fortune was Bottomley's, and later on de Stern's.

Horatio Bottomley was a company promoter. He specialized in forming speculative joint stock companies, floating the shares, and then judiciously manipulating the share prices so that they briefly rose, when he would sell out and the company would then crash to bankruptcy with monotonous regularity. The companies nearly always operated in the remoter parts of Australia or the American West, and were usually in highly speculative fields such as gold or silver mines. Their shares were foisted on a gullible public by word of mouth by scouts such as Cohn, who was adept at spotting the rich and stupid, and by constant recommendations in publications such as *John Bull* which Bottomley both owned and edited.

Bottomley had what he modestly called a 'cottage' at Dicker in Sussex. The 'cottage' had thirty bedrooms, eight gardeners and a private racecourse. It was here that he invited the newly married de Sterns and he was delighted when Cohn persuaded them to buy Michelham Priory at nearby Hellingly as their country seat. The de Sterns had already purchased Horace Walpole's famous Strawberry Hill and 26 Princes Gate in London. All three houses were furnished by Duveens.

Cohn also took the de Sterns to the bloodstock sales, introduced them to acquaintances of his who had promising horses for sale, arranged for those they bought to be trained by Bottomley's trainer, Harry Ware, and supervised their racing programme.

Cohn's tutelage was far from successful, and Herbert rapidly acquired the reputation of being the unluckiest owner on the turf. However, racing took him into the society he craved. Herbert became an acquaintance of the Prince of Wales and, when Queen Victoria died, was always available to give the Prince, now King Edward VII, the benefit of his financial advice, and probably his chequebook. In 1905 his grateful monarch created him first a baronet and then, a few months later, a peer; he took the title of Baron Michelham of Hellingly, and settled down to enjoy a life of semi-retirement at Michelham Priory with his wife and the two sons with which she had presented him: Herman, born in September 1900, and Jack, who arrived on Christmas Eve 1903. What the happy baron did not know was that Jack, his favourite, had been fathered by Jefferson Davis Cohn.

Herbert Michelham's semi-retirement was short-lived. In 1907 Horatio Bottomley faced the second bankruptcy proceedings of his career and moved swiftly to frustrate his creditors. His method was as heartless as it was effective. He married off his complaisant daughter, Florence, to the ubiquitous Cohn and transferred the title of his house at Dicker, plus all the furnishings, to the happy couple as a marriage settlement. He tried to transfer the racehorses as well, but his legal advisers had doubts about the legality of that particular stratagem, so the sixty horses were transferred first to Ostend and then to France, safely out of English jurisdiction.

Michelham helped in the necessary financial laundering largely, it may be supposed, at his wife's insistence. Furthermore, as Michelham's own horses were so involved with the Bottomley stable, they all went to the continent as well. Unfortunately, this inextricably associated Michelham with Bottomley among those in the know.

Florence Cohn stayed at Dicker with her mother, while Jeff Cohn leased a large house in Paris and an estate just outside the city which boasted ample stables and paddocks, a private racecourse and nine miles of gallops. It was a judicious move, as he had been warned off the London Stock Exchange and, to his deeper chagrin, the British turf. Neither the Inland Revenue nor the Bankruptcy Court nor Bottomley's frustrated creditors could stop Cohn. The carefully drawn up legal agreements between him and Bottomley were unassailable, chiefly due to the perspicacity of one of the Duveen family's stable of solicitors.

Bottomley's financial disgrace rebounded on the Michelhams. Polite society, into which Herbert and Aimée had so recently gained an entrée, now shunned them, and in 1910 his relations, led by his cousin Sir Alfred Stern, bought him out of the family bank. Lord Michelham took his family off to Paris, where Joe Duveen found them a vast apartment—three floors of a former mansion with twenty-six bedrooms, several suites of reception rooms, and a mirrored salon 120 feet long—in the rue Nitot. Naturally it had to be decorated and furnished in the style which Duveens had taught them was appropriate—at a cost of $1.8 million. In their absence from London, Lady Michelham allowed Ernest Duveen to refurbish entirely their London houses at 26 Princes Gate and 30 Arlington Street, next to the Ritz. The invoices, totalling a further $2.3 million, were written and paid in France to prevent any close inspection by the Inland Revenue.

During the autumn of 1910, Lord Michelham suffered a mild stroke. He made a partial recovery but his speech became slurred and there were disturbing signs that the insanity which had killed his brother was beginning to affect him as well. It was a propitious time to make a will, and once again a Duveen solicitor took care of matters. The will, dated 18 January 1911, was remarkable.

The fortune was left to the two young sons but Lady Michelham was to receive a life interest in the properties and the income from the capital, plus the contents of all the properties. Lady Michelham and Jeff Cohn were made joint executors and Cohn became trustee for the sons—then aged eleven and eight—at a salary of $15,000 a year. Cohn was also to receive a legacy of $125,000. In addition, Lord Michelham was persuaded that his affairs were now so complicated that he needed someone to manage them for him. That duty also fell on Jeff Cohn, at a salary of $125,000 a year plus out-of-pocket expenses.

The Michelham millions were invested in a new company, registered in Paris, called Herbert Stern and Co. Joe Duveen recommended an elderly American, Colonel Hunskie, a former president of the U.S. Steel Corporation who had retired to Paris, as a suitable figurehead, but he died shortly afterwards.

The next five years were immensely profitable to the Duveens. The Michelhams entertained widely while Cohn's style of living improved dramatically. Cohn leased a magnificent mansion in the Avenue Friedland and acquired the steam yacht *Alberta* from the Belgian royal family. His summer cruises, usually with either Ernest or Louis Duveen aboard, brought a great deal of business to Duveens. Some idea of the milieu in which Cohn now moved can be gained from looking at the guest list for a lunch given by Cohn in honour of the King and Queen of the Hellenes on 14 March 1914. Those present included Horatio Bottomley, still dodging his creditors, the Greek Crown Princess, Princess Charlotte of Prussia, Prince Alexander of Greece, Princess Helen of Greece, the Prince of Saxe-Meinigen, and a constellation of continental counts and barons with, naturally, the Michelhams and Ernest Duveen in attendance.

The entertainment in Paris was just as lavish. Edward Fowles, the manager of Duveens' Paris gallery, recalled in his book, *Memories of Duveen Brothers*: 'Lady Michelham complained that there was nowhere suitable for her to dance in their apartment. I rearranged the furniture, adding a number of small tables and commodes, and turned one of the rooms into a miniature ballroom. She paid our bill for £90,000 without a murmur'.

The dancing continued, although the outbreak of the First World War cast a slight shadow over the parties. Cohn lent the Avenue Friedland mansion to a succession of British political dignitaries, at least that is what the public was led to believe when he was granted the position of an honorary attaché on the staff of Lord Esher in Paris, with the rank of captain. In fact, the remainder of Cohn's lease was simply assigned to the British Embassy. Joe Duveen, as we already know, lent a substantial part of the Place Vendôme building to the Intelligence section of the British Expeditionary Force, which was presided over by Lord Esher's son,

Captain Oliver Brett, while many of Esher's servants metamorphosed from butlers and footmen into clerks and telephone operators. The Michelhams spent the entire war in Paris, and in their own way made substantial contributions to the war effort. They paid for the conversion of the Hotel Astoria into a convalescent home and made a floor of their apartment available to members of the British General Staff. The unfortunate, and by now largely comatose, Lord Michelham placidly accepted whatever happened around him.

BB, who, it will be remembered, had stayed in Paris after September 1917 at Joe's request while the Demotte scandal blew over, frequently attended Lady Michelham's parties as they were old friends. He now noticed the appalling deterioration in Michelham's condition and pointed this out to Duveens, suggesting that they speedily recover any monies owing. Berenson revelled in intrigue and was now as concerned as anyone at Duveens about what was going to happen.

The Michelham indebtedness to the firm at that time was almost $6 million, and with His Lordship largely incapacitated it was almost impossible to obtain a payment. True, Captain Jeff Cohn could and did arrange modest drafts from the Michelham bank, but he tended to deduct his 15 per cent from the gross first. With the $450,000 bill for decorating the ballroom, for example, the first payment on account was for $90,000, from which the gallant captain deducted $67,500—his commission on the whole $450,000. To add to the complications, Ernest Duveen had the right to draw an overriding commission on goods bought from or by clients he regarded as his own. The Michelhams fell into this category and, as Ernest and Jeff Cohn wre well-nigh inseparable, Jeff took care that Ernest received his commission in advance of the gross as well.

Lady Michelham now took up with a distinguished English Royal Flying Corps officer, Captain Arthur Capel, who, after a heroic if gruelling spell at the front, was being lionized in Paris in general and by Her Ladyship in particular. Capel temporarily began to supplant Jeff Cohn in Aimée's favours.

So taken was Lady Michelham that she invited his sister Bertha, thirty-nine years old and unmarried, to join her, ostensibly to assist her in her war work—visiting hospitals and convalescent soldiers—

but in reality as a chaperone. Bertha Capel had a third duty, which was to keep an eye on the elder Michelham boy, Herman, then aged seventeen, who had left Malvern School prematurely as he had begun to show the first signs of the mental deterioration which plagued his father's side of the family.

As if inspired by the Capels, Lady Michelham's parties now became a byword for their splendour and flamboyance. News of all this extravagance reached the ears of His Lordship's relations and made them determined to act, for they felt, with some justification, that he had once again fallen amongst thieves. Somehow they also managed to learn of the terms of the will which so conspicuously favoured Captain Cohn. BB told Duveens that they had been tipped off by Captain Arthur Capel.

Shortly after the Armistice several members of the Stern family visited Paris, and on 27 September 1918 they managed to gain Michelham's ear during one of Her Ladyship's frequent absences. A new will was drawn up and witnessed, which totally omitted Captain Cohn and which effectively took control of the capital sums away from both him and Lady Michelham. Lady Michelham would, on her husband's death, have to survive with the contents of the houses and a fixed income for life. This new will was kept a secret.

On 23 December 1918, Lord Michelham caught a chill which turned into pneumonia. On 2 January he was on his deathbed, and the household gathered together to await the end. He was attended by two doctors: Dr Thompson from the British Embassy and, at the Stern family's request, the eminent London physician, Sir Thomas Horder.

Sir Thomas examined Lord Michelham on the morning of 3 January; he found him to be 'febrile, breathing with difficulty and incapable of any intelligent response'. He formed the impression that death was at most only a day or two away and prescribed a mild dose of morphine to make His Lordship's exit easy for all concerned.

Duveens were desperate. They had learned the contents of the new will, partly from the solicitor and also from one of the new executors, Sir Lionel Salomons, a distant relation of Lady Duveen. A third source had been none other than Captain Capel. Joe Duveen, scenting that Jeff Cohn was currently out of favour, had

sounded out Capel as a possible conduit to persuade the Michelhams to settle their account. Through Sir Lionel's influence Captain Capel was made a co-executor of the still secret will.

Unhappily, at least for the Stern family, Capel also told Her
Ladyship of its contents shortly after Sir Thomas Horder left the
apartment. She responded immediately, calling in an English solicitor, a Mr Chance who was currently in Paris, and Dr Thompson, the Embassy doctor. She persuaded them that His Lordship
was still in possession of his faculties and wished to add a codicil,
which Mr Chance obligingly drafted. In effect, it was to substitute
herself in place of the Stern cousins as executor and to place the
entire capital sum—estimated at $75 million—under her control
until the boys reached the age of thirty. They were then aged
eighteen and fifteen.

Dr Thompson recounted what happened next in an affidavit
submitted to the Chancery Court:

> I attended Lord Michelham at 6.15 P.M. on 3rd January. At
> Lady Michelham's request I asked his Lordship if he wished
> to see Mr Chance the Lawyer. He distinctly replied 'yes'. I
> then told Mr Chance that his Lordship wished to see him.
> Mr Chance explained to him that he understood that he had
> expressed a wish to make a codicil and inquired if that was
> his wish. His Lordship again replied 'yes'. At Mr Chance's
> request I then asked if he understood the document and did
> he wish it to be executed. He nodded his head. Mr Chance
> then said that as the patient was not very well, he (Chance)
> could sign for him if he wished. His Lordship again replied
> 'yes'. Mr Chance then signed and we went downstairs. I left
> the premises at 7.30 P.M. and returned at 10 P.M. to see my
> patient.

When the obliging doctor returned he found the house in an uproar. In one room were the Stern relations and their London lawyers, in another, a Mr Jocelyn Brandon from the London firm of
solicitors Brandon and Nicholson, who occasionally acted for Her
Ladyship. In yet a third room were Captain Capel and his sister
Bertha.

According to Dr Thompson, Lady Michelham and Mr Brandon
were moving from room to room having 'animated discussions'.

Shortly after Dr Thompson arrived, she asked to speak to him privately. She said that she and her husband were most anxious that the 18-year-old and slightly dotty Herman should marry the 39-year-old Bertha immediately. Lord Beresford was arranging for the ceremony to take place by special licence the following afternoon at All Saints Church, Knightsbridge, Captain Capel had agreed to fly Herman and Bertha to England at first light, and Lord Beresford was to give the bride away on Lord Michelham's behalf. Dr Thompson declared himself 'stunned'.

He asked to speak to both the prospective bride and the groom. Bertha was prepared to accept the marriage 'provided the settlement was satisfactory'. Herman was perfectly happy: 'He was too excited at the chance of a ride in an aeroplane to think of anything else'. Thompson then reported that 'there was an equally animated discussion as to the size of the settlement'. All the separate factions except the Stern relations took part, and the final figure agreed upon was a sum which would generate an income of $125,000 a year for Bertha, free of all present and future taxes. The sum required for such an annuity was coincidently exactly the amount of the Michelhams' indebtedness to Duveens—$6 million.

The result of this marriage settlement, under French law, would be that though the monies would technically be Bertha's, they would be administered—or at least seen to be administered—by her husband, Herman.

The doctor was then asked to witness the marriage settlement as he had witnessed the earlier codicil. The Chancery Court transcript of Dr Thompson's examination by Sergeant Sullivan takes up the tale:

The witness [Dr Thompson] did not remember if he inquired into his Lordship's capacity. He protested against going upstairs to sign as he felt the family lawyer should be present. Lady Michelham, Mr Brandon and the witness then went up. Lady Michelham said to Lord Michelham 'You gave your consent to the marriage with Bertha—do you now wish it?' Lord Michelham moved his head in affirmation. She then said 'Do you wish to sign the settlements?' He again affirmed. She then took his hand in hers and, putting a pen between his fingers, guided his hand and the signature was made. He was in his usual drowsy state. The witness then signed as the witness to the signature on the settlement.

Thereafter all went as planned. Bertha and Herman were married at 4 P.M. on 4 January 1919 at All Saints, Knightsbridge. Lord Beresford gave the bride away and Ernest Duveen paid for the flowers. The bride's posy contained the note, 'Love will find a way'.

Lord Michelham died three days after the wedding. Jeff Cohn now did his best to ensure that Aimée, now the Dowager Lady Michelham, ran into problems. He filed a caveat or legal warning against the September 1918 will, the January 1919 codicil and the marriage settlement. This had the effect of asking the English and French courts to decide which of the wills was valid, but before that issue could be decided, the validity of the deathbed marriage settlement had to be settled.

When the case came up for trial the affair would, as the *Sun* newspaper declared, 'contain sensational revelations which would astound the public'. The *Sun* continued: 'It is expected that enormous sums will be swallowed up in lawyers' fees. Practically all the famous counsel at the Bar have been engaged—men who consider their appearance in court cheap at £5 a minute'.

The preliminary pre-trial skirmishes took place during May and June 1919 before Mr Justice Eve, who declared that such were the allegations that he would hold the proceedings in camera if the matter came to trial, and urged all the parties to come to an agreed settlement. The chief casualty of any such hearing would be Aimée, the Dowager Lady Michelham, and she now appealed to Duveens for help.

They were only too anxious to oblige as the Stern family had already introduced an affidavit into the case stating that Christie's independent valuation of the paintings and furniture purchased from Duveens was no more than $1 million, as opposed to the $6 million charged. Once more Ernest Duveen was asked to see what he could do.

Ernest discovered that the solicitor, who was negotiating the settlement urged by the judge, collected snuff boxes. He and Joe arranged a mouthwatering display of them in a glass vitrine in Ernest's Grafton Street office and invited the solicitor for a working luncheon. They ate smoked salmon, plovers' eggs and chocolate cake, washed down with Château d'Yquem. The luncheon finished with an agreed settlement which the solicitor persuaded all the parties to accept. At the same time he was allowed to purchase the snuff boxes at what Ernest and Joe insisted was an independent valuation.

The result was that all the parties' costs and Duveens' bill of $6 million were paid for out of the estate. The marriage was held to be valid, but the marriage settlement was cancelled. Bertha, now Lady Michelham, was granted a modest annuity and a small country estate at St Germain-en-Laye. Duveens gave evidence that all the items purchased from them had been gifts from His Lordship to his wife at the time of purchase, so did not rank for probate and therefore independent valuation. Aimée, the Dowager Lady Michelham, received the Arlington Street house and its contents plus the contents of the Paris apartment and a fixed income for life.

Herman, now Lord Michelham, together with his brother Jack, became Wards in Chancery and the Chancery Court allowed Herman to retire quietly to Switzerland, where he lived happily until he died in April 1985. The balance of the $75 million was administered by Herbert's cousin Sir Alfred Stern, assisted by Mr Whinney, a leading London accountant, while the minor figures such as the compliant solicitors and Dr Thompson were given written indemnities from all the parties concerned. Outwardly the only loser was Captain Jefferson Davis Cohn, but privately he was allowed to keep the Michelham racehorses. Nor did he lose any time in re-establishing himself in the favours of 40-year-old Aimée, the Dowager Lady Michelham.

Once the estate was settled Aimée, aided and abetted by Jeff once more, began to buy from Duveens. Again she bought none too wisely. She paid $70,000, for example, for a full-length portrait of Lady Peel attributed to Lawrence which, after her death, was sold for $150. By 1922 Aimée owed Duveens almost $1.5 million. She delighted in prevaricating over payment, claiming that she needed the permission of the trustees to realize capital, though her income was $2 million a year.

By the end of 1925 Aimée's romance with Jeff Cohn had finally cooled. On 6 February 1926, she made a hasty marriage to a tolerably wealthy 28-year-old Texan called Frederick Almay and left England to live in Florida. She returned to France the following July and was taken seriously ill with alcoholic poisoning at Deauville races. When it became plain that her liver was so damaged that she had not long to live she returned to Arlington Street to begin her final bout with Duveens.

She was well aware that the last thing Joe wanted was for her collection to be exposed to public auction. In order to keep his reputation he would have to rig the sale to ensure that respectably high prices were paid. She resolved to take advantage of his fears.

A few months earlier Joe had offered Aimée Almay, as the Dowager Lady Michelham had now become, $325,000 for Sir Thomas Lawrence's portrait of Miss Sarah Moulton-Barratt, known all over the world as 'Pinkie' and one of the most charming and powerful of that artist's early portraits. He had sold it to her some years previously for $250,000 at a time when Lawrence had not begun to appreciate in value, and almost any other dealer's price would have been around half that figure. She speedily found out from Jeff Cohn what Joe was up to.

She learned that Joe was anxious to make the American millionaire Andrew Mellon one of his customers. Hitherto, Mellon had dealt exclusively through Knoedlers of New York, and Joe dearly wished to capture Mellon from Knoedler, whom he regarded as his greatest American rival. Mellon had admired 'Pinkie' from afar, and on hearing of this Joe had rashly promised to obtain the picture for him. Jeff Cohn on Aimée's behalf then devised the following stratagem.

Cohn suggested that Aimée ask Hamptons, the auctioneers, to sell her entire collection, less 'Pinkie'. He would leak to Knoedlers what Joe was prepared to pay for the picture. In this way Mellon, in turn, would learn Joe's price and Joe would have to be straightforward with him. Mellon would get the picture but Joe would be denied his customary profit.

Aimée at first demurred. She was already heavily indebted to Duveens and felt that she should pay off some of the debt before she took such a decision. Jeff then came up with an idea which was wholly in character. She had, he explained, an insurance policy for $1.25 million. Its surrender value was $425,000 but the insurance company was unaware that she was mortally ill. He could, he felt, persuade Joe to credit her account with Duveens with $500,000 if she would assign the policy to Duveens. She agreed to do this and Cohn, with Joe's agreement, told the insurance company how near to death Aimée was. The company hastily bought the policy back for $625,000.

In the event, she was too ill to take the 'Pinkie' negotiations any further, and to Joe's chagrin Hamptons announced that they would sell the complete collection, including 'Pinkie', on 24 November 1926.

The rapidly sinking Aimée sailed for New York before the sale and died a few weeks later, on 2 January 1927. She had made her final will shortly before she left, and the obliging solicitor had furnished Duveens with its contents. She left her personal monies and jewellery, plus the proceeds from the sale of the Arlington Street house, to her elder son, Herman. Her younger son Jack Stern was to have half the net proceeds of the auction of her collection.

At a conference just before the sale, Joe Duveen, Jeff Cohn and young Jack Stern, now freshly graduated from Oxford, decided on the following plan. Jack was to bid up the pictures and Joe would always top his bid until he took a watch out of his waistcoat pocket. As far as the furniture was concerned, Jack was to buy as lavishly as he wished, while Joe would store it free of charge and try to place it amongst his other clients at no profit to himself. This was in Jack's interest as he would receive half of whatever prices were paid and the furniture would certainly appreciate in value.

The scheme worked well. Jack bid the pictures up so successfully that Thomas Gainsborough's 'The Master of Heathcote' and George Romney's 'Anne, Lady Poole' fetched record prices. Knoedler opposed Joe in the battle for 'Pinkie', which Joe eventually purchased for 73,000 guineas, a record price for a Lawrence. Joe then sold it to Henry Huntington of Pasadena, thereby teaching Mellon the lesson that if he wanted a Duveen picture he must pay a Duveen price.

On the whole, Duveens escaped relatively lightly. The record picture prices obscured the remarkably low sums the furniture realized. So low, in fact, that a few months later Jack and Jeff, working in unison, had no difficulty in selling most of it to Mrs J. D. Rockefeller at a profit of $150,000.

Jack dabbled in the art market for most of his life before he settled in Mexico. Jeff was not so lucky. Horatio Bottomley had been sentenced to seven years' penal servitude in 1922, and in the final winding up of his affairs Cohn's true role became widely known. Lloyds Bank, Paris, had him adjudged bankrupt in 1931, and he slipped out of the twilight world of Joe Duveen as surreptitiously as he had entered it.

❧ 16 ☙

Thin Ice

It will be remembered that when Joe Duveen finally gained control of the firm, he had been left with several problems: the death of Lord Michelham had been one, the death of Henry Frick another, the Demotte scandal a third. But an unforeseen fourth problem of major proportions was suddenly created by the death of William Salomon.

William Salomon had been a banker and a minor client of Joe Duveen's for some time. He had frequently discounted the bills of Duveens' larger customers and had gradually grown interested in Italian pictures. In 1913, he had decided to emulate Henry Clay Frick by furnishing his house as a living museum and had asked Joe to create a suitable collection for him. Salomon bought his Italian collection in two batches. The first group of six paintings, which were all selected by Bernard, cost Duveens $145,000 delivered in New York. Salomon was charged $650,000. Bernard then selected six more, and a further three were certified as genuine by a Swedish expert called Dr Oswald Sirén. Joe told Salomon that Bernard had passed all fifteen. The entire collection cost Salomon $1,100,000.

Salomon died suddenly in 1919. His family had no wish to maintain a museum and asked the then leading New York auction house, the American Art Association (AAA), to sell the fifteen paintings. Delighted at such an important sale, they engaged Maurice Brockwell, a one-time secretary of Bernard's, to prepare the catalogue.

When Brockwell examined the pictures he was horrified. He told Joe that he could not accept certain of the attributions, in particular an improved Giovanni Bellini Madonna and two dubious Catenas from Bernard, and a Luini and a Botticelli authenticated by Sirén. Apart from these five problem pictures, he advised the auctioneers that there was no hope of obtaining anything approaching the prices which the late Mr Salomon had paid.

Mr Kirby, the principal of the AAA auction rooms, had a series of what must have been embarrassing interviews with Joe. He asked to see the letter of attestation from Bernard Berenson which Salomon had been led to believe existed for all fifteen pictures. Joe blustered, then promised to obtain it. He delegated the matter to Edward Fowles, who recalled:

> 26 August 1922.
> Joe nagged at me for a whole day, telling me that without the letter he would lose his reputation and be ruined. Only I could save him and he was sure that Bernard would not refuse such a favour . . . I finally agreed to try.

Fowles already had an excuse for meeting Bernard, for he had been asked to renegotiate the Doris-Duveen contract which was due to expire on 25 September. Edward arranged to meet Bernard at a Berlin hotel where he was holidaying with his secretary, Miss Nicky Mariano. There have been two accounts of what happened at that meeting, and they contradict each other.

In her book *Forty Years with Berenson* Miss Mariano states that 'The Chief assistant to Sir Joseph appeared with an urgent request . . . Duveen wanted B.B. to endorse the attributions of several pictures sold by him during the war . . . over which he was in some trouble. B.B. refused categorically in spite of the financial advantage'.

Fowles tells a different story. He says that at first Bernard refused. Later that evening it was Miss Mariano who persuaded him to change his mind. In due course she received a pair of emerald earrings and a check for $1,250 from a grateful Fowles. Bernard's final words on the subject of the fifteen paintings, Fowles noted, were, 'Don't forget to put them in the X book'.

The acid test as to which account is correct seems to be: are they there? The 'X' book does in fact list all fifteen of the paintings (Nos. 188–202), including the disputed Botticelli, which has a note attached to it to the effect that, while BB had certified it as a 'late Botticelli', he really believed it was by Jacopo del Sellaio.

Joe had to pay for this concession from Bernard by easing the terms for the renewal of the Doris-Duveen contract. In addition to collecting 25 per cent of the profit that Joe had made when he sold the Sirén pictures to Salomon in the first place, Bernard was brought fully up to date on the state of the 'X' sales, and all arrears of commission were paid off. Bernard now insisted that he be permitted to deal on his own account if Duveens were not interested in the pictures concerned and that his relationships with other dealers should not be held against him. Finally, and at his own insistence, Bernard was allowed to buy for the firm on his own initiative without reference to Paris or New York.

Once Joe had Bernard's authentication of the Sirén pictures he preempted the auction by agreeing to buy all fifteen back from Salomon's executors for $1,100,000 plus a percentage of whatever he managed to sell them for in the future.

A 'Portrait of a Young Man', then wrongly thought to be by Alvise Vivarini, was sold to Andrew Mellon with a Berenson certificate that it was a Giovanni Bellini. Mellon returned the picture after a few months, so Joe sold it to Jules Bache, still under the ironically more accurate Bellini label. Today it hangs in the Metropolitan, described as by Jacometto Veneziano.

Samuel Kress bought Bernardino de' Conti's 'Portrait of a Lady', which the National Gallery, Washington, now attributes to an anonymous imitator of Leonardo da Vinci.

The collection included a so-called Baldovinetti, which had been one of Bernard's first purchases for Duveens. This is a palpable fake, being nothing more than a wreck of what might once have been a Pseudo Pier Francesco Fiorentino, totally repainted to look like a Baldovinetti. It had been purchased from Icilio Joni the forger in Florence in 1910 for $5,000 and sold to Salomon for $62,500. Joe resold it to Clarence Mackay for $105,000. When Mackay was ruined during the Depression Joe resold it in 1936 to Samuel Kress, who gave it to the National Gallery of Washington. It is now in storage.

Palma Vecchio's Annunciation, which had cost Bernard $25,000 and for which Salomon had paid $105,000, went to Mrs Duke of Newport, while a Pollaiuolo portrait of a woman, which cost $35,000 and had been sold to Salomon for $60,000, was purchased by Nils B. Hersloff of New Jersey for $75,000. The contentious

Botticelli, two Francias and a Catena were sold off to the dealer Kleinberger. The remaining six pictures went to none other than the gullible restaurateur who had bought the Arch of Constantine from the enterprising von Kopp many years previously, John R. Thompson of Chicago, who, according to the late Louis Levy, paid $1,000,000. Levy, who was present at the time, described the sale to Sam Behrman, who published the account in his hilarious if unreliable book *Duveen*.

According to the Levy-Behrman account, Thompson had begun to collect pictures with the help of a Chicago dealer. After a suitable period of tutelage he expressed a wish for rather better pictures than were available in Chicago; the dealer then approached Joe and arranged that in exchange for delivering Thompson and his chequebook he would receive a suitable commission. 'But', Joe warned him, 'don't be shocked by my tactics'.

When they arrived Joe kept them waiting for an hour; then, after the introductions were complete, he launched into a lengthy homily on the economics of the restaurant business. He spoke of restaurants as a social service; he inquired about turnover, the price of food, the need for refrigeration. At length the wretched Thompson interrupted, saying that he had come to buy pictures, not to receive a lecture on running restaurants. Behrman's account continues, 'Snapped back so rudely to an activity so marginal, Duveen made a quick adjustment. "Oh, paintings!" he said, as if recalling an almost forgotten acquaintance. "Of course, paintings! Oh, well, now if you're interested in pictures come upstairs with me and I'll show you some." '

When they came out of the lift, Thompson found himself in a dimly lit room that contained the six remaining Salomon pictures. Duveen made as if to walk straight through to yet another room when Thompson made the mistake of looking back.

He lingered; from the blur of the six pictures he got a quick impression of infinite desirability. He called the hurrying Duveen back. 'Here are some pictures', he said. 'What about these?'

Duveen took his arm. 'My dear Mr Thompson', he said gently, 'there is nothing in this room that would interest you in the least'.

'Why not?' argued the new pupil. 'Of course they interest me. What would I be doing here if they didn't interest me?'

'These pictures, my dear fellow, I am reserving, as a matter of fact, for a favourite client', Duveen said. 'They will interest him far more than they could possibly interest you'.

Thompson protested; he would yield to no one in acuteness of interest. 'Why do you think they wouldn't interest me?' he asked. 'I want you to know, Sir Joseph, that I own some pretty good pictures'.

'I am sure you do', Duveen said soothingly. 'And if you will just follow me, I am sure that I can add to your collection and, if I may say so, improve it. But not these. You are a busy man, and I don't want to waste your time. Not with these'.

'Why not?' repeated Mr Thompson.

Pushed to the wall, Duveen dropped all pretence of tact. He made it plain that he thought the pictures were over Thompson's head, both aesthetically and economically.

'How much for the six?' Thompson demanded.

'A million dollars, I am afraid', said Duveen, as if pained at having to demonstrate the truth of an unflattering statement.

Thompson was ready with an answer. 'I'll take them', he said vindictively.

The methods used in the sale, repurchase, and resale of the Salomon pictures show how ruthless Joe Duveen had become and demonstrate the final corruption of BB's integrity. BB never forgave himself for the lapse and both he and Miss Mariano remained bitterly ashamed. After this episode BB decided to make posthumous amends by earning enough money to bequeath I Tatti, his art collection, and his library to Harvard, together with sufficient endowment to maintain the bequest.

He was now fifty-seven, comfortably off, distinguished-looking in a continental way, but plagued by a nervous dyspepsia, probably due to the tensions created by Joe's demands and his own acquiescence in them. His wife gave him little support. She still helped him with his writing but had a habit of provoking his temper by her total lack of interest in either running the household or the state of their finances. She allowed Miss Mariano to assume almost all of her role as wife/lover and housekeeper and remained a noisy presence in the background.

In this uneasy household, all three of them were terrified of one thing—discovery—and the fear that sooner or later Joe Duveen would precipitate their downfall.

Joe, on the other hand, four years younger than BB, appeared to thrive on the subterfuge involved. It made him feel ebullient and over-confident. Self-assured, certain that he could both out-deal and outwit all his competitors, he decided in 1922 that the time had come to precipitate the long-awaited showdown with Demotte over his so-called 'antique' sculptures.

Joe had already begun to cultivate the manager of Demotte's New York gallery, a young man called Jean Vigoureux, in the autumn of 1921. Exactly what Joe had learned from him is not recorded, but, whatever it was, it provided Joe with what he thought was the opportunity to destroy his rival.

On 8 January 1922, the Trustees Department of the Fifth Avenue Bank asked Joe to make a probate valuation of the collection of one of their clients, the late Michael Dreicer, a wealthy New York jeweller. One of the items was a gold, jewelled communion vessel, known as a monstrance, decorated with an enamelled picture of the Madonna and Child in the style known as champlevé. The accompanying documents showed that Dreicer had purchased it from Demotte for $100,000 and that it had formerly been in the collection of Prince Antoine de Bourbon.

This provenance, and probably Vigoureux's information, was enough for Joe. He promptly declared the monstrance to be 'a thoroughly modern fake'. Demotte brought an action for defamation.

Joe countered rather foolishly by persuading Vigoureux to leave Demotte's and bring his firm's New York ledgers with him. These Joe handed to the U.S. Revenue, claiming that they showed that items had been entered as sold for considerably less than they had in fact realized. The implication was that Demotte was defrauding the U.S. Revenue. Joe's plan of course was to have Demotte banned from trading in the United States, as had nearly happened to Duveens themselves after the great customs scandal a decade before.

Demotte responded by bringing an action in the French courts against Vigoureux for embezzlement, claiming that the unfortunate manager had pocketed the difference. In fact as both parties knew perfectly well, and as the numerous pre-trial affidavits make clear, the differences could be explained by the numerous bribes and commissions Demotte had had to pay to his agents and intermediaries.

Demotte's affidavits detail payments made to officials of the

Metropolitan, BB, George Barnard and many others. Joe was named as having bought a head of Christ manufactured by the sculptor Boutron from some surplus Parthenay stone and as having sold it as thirteenth-century sculpture to a Mr Hawley MacLanahan of Philadelphia for $16,000. This pre-trial skirmishing in Demotte's civil action against Joe should have made it clear that the case should never come to court, for if a fraction of the allegations they made about each other were true—and I have only chosen an example whose truth could have been proved—both men would have been ruined.

As a final ploy Joe entered a new defence, asking that the issue to be tried should be confined to the authenticity of the monstrance, and cabled Fowles in Paris ordering him to offer a reward of 10,000 francs for the name of the forger. Fowles warned him not to: 'If we inquire too deeply, the firm will be harmed beyond redemption'. Joe insisted that the forger must be found and, as Fowles had warned, the storm broke.

Fowles' inquiries were deeply resented. 'They are all afraid to talk', he cabled to Joe. 'The best fakers say it is old'. He again advised Joe to settle the case as quickly and quietly as possible, pointing out that Joe had a great many enemies, particularly in America. 'We are told here [Paris] that Demotte's process is financed by Walters of Baltimore and George Blumenthal and that it makes no difference to Demotte whether he wins or loses'.

Joe now had his back to the wall, for others had joined in aiding Demotte. These included the dealers Durlacher Brothers, Emil Rey and Jacques Seligman and a lobby of the French nobility led by the Duc de Trévise.

The Duke became involved by accident. Under French criminal law, Demotte's accusation of embezzlement against Vigoureux was sufficient for the unfortunate manager to be committed for trial. Vigoureux had willingly returned to France, confident that Joe would help him have the charges dismissed. Foolishly Joe ignored his pleas for help. Vigoureux, desperate and on bail awaiting trial, decided to tell all he knew to Henri Lapauze, the director of the Petit Palais and a friend of his family. Lapauze informed the Duc de Trévise, who was chairman of his Board of Administrators, and the Duke in turn took advice from the Vicomte d'Andigne, who was on the board of the newspaper, Le Matin. They evolved a subtle plan, designed to bring the matter into the open.

On 22 May 1923, *Le Matin* published an innocent letter from the Duke which illustrated the original engraving of the Magi— the Three Wise Men—made when the Parthenay figures were documented by the Louvre (see Chapter Thirteen). Beside the 1830 engraving were photographs of the two sets of kings owned by the Louvre and Isabella Stewart Gardner. Isabella was not mentioned, the Duke merely said that one set was 'in an American museum'.

The Duke's letter then asked the Louvre to explain how the transformation had taken place, and invited the Minister for the Arts to comment on how Isabella's figures had travelled to America. In a playful reference to the Three Wise Men, the Duke wrote that he found it hard to believe that they had 'followed a star'.

The French press pursued the story with delight. By 3 June they had traced the priest who had sold the crumbling wall at Parthenay, and he had named Henri Boutron as the man who had collected the rubble with 'an American'. On 9 June Henri Boutron was found dead in his studio with a bullet in the back of his head, an army cavalry pistol nearby. The butt of the pistol was inlaid with a silver monogram of the letters GR. Edward Fowles had no difficulty in recognizing both the pistol and the monogram, which stood for Gilbert Romeuf.

The investigation into Boutron's death was conducted by M. Hameline, a magistrate attached to the 7th Arrondissement Correctional Court. He was advised that it was just possible for a 'suicide' to aim a pistol at the base of his own skull, though it was pointed out that this was not an easy matter when the weapon employed was a cavalry model with a nine-inch barrel. Further doubt on the suicide theory was caused by a statement made by a friend and neighbour of Boutron's, Monsieur de Stocklin.

De Stocklin explained to M. Hameline, the magistrate, that he had become friendly with Boutron, though Boutron would never do even the most minor sculpture repair for him as he was exclusively employed by Demotte. On a Sunday morning, when the staff were absent, he would show de Stocklin his new productions. 'Find the restoration and I will give you a dinner', he would say to de Stocklin, who could never unmask his work. 'I have had more luck than the great artists; I am the only sculptor represented at the Louvre in my lifetime; I ought to say, anonymously, and with an old collaborator, but anyhow, there I am'.

Several times he would say, 'I do not know what Demotte would do without me, for he knows nothing, and he relies on my documents when I work for him. He had me make the barefoot Kings which are in the Louvre! I protested against this absurdity; it was often so! Demotte wished me to do things which I did not wish to do, because they were archaeological nonsense'.

De Stocklin went on to say that every time Demotte came to the rue Dutot, Boutron asked him to go quickly into the next studio.

> I had a feeling that Boutron trembled before Demotte, so he obeyed him fearfully, treating him as a clever dealer who was selling for fabulous sums that which he bought for nothing . . . The last time I saw Boutron was the Sunday in May. He said that Demotte was angry with him . . . that he had threatened to kill him . . . he was much concerned and asked for my advice and protection. Like many stoneworkers he was a thirsty man and I concluded that he was talking through the wine. He said he wanted to retire and just work for himself at a new studio he had found, but was fearful that Demotte would follow him.

The magistrate sent copies of the relevant paragraphs of de Stocklin's statement to the authorities at the Louvre. Fowles and Joe's nephew, Armand Lowengard, who was a director of the Paris company, were sent for and told bluntly that the Louvre were 'displeased with them'. Fowles wrote in his journal: 'Louvre staff consider Joe morally responsible for their troubles, as his quarrel with Demotte began the whole business. Many will lose their jobs. Dreyfuss is bitter'.

On 22 September 1923, Joe and Demotte were both served with a notice asking them to attend before Magistrate Hameline and be questioned on their joint and individual relationships with Boutron. Three days later Demotte was found dead in a wood on the outskirts of Versailles with a bullet in his head. 'A victim', reported *Il Monde*, 'of a tragic ricochet from one of the hunting parties who were shooting nearby'.

The police and judicial inquiries into both deaths lapsed as quickly as they had arisen. Demotte's was judged to have been an accident, despite the fact that the shooting season had yet to start. No effort appears to have been made to identify the members of the alleged hunting parties.

In Boutron's case, the verdict was suicide, despite a mass of evidence that he had been in fear of his life, and that a strange pistol had been used rather than his own wartime souvenir which was found amongst his effects. Neither the police nor the magistrates appeared to see a connection between the two deaths and no attempt was made to investigate the double tragedy as one despite the much publicised connection between the two men. It was as though someone had decided that matters should be hushed up as quickly as possible. Fowles did not volunteer that he believed the pistol was Romeuf's, but always suspected that somehow or other Romeuf could have thrown a deal of light on the matter. He knew, and everyone else knew, that further investigation could have been damaging to the firm, and that the deaths had been highly convenient to Joe.

Despite the fact that the investigations had taken place separately, the verdicts were announced on the same day. Joe was lunching at the Ritz in Paris with Mrs E. T. Stotesbury. 'Tell me, Sir Joseph', she asked, 'am I a friend of yours?'

'Of course, my dear lady', he replied.

'Oh dear', she sighed, 'all your friends appear to get shot'.

On 12 October 1928, the Venetian dealer Balboni called at the Duveen Paris gallery. He made a detailed statement setting out his and Demotte's relationship with Dossena and a cabal of Italian dealers. He confirmed that they had merely used BB as a means of obtaining introductions, and that, though Berenson had been well paid for his efforts, he was unaware that he was dealing with forgeries. Balboni also gave the provenance of Michael Dreicer's monstrance. It had been made around 1875 by a goldsmith called Rheingold Vasters, then employed as a restorer to the cathedral treasury at Aachen. It had been sold to a collector called Spitzer, who had returned it when he discovered that it was a copy of one in the collection of the Duc de Galleria Montpensier.

It had then turned up in the hands of an Italian dealer called Palesi of Bologna who, in parternship with Demotte, paid Prince Antoine de Bourbon, the Duc de Montpensier's nephew, who was notoriously short of money, to say that it was a family heirloom. Once more Joe wished to publicize the matter but Fowles urged him to stay quiet. 'Demotte is dead', he cabled, 'but you are keeping his memory green'.

Five months later, on 29 March 1929, the *New York Herald* stated that a metallurgical investigation had proved that the monstrance was authentic and that it had been purchased by a Boston collector for presentation to the Boston Museum.

❧ 17 ❧

The Hamilton Hype

The problems generated by the deaths of Lord Michelham and William Salomon, coupled with the Demotte débâcle, meant that everyone at Duveens had to adopt a much lower profile for a little while. BB spent most of his time travelling while Edward Fowles scouted quietly amongst those European families ruined by the war who might have pictures to sell, but he delayed concluding any deals until the fortunes of the firm improved. Henry Frick's death alone had meant that a million dollars' worth of items on approval had been returned. Until another purchaser of his calibre appeared, Fowles judged it best not to take on any more commitments. However, Joe thought he had a prospective major client in a young man who called himself Carl Hamilton.

Hamilton's background is a mystery, but as an orphan in Philadelphia he had somehow attracted the attention of Mrs E. H. Harriman (the mother of Averell Harriman), who had partly financed his education. He was a strange combination of religious fanatic and unscrupulous financier, but blessed—or perhaps cursed— with a devotion to religious works of art that bordered on mania. Today he would be recognized as a psychopath, for he genuinely believed his own fantasies, one of which was that he was a millionaire.

Hamilton had spent the early part of the war in the Philippines, where he worked as an accounts clerk in a large copra plantation. When the United States entered the war in 1917 the oil shortage led to a boom in coconut oil. Using his inside knowledge, he had persuaded several plantation owners and merchants to pool their production, corner the market, and hold their customers to ran-

193

som. On the strength of the record harvest he floated a public company, which was fourteen times over-subscribed.

Despite the over-subscription, Hamilton issued shares to everyone who applied and diverted the cheques which accompanied the excess applications to his own pocket. In this way he netted $2 million. The first accounts were due for publication in January 1920 and the dividend would have to be paid. Since the company had fourteen times as many shareholders as the register showed, he was living on borrowed time. This did not appear to concern him. Hamilton was well aware that, since he had committed his swindle in the Philippines, he was safe from the jurisdiction of the American courts. He arrived in New York, took a suite in the Plaza, and inevitably came to the attention of Bert Boggis.

In December 1917 Bert persuaded Joe to attend a revivalist meeting sponsored by Mrs Harriman to pray for an early end to the war. Carl Hamilton gave the address, which apparently so moved Joe that he invited his new-found friend to dine. Joe appeared to believe in Carl's fantasies. 'Carl knows the Bible and the stock market backwards', he later told BB. 'He is the first really good man I've ever met'.

Soon Duveen had fired his guest with the idea that nothing brought a man closer to the Almighty than the study and perhaps the acquisition of the finest examples of Christian art. Hamilton was as eager a student as he was to be a customer. A crash course in art books given to him by Joe led to his first purchase, which Joe was wise enough to leave to the aging Uncle Henry. It was a Louis XII period tapestry of the Deposition of Christ, which had cost, including bills for restoration, a total of $8,772. Carl paid $150,000 in cash.

In quick succession Hamilton then bought four paintings. First, at $50,000, a pair of panels cut from a large Annunciation which BB had bought in 1911 from Icilio Joni for $5,000 and attributed to Fra Angelico. His second purchase, also for $50,000, was a Madonna and Child, again from Joni and attributed by BB to Fra Filippo Lippi. It had cost $3,000 and had been entirely repainted. The wreckage from which it had been reconstituted came from the Carmine Brethren of Florence. It was accompanied by a certificate from BB stating: 'It is in my opinion one of this master's finest works'.

This picture, together with the fourth one, were to rise up and haunt the Doris-Duveen partnership in the future. The fourth painting was a crucifixion scene which BB had purchased from Luigi Grassi in Florence in 1914 at a cost of $10,000 delivered to Paris. Astonishing as it may seem, BB genuinely believed it to be by Piero della Francesca.* He had once tried to sell it to Isabella Gardner for $95,000. Hamilton paid $65,000.

Joe took a paternal interest in what he sold. It grieved him that such monumental examples of the Christian ethic had to bloom in a Plaza suite—in those days not quite so stultifyingly respectable as Plaza suites are today. He persuaded Carl to take an extended trip to Europe, furnishing him with introductions to Edward Fowles and BB, while he searched for a suitable apartment for him. Joe found one on the corner of 46th Street and Park Avenue, which he promised to decorate in Carl's absence. As it contained fourteen rooms, apart from bathrooms and servants' quarters, there can be no doubt that he not only hoped that Hamilton would return with a collection, but expected it.

Hamilton arrived in Paris in the spring of 1919 and lost no time in introducing himself to Fowles and BB. Neither of them took to him as a person, although they had been well briefed. BB contented himself with scribbling a note of introduction to Mary asking her to take him on a tour of I Tatti.

Fowles was cannier. He took him to see the Spiridion Collection, which was rumoured to be on the market, and was slightly shocked when Carl instructed him to offer $2.8 million for it on his behalf. Since all Carl's bills were being sent to Duveens for payment and he asked for a few hundred francs petty cash almost every day, Fowles decided to soft-pedal.

Carl's requests soon became even more esoteric. He asked to be allowed to preach in Notre Dame, which not even Bert Boggis could arrange. Then he turned out to have an even greater interest than sacred art—young boys. He wrote a memo asking the firm to find him some 'young fellows—about 12 to 13 years old', whom he would like to adopt, take home to America, and bring up as a ready-made family. Duveens obliged. Two comely young men, one from France, the other from Spain, were recruited. Fowles had to

---

* It is now attributed to 'A Northern Master'. A Frick loan to the Fogg Museum.

obtain their parents' permission, arrange their passages to the United States, and buy them clothes suitable for their new life.

Fowles did not relish the assignment and wrote a guarded cable to Joe voicing his reservations. When Carl asked him for 'two youths of oriental appearance and from good families of the servant class' Fowles put his foot down and tactfully refused. However, Boggis located two Japanese orphans and installed them in the apartment to await Carl's return.

Before Carl left Paris he bought several pictures from Duveens' Paris stock. Amongst them (the original cost to Duveens is in parentheses) were 'Christ between Saint Peter and St James', attributed by BB to Cimabue, $150,000 ($16,800); an Adoration of the Magi by Benevenuto di Giovanni, $90,000 ($6,800); a Nativity by Utili da Faenza, $90,000 ($2,500); Sassetta's 'Procession to Calvary', $25,000 ($4,500), and Andrea Mantegna's 'Judith', $160,000 ($70,000). His total Paris purchases came to almost $1 million. Having briefly slaked his thirst, Carl headed south for Florence.

Mary Berenson was delighted with him. She found him 'exhilarating, semi-intoxicating, with laughing languid eyes and a keen quick-witted brain'. After a week of showing Hamilton around, Mary wrote BB that she was amazed by this seemingly paradoxical man. Though he was brilliant, he also appeared to be terribly naive to the point where Mary almost felt sorry for him. But he *was* a potential client.

Mary was so determined that some of his seemingly untold wealth was to come to I Tatti that she almost caused the immediate end of the Doris-Duveen partnership. Early in 1916 the Duke of Northumberland had decided to sell his famous picture, 'The Feast of the Gods' by Giovanni Bellini and Titian. He had asked BB, who had identified the painting for him many years before, for his advice. BB had valued it at $250,000 and had suggested that he offer it to the dealer 'Silent' Sulley. The Duke had done so and Sulley had obtained an option. Neither the Duke nor Joe knew that BB had a fifty-fifty profit-sharing agreement with Sulley.

In January 1917 BB had offered 'The Feast of the Gods' to Isabella for $500,000 payable over two years, again claiming that he was neither 'peddling' nor had any interest. Isabella had tried to raise the money for several months but had been unable to do so.

During September 1919, while Hamilton was *en route* to Florence, BB told Joe about Sulley's option but omitted to mention his own interest in the deal. He suggested that Joe buy 'The Feast of the Gods' from Sulley and sell it to Carl. In this way BB secretly hoped to have 50 per cent of Sulley's profit *and* his share (25 per cent) of Joe's. Joe agreed. Unfortunately for BB he did not tell Mary.

Mary innocently told Carl about 'The Feast of the Gods', not mentioning BB's interest. Carl immediately telegraphed Sulley offering $500,000. His offer, which he confirmed in writing the next day, was accepted. A delighted Mary, believing that she had just earned the family their $125,000 share of the profit, presented Carl with a picture from BB's private collection, Domenico Veneziano's 'St John the Baptist in the Desert'.*

The sequel was even funnier. A few weeks later Hamilton was Joe's guest at Claridges in London, when 'The Feast of the Gods' was mentioned. Joe said that he planned to purchase it. Hamilton kept quiet, but after dinner he wrote a note to his host telling him that he had already bought the picture and that it was on its way to New York: 'Only my agreement with Mr Sulley to keep the matter a secret until the picture reaches my house kept me from launching forth and telling you all about it'. Then Hamilton offered to let Joe buy it from him for the same price if he wanted it, adding in the cloying tones which characterized much of their correspondence, and which made Fowles suspect that their relationship was closer than that of dealer and customer, 'If you need it, I will at least have the genuine satisfaction which comes to one who parts with a thing which he loves most dearly, to a friend whom he loves infinitely more'.

The inevitable three-sided row between BB, Mary and Joe took weeks to simmer down. Mary's role was kept a secret from Joe so BB could truthfully write that *he* had never mentioned the picture to Hamilton; but Joe learned about BB's relationship with Sulley. However, Joe was considerably mollified when he learned that BB had been outsmarted by Mary's gift of his 'St John the Baptist in the Desert'.

Early in 1920 Joe discovered that Hamilton was unable to pay

---

* When they acquired the picture—as a fee for appraising the Panciatichi Collection—both BB and Mary believed it to be by Pessellino.

for any of his purchases, let alone the fourteen-room apartment Joe had just furnished so expensively for him. Apart from the first four items, which Hamilton had paid for during Uncle Henry's lifetime, he owed $1,725,000 for pictures and almost $600,000 for furniture, rent, travelling expenses and petty cash advances. His copra company went bankrupt and he could not return to the Philippines where, he claimed, he held substantial assets, as he would have been arrested for fraud. To add to these problems Carl then unwittingly drove another wedge between BB and Joe. Unaware of the partnership between them, Carl sent BB a complete list of his collection, including the Italian furniture, majolica dishes and other Italianate items with which Joe had furnished him.

Both the Berensons realized that most of Hamilton's collection had not been entered in the 'X' book as it should have been under the terms of the Doris-Duveen contract, so Joe now owed them a considerable amount of money. They demanded their share, and Mary travelled to London to have it out with Joe. Once in London, Mary learned that Hamilton was unable to pay up and was told the full extent of the disaster. Desperate methods were called for and Mary, with her love of the dramatic, devised what she thought was a most original plan.

Her idea was that Hamilton should stay in his apartment and show off his collection to New York society in the hopes that someone would be tempted to buy it *en bloc*. To bait the trap Mary and BB agreed to spend a few months in New York, living and holding court in Hamilton's apartment.

In numerous letters in later years, both Berensons denied that they were parties to this plan, but there is no doubt from the documentary evidence available, from some of which I quote below, that, from the outset, they knew exactly what they were doing.

One of the first people invited to 'sniff the bait' was Miss Alice de Lamar, who was living in the same apartment block as Hamilton. In 1973 she wrote a detailed account of her experiences to the present author; the following extracts are taken from this account.

Alice de Lamar
The hostess who greeted us was Mrs E. H. Harriman (the mother of Averell Harriman) and the rooms I wandered

through, dumbfounded, were filled with treasures I could scarcely have dreamt existed. Bellini's incredibly enchanting 'Feast of the Gods' looked down at me. A little further to the left hung Botticelli's lovely portrait of a blond youth in a red cap, and to the right hung Mantegna's 'Judith and Holofernes' —further along were Fra Angelico's 'Madonna' and 'The Angel of the Annunciation', two companion pieces, further along a Sassetta, a fan-shaped Cimabue altarpiece, and the crucifixion scene by Piero della Francesca. Each of the several rooms—the living room, the entrance hall, the dining room and library—were filled with paintings of top museum quality and value . . . The walls were a sand colour finish and texture, the furniture was all of it authentic fifteenth century Italian, the rugs on the floor were seventeenth century Persian, the parchment lamp shades cast a soft and pleasant light on this scene of well studied beauty and elegance . . . Carl Hamilton, our host, was a busy and eager young man of about thirty, short, slim, round faced, with dark hair stiffly parted in the middle, and neatly plastered down. There were two Japanese servants in attendance . . . Next day a bunch of roses arrived from Hamilton, and later in the afternoon, on my doorstep stood 'Eager-beaver' Hamilton himself, with an arm full of large and obviously very valuable art books he insisted I accept. I had no intention of accepting presents from a young man whom I had, as yet, so slight an acquaintance with, so I protested that I would be glad to borrow them and bring them back in several days. 'Oh, you must come over for lunch the day after tomorrow', said Carl. 'Oh but you really must, Bernard Berenson and Mrs Berenson will be here and you must meet them . . . '

Mary wrote on 17 December to her daughter that she and BB were trying to match Hamilton and Alice de Lamar, whom she valued at $15 million. She told her daughter that Hamilton was in love—for the first time in his life—and that they were most suitable for each other, coming from the same social stratum—the lowest.

Four days later, she wrote to her sister, Mrs Bertrand Russell, that she and Bernard were working very hard on their Squillionaires. Among their heartily endowed prospects were Miss Frick, Mrs Otto Kahn, the Rockefellers and Archer Huntington. Business looked good.

Alice de Lamar

I was often aware of BB's lack of patience at Mary's constant defence of Carl, and if she ever had any well intentioned match-making idea in my direction, she was, I think, soon aware of my total lack of interest. My idea of Carl as a potential suitor could only be summed up by a 'God forbid!' . . . Duveen, of course, turned up from time to time. I found his arrogant manner definitely vulgar. I could see dear Mary's eyes cringe a bit at times when he talked too much and too loud, but BB kept a countenance serene and impenetrable, and a poker face, and yet instinctively I never doubted the irritation they both must have felt in Carl's presence. One day we visited Duveen's establishment, and as a special treat he opened the vaults and brought out all his treasures, one by one. There was nothing that he showed us that day to compare with what was hanging on the walls at Hamilton's apartment, and it was useless for him to pretend that there was. Before we left, he brought out a large and striking cinquecento [sic] bust, undoubtedly a portrait of Lorenzo.* 'I have just recently acquired this', he said, removing the cover from it with a flourish. 'We have no actual attribution for it, but I have my own idea. To my way of thinking this must be the work of Pollaiuolo.† In fact', he said, with a dramatic gesture, 'I would say, the greatest Pollaiuolo in the world!' In the taxi returning from the visit to Duveen's BB remarked, 'A very fine piece he has got there, that bust, an exceptional find. Of course, it isn't a Pollaiuolo by any means, but if it makes him happy, let him think so . . .

BB said one day, 'You know, I have been thinking a lot about Mrs Gardner. We saw her last year, but this might be

---

* The bust is quattrocento.
† Sold to Samuel Kress as a Verrocchio for $150,000. It cost Duveens about $10,000 at Sotheby's, 16 July 1920. Now in the National Gallery, Washington.

the last of our visits to America, one never knows—and Mrs Gardner now is very old, in fact she's said to be at times a little "gaga" as the French so aptly say, and her health, we have heard, is failing fast' . . . He wrote a letter up to Mrs Gardner and said . . . It would give him great pleasure to come to see her, and to bring up some very wonderful treasures for her to feast her eyes on . . . Carl assembled bath towels as the softest wrapping and tied them up with string, on the dining room table. The Mantegna, the Piero della Francesca, the Alvise Vivarini portrait, and the two Fra Angelicos—four large suitcases contained them all with ease, and we set forth on the Boston train, the two Japanese servants carrying the four cases . . .

Isabella did not express any interest in Hamilton's pictures. Desperate to sell something to someone, Mary and Bernard tried another tack. They spotted a Bellini in the Henry Rheinhart Gallery for $30,000. Mary wrote to Isabella on 21 March that she needed a Bellini to round off her collection, that she and BB had spotted just the right one for her, and that the price had dropped from $100,000 to $75,000.*

Mary's brilliant idea of how to sell the Hamilton collection had not been a success. 'The Feast of the Gods' was returned to Sulley and Duveens repossessed most of Hamilton's purchases under a 'consent judgement' on 9 February 1922. Hamilton managed, however, to hang on to the repainted Fra Filippo Lippi, the Piero della Francesca Crucifixion and Mary's gift of 'St John the Baptist in the Desert' until his creditors forced him to auction the first two in May 1929. Joe bought the Crucifixion for Mrs Rockefeller for $375,000, the exact sum Hamilton owed him. The Lippi, which was little more than a forgery, was bought by the dealer Schinasi of New York for $125,000.

Hamilton, who had expected twice as much for them, accused Joe of rigging the sale and sued him for $1 million. He was amply justified in his suspicions. The preliminary trial proceedings dragged

---

* Isabella eventually purchased it for $50,000 from Rheinhart, who paid a commission to BB.

on until 1939. Hamilton accumulated documentary evidence that Bert Boggis had bribed the auctioneer, and that Joe had spread the word that his Lippi had been ruined in an accident and had been repainted by Hamilton himself. By now a very sick man, and unable to face the tensions and probable disgrace of a court case, Joe settled out of court for $500,000. He died two months later.

❧ 18 ❧

The Artistic Education of Jules Bache

Jules Bache, the American financier, and his daughter Kitty were BB's guests for luncheon at I Tatti on 28 May 1927. They were fortunate in that, having served an expensive apprenticeship as Duveen customers for such household names as Rembrandt, Romney and Van Dyck, they were now to be initiated into the arcane world of Italian Renaissance art by none other than Mr Berenson. In fact, they were doubly fortunate as the precious introduction had been arranged for them by Sir Joseph Duveen himself, who, apparently, was on first-name terms with the famous expert. Berenson was now sixty-two and Duveen fifty-eight. To Bache they were an awe-inspiring pair. The next day Mary Berenson wrote formally to Duveens that Bache wanted a Crivelli and a Bellini.

The education of Jules Bache had begun some fourteen years earlier, when, on 3 April 1913, he had slipped into Duveens' New York gallery and, after some embarrassed haggling, had purchased a small Viennese snuff box with a mildly indelicate painting of a young woman on the inside of the lid. He had a weakness for such bibelots and from time to time added to his collection.

He was a congenial man with a great sense of humour and a fund of 'darkie stories', for which Joe had a well-known weakness. Although only a minor customer Bache was a frequent and welcome visitor to the gallery, sometimes asking for assistance with insurance valuations but rarely expressing an interest in anything but the stock market prices. He was not regarded as a 'major prospect'. He had lived in Paris for several years before the war and, guided by the Lowengard family, had formed a small and choice collection of fine continental furniture for his house in the

Avenue d'Iéna. Duveens mistakenly regarded him as too 'Europeanized' to pay their prices.

Two factors led to his becoming a major customer. The first was that Joe was knighted in 1919 and happily discovered that Bache was fascinated by titles and the intricate pecking order of the aristocracy. Again and again Joe stayed late at the gallery, giving for the umpteenth time a blow-by-blow account of his investiture. Bache would listen as a child to a favourite bedtime story. 'Get to the bit where the King takes hold of the sword, Sir Joe', he would say, and, when Joe got there, would always interrupt, 'Sir Joe—it was surely a gold sword?'

The second factor was that, in the post-war stock-market boom, Bache's brokerage house became one of the richest and most dominant on Wall Street. Bache, like many others of his kind, had money to burn. To tempt him, Joe sent him round a full-length Romney of a suitably aristocratic lady, telling him to keep it on his walls and see how he got on with it. It hung there for two years until Bache returned it, saying it had begun to bore him. Joe reasoned that the sitter was probably not sufficiently aristocratic.

Joe's chance came in the spring of 1924 when he casually mentioned to his friend that he would be visiting England that summer and that the Duke of Grafton had asked him to bid for one or two of his better pictures. The ducal cachet proved to be the correct bait, and by September Bache owned his first major picture, a self-portrait by Anthony Van Dyck for which he cheerfully paid $130,000.

Bache's entry into the major league generated considerable jealousy amongst Duveens' rivals. A. S. Drey, an immensely respectable Munich dealer, sold him a fine eighteenth-century terra-cotta bust which Nathan Wildenstein promptly dubbed a modern copy. Bache called in Sir Joe to arbitrate. Rather than give a written opinion Joe offered to take it in part payment against George Romney's full-length portrait of Elisabeth, Countess of Derby. 'It's the most beautiful Romney I've ever owned', he told a grateful Bache, murmuring the price of $225,000. In fact it was not his at all as he had borrowed it from Knoedlers of New York.

Bache must have been delighted with Elisabeth, for three weeks later he was back, begging Sir Joe to sell him Van Dyck's imposing full-length portrait of Robert Rich, Earl of Warwick, as his Countess needed someone to keep her company on the walls of 814 Fifth Avenue. Duveens had bought the portrait from Mrs Baillie Hamilton for $100,000. Bache offered $250,000 but he had to increase his offer to $275,000 to make it worth the firm's while to sell.

It was still touch and go whether or not Sir Joe would sell. He had become very attached to the Earl in the three weeks he had owned him, and apparently the Earl had become equally attached to a small painting attributed to Jan Vermeer called 'Head of a Young Boy', which Duveens had on approval from a French dealer called Yves Perdoux. Bache solved the problem by buying the Vermeer as well—for $175,000—specifying only that they had to be framed and hanging in his house by Christmas Day.

Sir Joe was invited to the reception Bache gave for his new arrivals and noticed a space on the walls that seemed to cry out for attention. The matter was speedily remedied. Bache bought Rembrandt's 'The Standard Bearer' for $60,000, a picture which Duveens had previously sold to George Jay Gould of New Jersey, but had been asked to repurchase a few weeks before. It was framed and hanging in Fifth Avenue by New Year's Day.

The problem with Bache was that his taste appeared to be concentrated on the Flemish and German schools of painting, leavened with a dash or so of languid portraits of the English aristocracy. Many of the best examples of this type of painting that were on the market were already spoken for, to dealers such as Agnews and Knoedlers who were powerful competitors of Duveens. Occasionally Joe went into partnership with them, as he did with Wildenstein, but it was a practice he abhorred. It was therefore imperative that Bache, having proved himself by spending almost $1.6 million, should now place himself entirely in Duveens' more than capable hands. Joe reverted to Uncle Henry's dictum of first sell the man a house and his furnishings, then—and only then— start selling him pictures.

A house was found at Palm Beach and much of 1926 was spent helping Bache and his daughter Kitty choose the soft furnishings and decorations to set off and occasionally augment his collection of French furniture. By Duveen standards it was a modest operation: rugs, the odd Sèvres vase, and a fine sculptured bust by Lejeune of Bache himself cost a modest $45,000, though in October that year Joe could not resist slipping in a finely detailed

Dutch portrait group by Gerard Ter Borch for $35,000, if only to cover the costs of his frequent train journeys to Florida.

Bache, at this time, was under the influence of his daughter Kitty, and in October 1926 she began to justify the considerable investment Joe had made in her father's education. On one of her frequent visits to the gallery she admired Francisco de Goya's famous little portrait of the infant Don Manuel Osorio de Zuniga, better known as 'The Red Boy', which had formerly belonged to the well-known Parisian actor-playwright, Henri Bernstein. Bache humoured her by paying $275,000 for the picture.

Duveens had not had the picture very long, though they had been angling for it since 1921 when they purchased Gainsborough's 'The Blue Boy' from the Duke of Westminster for Henry Huntington. There had been a great outcry in London against the export of this picture, so to assuage public opinion Joe had exhibited it at the National Gallery for a month. An enterprising print-seller had capitalized on the artfully contrived ballyhoo surrounding 'The Blue Boy' by making thousands of reproductions of Goya's sentimental study and calling it 'The Red Boy'. These had sold in great numbers, making the Goya famous, and because of this Duveens had been determined to possess it.

Unhappily, Henri Bernstein had been reluctant to sell. Instead he, in turn, capitalized on his picture's notoriety and wrote it into his latest play, 'La Galerie des Glaces', which starred Charles Boyer. The painting was the centrepiece of 'the set' and received almost as much press coverage as Boyer which, to Joe's chagrin, kept raising the price.

The play's success in Paris went to Bernstein's head. He began to live far beyond his means, gambling long into the night. On the evening of 22 November 1925, he lost $100,000 and authorized an art dealer acquaintance called Henri Bardac to get the best price he could from Duveens for his Goya. The problem was that Bernstein had to raise his gambling debt of $100,000 within twenty-four hours to cover his cheque or face not only social ruin but probable imprisonment, as issuing a dishonoured cheque was a criminal offence in France at the time.

Duveens agreed to pay him $90,000 in gold francs the same day, plus a further $45,000 to his wife in London. They also agreed that the picture could stay on the stage until the play closed, which it did not do until June 1926. The picture had only just arrived in New York when it caught Kitty Bache's eye.

At this stage it is well to dismiss the story contained in Sam Behrman's biographical romp *Duveen*. Behrman states that Kitty's husband, Gilbert Miller, the theatre producer, immediately recognized the picture as a former stage prop and learned from Bernstein what it had cost Duveen. As a result, claims Behrman, he prompted Bache to demand and get a discount of $115,000. This is untrue: Kitty Bache did not even meet Gilbert Miller until some months after the picture entered the Bache collection and no discount was ever asked for or given.

'The Red Boy' became a major talking point in the Bache household and, shortly before Christmas 1926, Kitty persuaded her father to buy himself a Velázquez self-portrait from a reluctant Joe for $1,125,000. Joe was reluctant to sell because he wanted to include a second Velázquez, a small portrait of the Infanta Maria Theresa, who became Louis XIV's bride, for a similar price. He argued that the Velázquez would match the Van Dyck self-portrait and the Infanta would be a suitable companion for 'The Red Boy'. Both of them, argued Joe, deserved a Christmas present as much as Bache himself. This time Bache refused to see the logic of Joe's arguments, but at Kitty's insistence he purchased the Infanta eighteen months later, though at the reduced price of $175,000.

Kitty received a Christmas present from Joe—a fine statue of the goddess Hebe by Falconet. At the same time she received a hand-written letter from him in which he proposed that, during 1927, the entire Bache family should make a major European tour. They should take the cure at Carlsbad, visit Italy, lease a mansion in London with a suitable ballroom and 'do' the London Season. It was time, he argued, for her to see as much of Europe as her father had as a young man; Joe's numerous friends such as Lord Esher would of course arrange such matters as a box at Royal Ascot and such invitations as would be 'appropriate to a young lady of your presence and social standing'.

The unstated attraction to Kitty was that it was a chance to find an eligible husband acceptable to her father. Bache had somewhat Victorian ideas and had erected some formidable barriers around his heiress daughter. Furthermore, Kitty possessed a sharp intelligence which deterred many a fortune hunter, and at the age of twenty-nine, could fairly be described as comely rather than beautiful. She welcomed the prospect of what was undoubtedly a fishing trip for a husband, and that is how it was euphemistically described in the Duveen code-book. Kitty now became 'Redsails', a reference to the numerous fishing boats in her father's beloved minor Dutch pictures. The equally unstated attraction to Duveens was that they would arrange the itinerary, and great pains were taken to see that it did not include any of their rivals' premises. The high point of the trip would be a visit to BB, with the intention of persuading Bache that now was the time to form a major collection of Italian paintings.

Now that Bache had been elevated to 'major customer' status there were other, more mundane, matters to be attended to. Did he, for instance, prefer to travel on a train facing the engine or with his back to it? What type of cigars, shaving soaps and other toiletries were needed? Were there any special dietary habits or tastes for delicacies? Did Bache and his wife prefer separate bedrooms? These and dozens of other details were quickly established by the redoubtable Bert Boggis, Joe's egregious 'fixer', who established his customary relationship with his customary source, the client's butler.

In Bache's case, the butler was a former English actor called Gilmore, who gave Boggis such excellent service that he managed to put his son through Harrow School on the 'presents' he earned from Duveens. Gilmore reported on all his master's telephone calls and appointments and logged every approach from any rival dealer. Boggis, reminiscing years later, put him second only to Mellon's Flore, who was diligent enough to sift through his master's wastepaper baskets and transcribe his diary entries.

From Christmas until February 1927, Bache's personal file amongst the Duveen archives is dominated by the arrangements for caches of ten kilos of his favourite cigars to be stored in suitable condition along his proposed itinerary. These arrangements were momentarily interrupted when Gilmore telegraphed that Knoedler had granted Bache an opinion on an important Holbein.

There was obviously little time to be lost. Joe called on his friends Lord Esher and Viscount Lee of Fareham for assistance. Esher arranged a suitable London house, Ascot tickets for Kitty and her mother, boxes for the opera and ballet, and a promise of invitations for at least one royal garden party. Lee artfully suggested that Bache might care to meet the Prime Minister, Stanley Baldwin, and possibly stay at Chequers while he was over in England.

The 'invitation' was accepted and the unsuspecting premier was somewhat surprised to receive a fulsome note from Jules Bache, together with a case of fine old brandy.

Bache was overwhelmed by Joe's solicitude and influence. So overwhelmed, in fact, that he purchased—solely on the basis of a photograph—Rembrandt's life-size portrait of 'Christ with a Pilgrim's Staff' for $300,000, which Joe had persuaded Count Eduard Raczynski to part with for exactly half that price. Knoedler had previously turned it down as too expensive. This was an eloquent rebuke to Knoedlers for daring to interfere with a Duveen customer, if somewhat expensive for Bache.

Bache still had a hankering for Knoedler's Holbein, however. Joe obtained a set of photographs of the Knoedler picture, taken both before and after its restoration. He arranged for a well-known but distinctly malleable expert from Basle, a Professor Ganz, to show the photos to Bache who then, as he had over the Drey-Wildenstein bust, asked Joe for his opinion. Joe hemmed and hawed. Knoedlers were an excellent firm, he explained, but perhaps did not have the access that he did to the greater houses of England and the Continent. As it happened, Joe explained, he had that very morning received a confidential letter from their mutual friend, Viscount Lee of Fareham, who also had a Holbein.

Joe showed Lee's letter to Bache, carefully explaining that, of course, His Lordship was a Trustee of the National Gallery and could not be publicly seen to be disposing of his pictures without giving the Gallery first choice. Lee's letter explained that an American dealer had recently offered him $150,000 for his Holbein, a small jewel-like portrait of Edward VI as Prince of Wales, at the age of six. While he was tempted, he felt that he could not sell it publicly, and asked Joe if he could find a discreet customer and, if successful, provide him with a really good copy so that no one would know that the picture had left his collection.

Neither Joe nor Lee's letter explained that Lee had bought the picture from Duveens some five years earlier, that it was of uncertain provenance, and, though it had never been publicly disputed, that it was only by way of a substantial fee that Professor

Ganz had overcome his reluctance and given Lee his written opinion that it was by Holbein. Even then he had covered himself by saying that it was a very late work, possibly the last picture he had ever painted. This opinion made curious sense, however, as the young prince's sixth birthday was on 13 October 1543, and Holbein was sick with the plague at that time, having made his final will on 7 October. He was buried on 29 November 1543. It is unlikely that in his condition he would have been allowed near the young prince. The picture is now regarded as being by a follower of Holbein.

Bache was enchanted both by the portrait and by the Viscount's invitations to his country estate and to a personal tour of the National Gallery. Bache agreed to buy the portrait, and Joe was adamant that he purchase it direct from Lee for Lee's original price of £30,000 ($150,000). For some years Bache believed that, thanks to Joe, he had outsmarted both Knoedlers and the National Gallery, who in fact had never evinced the slightest interest in the painting.

From England, Bache moved on to I Tatti, where his visit to the Berensons in May 1927 was an unqualified success. Though Mary, in her report to Duveens, mentioned at the beginning of this chapter, was scathing about Bache's lack of knowledge, there is no doubt that he left I Tatti fired with ambition to form an outstanding collection of Italian paintings in the shortest possible time. Unhappily for the plot, Bache at first refused to realize that one of the rules of the game was that he should only buy through the Doris-Duveen partnership.

He was in Venice the following week, and from there he wrote to Joe saying that he had met Dr Lionello Venturi, the Italian scholar, who had offered him an important Titian which he proposed to buy. However, he wrote, 'I would like your opinion of the picture and of course would pay the appropriate advisory fee'.

Joe did not like to be called an adviser, particularly when it meant being asked to encourage Venturi, whom he regarded as a rival to BB. 'Venturi is a nice enough fellow', he wrote in reply, 'he was a good student in his day, but perhaps at his age you should be careful, and take the opinions of others. Should you wish I could ask Mr Berenson, who advises me occasionally on important paintings . . . of course, there is no question of a fee'.

Finally, doubtless remembering Mary's letter, he gently suggested that Bache should bide his time: 'I have the greatest little pearl to offer you when you are in Paris, none other than Lord Northbrook's Madonna and Child by Carlo Crivelli'.

This is one of the most sumptuous of Bache's purchases and it remained his favourite picture until his death. It is also one of Crivelli's most important and characteristic pictures and, at the time Joe purchased it, was in such superb condition that not even he had the slightest reason to 'improve' it. Today it is one of the stars in the Metropolitan in New York and, compared with the prices usually charged by Joe, Bache acquired it cheaply for $230,000.

Joe was angry at having to sacrifice such a fine picture and roundly berated the Berensons for allowing Bache even to meet, let alone deal with, Venturi. He suspected that BB had deliberately let slip Bache's secret itinerary to Venturi. He urged them to be more careful in future and to take Bache firmly in hand.

Mary replied on 1 August 1927 that BB was taking another angle to beat Venturi. Four days later she wrote again saying that Bache still wanted a top-notch Giovanni Bellini. BB recommended the Oblong Madonna and Saints from the Benson collection.

This is an example of how frequently and dramatically BB could change his mind about a picture. The Benson Bellini, though it bore the artist's signature, had not, at that time, been accepted as an autograph work by the master. Most experts dubbed it a workshop picture, while Berenson's mentor, Morelli, had written that the signature was a fake and that it was probably the work of a minor Venetian artist and follower of Bellini called Francesco Bissolo.

BB had himself 'written' in two of his books, *Venetian Painters* in 1894 and *The Study and Criticism of Italian Art* in 1916 (drafted by BB and doctored by Mary), that the Oblong Madonna was the work of Marco Basaiti and the signature a fake, and he had put forward the idea that Basaiti might have worked in Bellini's workshop. In a more recent magazine article in 1924, he had even withdrawn the attribution to Basaiti and said it was nothing more than a workshop Bellini, executed by studio assistants.

Once BB had recommended the painting to Bache as a top-notch Bellini he wrote to both Joe and Bache himself, congratulating them on securing the picture and giving his opinion that it was an exceptionally fine work of the master painted between 1510 and 1512.

Jules Bache was delighted with the Oblong Madonna and happily signed promissory notes for it to the value of $350,000. It was some consolation to the partners for the sacrifice of the Crivelli. Today it is in the Metropolitan, correctly catalogued as by Bellini *and* his workshop.

All parties voted the Bache family's 1927 European tour a complete success. Kitty met and married her husband, Gilbert Miller. Jules Bache had spent $1,613,000 by Christmas and was so delighted with his purchases that, on BB's cabled recommendation, enclosed in a New Year greetings telegram, he paid $350,000 for Domenico Ghirlandaio's heavily repainted portrait of the Florentine banker Francesco Sassetti with his young son and $150,000 for Cosimo Tura's 'Flight into Egypt'.

A discordant note that might well have soured the relationship came from a colourful English country squire called Sir Robert Abdy, a west country baronet with a taste for horse-racing. He had inherited a splendid collection from his family but in 1922 he lost most of his money to the bookmakers.

He was forced to start selling his pictures and, being chary of the dealers, decided to do it himself. He developed a taste for the game and over the next few years became what was called a gentleman dealer, selling from the walls of his country house. What many of his customers did not know was that many of the 'heirlooms' he felt 'compelled to sell' were actually purchased by him on the Continent or given to him on a sale-or-return basis by Wildenstein and the Florentine dealer Contini.

While in Bache's apartment during a visit to New York he recognized the Vermeer portrait of a boy which Joe had obtained from Yves Perdoux of Paris and which had been one of Bache's first purchases.

Sir Robert spoke to Bache as one gentleman to another. The picture was not a Vermeer, he said. It had been sculling around the French dealers' network for years and Perdoux had offered him a half share in it if he would pay the then leading Vermeer expert, Dr Hofstede De Groot, the 25,000 French francs that he demanded in exchange for certifying it as genuine. Abdy said that of course he had refused but that it was well known in the trade that Joe had paid De Groot, which was why he had the picture from Perdoux. Bache did not believe him at the time and warned Joe of Abdy's 'lies'.

Bache continued to buy from Joe in 1928. The first painting which Bache accepted that year—as usual on BB's suggestion—from a photograph in the Benson catalogue, was a modest-looking painting called 'Portrait of a Young Man', attributed to Vincenzo Catena, a minor Venetian contemporary of Titian and Giorgione. Bache bought it for the appropriately Catenesque price of $40,000.

It had hardly been delivered before Joe received a frantic telegram from Agnews of London. The Catena, they believed, was in fact by Giorgione himself. They proposed that Agnews and Duveens should each buy a half share in the picture. Since Giorgione commanded up to ten times the price of Catena, this was attractive arithmetic, and the problem of prising the picture back from Bache was neatly solved by Joe, using BB and the promise of further Bellinis from a hitherto unknown Italian collection.

On 21 February Joe wrote to Bache suggesting that he should visit BB again that summer as some remarkable items from 'certain collections' were due on the market and he wished him to have first refusal as he was his most favoured customer. Almost as an aside he wrote, 'on reflection I am convinced that the Catena is not up to the high standard that you and I have set ourselves' and offered full credit if Bache cared to return it. Bache obliged and the picture was quickly despatched to Paris where Edward Fowles was told 'to hide it for a while'. It was later sold by Agnews, and today it is in an English private collection.

The 'certain collections' were, in fact, various paintings lying in the basement of Duveens' New York gallery. Among these were six 'Bellini type' pictures which, at different times, BB had attributed to Bellini or to differing members of his workshop. They and many others were known as the 'old stock' and were a source of constant friction between Joe and BB.

Joe insisted that mistakes—usually pictures which had to be disposed of at a loss—should be included in his accounting with BB. He expected BB to share any losses in the same proportion as he shared the profits. BB disagreed. However, he accepted Joe's plan to off-load the old stock on to Bache—though evidently with some concern. On 1 April 1928 he wrote to Edward Fowles in

Paris to complain about how difficult it would be to come up with the six Bellinis at the right time for Joe to show Bache. Bache duly arrived in Florence on 23 August 1928, and entertained BB and Mary at dinner at his hotel that evening. He arranged to visit I Tatti on the 25th to study the photographs of the secret collection and hear BB's opinions of them all. The following morning Mary dutifully reported to Joe, who was staying at the Lido in Venice.

She and BB thought Bache had great potential as a collector. But Bache had complained to Berenson about the Duveen prices. Mary wrote to say that BB saved the day, telling Bache about all the good reasons why it would be worth his while to stay with Duveens. Bache, she reported, was quite impressed.

The lunch must have been a remarkable success, for in the following weeks Bache reserved pictures to the tune of $1,195,000. A portrait, in the style of Bellini, which has since disappeared, was the cheapest, and what BB described as an important and genuine work of Botticelli was the most expensive at $350,000.

This picture, known as the 'Coronation of the Virgin', had been taken on consignment by Duveens from the Berlin firm of art dealers J. and S. Goldsmidt some eighteen months previously. It had spent some time before it was shown to Bache being 'tidied up' by the energetic Madame Helfer in Paris.

It is unusually lifeless and stark, embodying the figure of the Virgin as shown in Botticelli's 'Coronation', now in the Uffizi Gallery in Florence. It cannot be by anyone of any merit and the attribution to Botticelli himself can only be described as either wishful thinking or downright dishonesty. It is currently in the Metropolitan Museum, New York, where it is listed as by a 'follower of the artist' who probably never worked in Botticelli's workshop and in 'remarkably bad condition' with 'substantial losses of paint and repeated and clumsy restorations'. It was sold to Bache, always a lover of titles, as the property of Prince Charles von Lichnowsky of Kuchelna Castle in Eastern Prussia.

In April 1929 Bache acquired Dürer's 'Portrait of a Venetian Lady' for which he paid Joe $95,000. Bache had been told that his new painting had once belonged to the 'Kings of Wurtemburg' and had innocently begun to ask scholars about this royal line. Bache was still more fascinated by the distinguished former owners than by the pictures themselves.

Unhappily, Joe had bought the Dürer for $25,000 from a minor if slightly discreditable scholar called Dr August Mayer and the royal provenance was probably the Doctor's invention. Included in the price had been a promise from Mayer that he would write a scholarly article about the picture in the leading German magazine *Pantheon*, in which Duveens were profligate advertisers.

Joe had convinced himself that the Dürer was genuine and had enthusiastically shown it to Berenson who had been so skeptical that he had christened it 'Cold Pig'. On 10 February 1929 Mary Berenson had written to Fowles in Paris asking him not to allow Joe to sell it to anyone important. Joe had ignored her advice. Despite Bache's pleadings during 1930 and 1931 little was done to validate the picture or its allegedly distinguished history.

The picture itself can at best be described as Dürer style. BB always believed Dr Mayer painted it himself and had modelled it on a stylistically similar portrait in the Berlin Museum. News of this view reached Doctor Mayer, who wrote to Bache saying that the Dürer he sold Duveen had no relationship with the 'very similar picture which you have purchased, unless most of the paint has been removed and repaint added'. He proved his point by enclosing a photograph of the painting as it was when he sold it, which, it must be conceded, looks rather more like a Dürer than it did after Joe's restorers had finished with it.

Bache's picture buying was eventually overtaken by the Wall Street crash, which began in October 1929. For once Bache did not allow himself his usual Christmas extravagances. His fortune was decimated and he still owed Duveens slightly over $4 million. Paradoxically, the panicky state of the market worked in Joe's favour. As long as Bache kept the pictures he would be sure to pay him in the end, and Bache dared not return the pictures as the word would spread that he was broke. Bache also used the pictures, though many were not paid for, as security for his indebtedness. He was by now beginning to suspect that he was being made a fool of, and he resolved to bluff Duveens along and exact as long a period of credit as possible. Bache was helped in this stratagem by information he received in a letter from a respectable German dealer called Kurt Bachnitz.

On his European tour this dealer had offered Bache a Raphael which he had much admired. Bache told the dealer that he would buy the Raphael if Joe Duveen passed it as genuine. Bachnitz then sought Joe's opinion. Joe was determined that only he would sell Bache Italian pictures, so he played the same game as he had when Bache had asked his opinion before: he suggested that Bachnitz consult BB. When Bachnitz said that he did not know Berenson and that he had heard that he did not give commercial opinions to dealers, Joe sent him a letter of introduction to the great scholar. At the same time Joe warned Bachnitz not to mention to BB that his client was Bache, explaining that BB disliked Bache and would certainly not do him a favour.

Privately Joe wrote to Fowles asking him to ensure that BB knocked Bachnitz's picture: 'It is more important to us that BB knocks it than it is to Bache to own it'. BB turned down Bachnitz's request, writing to him to say that he had no wish to be considered the judge of the last instance and that if the judgement of other reputable scholars was not enough for a collector, then he shouldn't buy pictures. Finally BB asked Bachnitz to conduct any further correspondence with his secretary, Miss Mariano. BB's letter arrived on 4 December 1930, and an infuriated Bachnitz promptly wrote to Bache and enclosed a copy of his own riposte to Miss Mariano.

In his letter to Bache he wrote:

> I received today a letter from Settignano in which Mr Berenson sincerely regrets having caused unpleasantness to me and assures me that it is not a question of being suspicious about me or the Raphael. His point is that he does not wish to be considered as the last instance and in this specific case he stated 'if the judgement of 80 connoisseurs like Professor Fischel or Dr Gronau is not sufficient for an art collector he should rather leave alone buying pictures'. I answered as per enclosed copy. There does not seem anything else to be left for me than to clear up the situation fully. It is deplorable that Sir Joseph acted thus and forces me to take the step which no doubt will stir up the entire question of expertise.

Bache, to his credit, ignored the letter, though he let Joe know that he had received it. Thereafter the relationship cooled. Early in 1932, Joe, with Bache's agreement, removed those pictures that had not been paid for and placed them in store so that they would not fall into the hands of his former client's creditors. In 1937 Bache's fortunes improved and by the end of that year he had settled his debts and was handed his pictures back.

It was Bache's rather endearing folly that he, as far as his art collecting was concerned, behaved with what he thought were the standards of the nobility and gentry who had previously owned his pictures. There is no doubt that once he was solvent again there were many 'Duveen' pictures he would have liked to buy, but it was a case of 'once bitten twice shy'.

PART FIVE

Rift

🌿 19 🌿

Break-up

The Doris-Duveen partnership was to collapse in 1937, but the powder train that led to the ultimate explosion had long been laid. Joe had meant to sever it at Uncle Henry's death in 1919 and then at frequent intervals ever since, but each time crises such as the Michelham, Hamilton and Salomon affairs prolonged the relationship. Bernard and Mary had become dependent on the income and wished the arrangement to continue, while Joe's intention was to string BB along for just one more deal and then call it a day. He also wanted to delay his promised accounting to BB under the 'X' agreement, which would entail paying what he owed to his partner.

By the autumn of 1926 the Berensons were desperate for money. In September Mary travelled to London to try and obtain payment of what was due to them. She stayed with Joe and his wife but found the atmosphere almost unbearable. She put up with it, as they needed an extra $25,000 to cover debts they had incurred. She reported to Bernard that she had been treated shabbily by the Duveen family, but that getting the money would be worth the humiliation.

There was a reason for Joe's attitude that autumn. For some years he had been troubled by acute indigestion and a series of irritating polyps on his throat. Shortly before Mary's arrival he had consulted specialists and asked them to find out exactly what was the matter. They had hinted at cancer and wished to perform an exploratory operation immediately. Feeling that he could not spare the time as the autumn was his major sales season, he had postponed their explorations until the following spring, when he would have the summer in which to convalesce.

In March 1927 the specialists diagnosed cancer of the stomach and insisted that, unless he submitted to fairly drastic surgery, including a colostomy, he did not have long to live. Even if the operation was successful they advised him that he should put his affairs in order. For this reason, more than any other, he had the 'X' accounts brought up to date.

He gave Messrs. Westcott Maskall and Co. all the information they needed, and in particular asked them to prepare two additional sets of accounts: first, the overall profit and loss account from 1912 to 31 January 1926, and, second, a similar set of accounts for the last three years of agreement, 1923–26.*

Losses amounting to $789,010 had been made on forty of the pictures they had handled, twenty-one on pictures purchased by Bernard on his own initiative, which showed a loss of $130,000, and eleven due to Carl Hamilton's default, which accounted for $630,000. Although the Hamilton pictures were back in stock, Joe deducted 25 per cent of the total losses from Bernard's share.

Having made these arrangements, Joe went into the hospital. His operation was partially successful, though thereafter he had to be attended by a male nurse wherever he went and scarcely a year went by when he did not have to undergo further treatment.

Despite, or perhaps because of, his failing health, Joe was determined to oust Bernard from the business altogether. Louis Levy was instructed to renegotiate the Doris agreement, due for renewal in 1927. It took him almost a year, for Bernard delegated most of the details to his secretary Nicky Mariano who, with Mary's blessing, was now a full partner in the I Tatti *ménage à trois*. Mary, plagued by cystitis and a series of other equally painful abdominal problems, happily allowed Nicky to take her place and retreated with undisguised relief to her own interests, writing a series of travel books, carrying on an immense personal correspondence, rewriting and editing her husband's correspondence and magazine articles, and in many cases giving attributions and opinions in his name.

---

* The accounts showed that between 1912–26, the 'X' dealings had generated a net profit after all expenses of $8,466, 935. Bernard's share was agreed at $2,366,730, of which he was still owed $250,000. This was in addition to his annual retainer. There was also unsold stock with a purchase value of $1,190,000, on which Bernard was to receive 25 per cent of the profits.

Nicky quickly learnt of Joe's illness and made a point of cultivating Louis Levy, whom she succeeded in charming into managing her own and Bernard's financial affairs. She suggested that, instead of taking a share in the profits, Bernard should convert the arrears due to him into a shareholding in the firm, the shares to be held by nominees. The idea was anathema to Joe. However, he realized that since Levy was becoming so influenced by Nicky, he was developing a conflict of interest. Joe also realized that if he was given a free rein, Levy would certainly compromise himself. His chance came when Levy forcefully put Nicky's arguments to him, adding that Nicky had threatened 'to destroy the firm' unless her demands were met.

To the surprise of everyone at I Tatti, Joe suddenly offered what seemed to be a generous compromise. He agreed to pay all the arrears due under the current Doris agreement, which totalled $250,000. He also offered a further $250,000 for Bernard's share in the unsold stock and a lump sum of $100,000 for work Bernard had done to date for him on the negotiations to purchase the Benson and Dreyfus collections. If they agreed to this settlement, then he promised an annual retainer of $50,000 plus a 10 per cent fee on the purchase price of any Italian paintings and drawings bought. The retainer was to continue for a period of five years, irrespective of the fact that one or other of them might die.

As he expected, Bernard agreed to his terms. For an outlay of $600,000 Joe had secured his operational independence from Bernard. What clinched the matter was that, on Levy's advice, neither BB nor either of his ladies believed that Joe would live to see the end of the five-year agreement. Joe encouraged them in this belief, seeking BB's advice only on such matters as which institutions he should endow and confessing that he would like to be remembered as both a peer and a trustee of the National Gallery.

The new agreement was signed in March 1928 and, at Joe's jocular suggestion, BB entrusted the $600,000 he received from Joe to Louis Levy to invest. 'Brutus', as Joe ruefully described the lawyer to BB, 'is not only an honourable man, but he's damned clever with other people's money'. Joe was not so jocular to Levy. He had calculated to a nicety the thinness of the ice on which his legal adviser was skating and now he threatened to create cracks. Under U.S. law a lawyer cannot act for both parties if he also handles either party's revenue returns. The result was that Levy, though he frequently wrote detailed letters to BB as to the type and calibre of investments he was considering, in fact lent the $600,000 back to Joe at 4½ per cent through the agency of Joe's financial comptroller and their mutual investment adviser, John Allen.

The result was that Joe paid off his partner without disturbing his cash flow. BB's $600,000 was wisely spent. Joe bought the Dreyfus Collection for $100,000 and made a down payment of $500,000 on the Benson Collection, promising to pay the balance of $2.5 million within two years. In due course Joe disposed of these two collections for an undivided profit of $3 million.

Joe did not begrudge BB the $50,000 a year retainer. He needed BB to buttress his sales pitch, but with the Dreyfus and Benson pictures under his belt, he had no intention of ever purchasing another major collection; he did not believe that he had long to live and, though in fact he lingered for another ten years, he bought very few pictures, confining himself to those for which he had a definite customer. Bernard had other ideas. He wanted his 10 per cent commission on purchases—and what was probably the largest art deal of all time was now in the offing.

BB had learned that the newly established Soviet government was anxious to dispose of some of the world's greatest pictures from the Hermitage. The information had come to him quite innocently in the course of his researches. He had been in correspondence with the Hermitage, and his contact there had mentioned in an elliptical way that 'the picture you once wanted to buy is on the market again;' he named Ilyn as the Soviet official charged with its disposal. The picture was Leonardo da Vinci's Benois Madonna, which Bernard had authenticated in 1913 when it had been offered to Duveens for $5 million.

BB told Louis Levy about it, remarking that, as it was a picture which they had dealt with before, he felt that, should Joe buy it, he should be treated under the more generous provisions of the earlier Doris agreement under which he would have had a slice of both the purchase and the sale prices. Levy certainly told Joe that the Benois Madonna was on the market in a letter dated 2 March 1928, but he did not say from whom he had obtained the information. At the same time Levy also told Calouste Gulbenkian, the

American art dealers Knoedlers, and the American oil millionaire
Armand Hammer, hoping no doubt to be rewarded by whoever
succeeded in purchasing the Leonardo.

BB followed Levy's example and told his old partner, Otto Gutkunst of Colnaghis.

Exactly how the Soviet government disposed of all the works
of art it sold at that time is not clear. But the detailed account
published by John Walker, former Director of the National Gallery, Washington, is far from accurate. Walker had an almost
pathological hatred of Joe, fostered by BB whose guest he was at
the time of the Soviet deals. In his account, Walker says that Joe's
failure to purchase the Russian treasures was the greatest disaster
of his life and that Knoedlers and their customer Andrew Mellon
outsmarted him.

It is true that Joe would have liked to purchase several of the
Hermitage pictures; he even made an initial written offer of $25
million for nine of them, including the five Mellon eventually
acquired for $3.4 million, six months before Knoedlers, Mellon
or Colnaghis entered the arena. The deal was to be financed by
his friend Calouste Gulbenkian. But Joe did not pursue his initial
offer for a very good reason.

Joe had just been advised that he was to be appointed to the
Board of Trustees of the National Gallery. His contacts at the
Palace—the Chairman of the Trustees was the Prince of Wales—
advised him that both the Royal Family and the government would
be dismayed should he traffic with the 'Bolsheviks', who had mur-
dered so many of the royal relations. Joe immediately dropped the
deal. However, he made this decision privately. Publicly, in the
United States at least, he made the appropriate noises, so that
many in the art world thought that he was an active bidder. Behind
the dealers' backs he did two things.

Joe knew that Knoedlers were bidding on Andrew Mellon's
behalf, so he signed a formal agreement with Carmen Messmore
of Knoedlers, which is preserved in the Metropolitan archives, that
he would stand aside in exchange for a share in their profit. His
second action was to contact Andrew Mellon. Joe explained that
his appointment to the National Gallery and his relationship with
the Royal Family had placed him in an invidious position, and he
assured Mellon that if Duveens and, by implication, the National

Gallery, London, were not to have them, then there was no finer home for them than the Mellon Collection.

In this way he further ingratiated himself with Mellon, whom he had long targeted as a major customer, and saved himself both embarrassment and the need to pay BB a commission, for by this time he was aware of the source of Levy's information.

Joe had had his eye on Andrew Mellon for twenty years, ever since Henry Frick had introduced them during a visit to the newly opened gallery on the corner of 56th Street and Fifth Avenue. Frick had said, 'This unassuming young man is Andrew Mellon. Some day he will be the greatest collector of us all'.

The accounts of both Sam Behrman and John Walker as to how the two men met are as inaccurate as they are hilarious. Behrman says that it was in 1931 and that the meeting was engineered by their respective valets at Claridges Hotel. Walker dates the meeting around 1930 and plays down Joe's influence. The facts are dramatically different.

Their personal relationship began in 1913. Shortly after Henry Frick had introduced them, Joe gave Mellon a series of introductions to collectors in London and Paris. During September 1913 he gave him a personally escorted tour of the major Paris collections. Fowles remembers that Mellon was entranced by a scale model of a small museum which Joe had designed to house the Edward Tuck Collection. The museum was to have been built at Concord, New Hampshire, and, though Tuck eventually changed his mind and left his Collection to the City of Paris, the model museum remained at Duveens. It was complete down to miniature light fittings and works of art. Mellon was enchanted by it and always asked to see it whenever he visited the gallery.

Mellon became a Duveen customer in 1918 when Duveens refurnished his Pittsburgh home. The following year he took a trip to California with Joe and was given a tour of the Huntington Collection. In the next ten years Mellon spent over $3 million at Duveens. They invited each other to their daughters' weddings and Joe made many of the European arrangements for Ailsa Mellon Bruce's honeymoon.

The relationship suffered a setback in 1927 when Mellon came to suspect that Joe had an 'inside' source of information on his affairs. He was correct. His valet, Flore, and butler, Tom Kerr, were both on Bert Boggis' payroll, but Joe's greatest source of information was the Paris representative of the Morgan Bank, Theodore Rousseau. He was a close friend of Joe's, while Mellon used him as a sounding board and confidant whenever he was in Europe. Mellon particularly enjoyed discreet candlelit dinner parties, complete with equally discreet feminine company, which Rousseau was adept at arranging, for Mellon in Paris was not the shy, austere, almost ethereal figure he appeared to be elsewhere.

Unhappily Joe let slip that he was aware of these assignations and Mellon jumped to the conclusion that the information had come from his valet; for a few months, he treated Joe with unaccustomed coldness. Joe could have remedied the situation by letting Mellon know that he too was an occasional guest at Theodore's secret apartment on the Ile St. Louis, but he preferred to keep Rousseau's role to himself.

The rift was healed in London in the autumn of 1928 when the two men visited the National Gallery together. It was at this time that Mellon conceived the idea of an American National Gallery, and it is possible to give its precise moment of conception. 'This', said Joe, indicating the galleries, 'will be my memorial'. He shyly confided that he was about to be created a trustee, and expounded his plans for improvement. He wanted sculpture courts, a study collection and travelling exhibitions. He wished to bring the place alive with concerts, make it a community centre instead of a morgue. In fact, he was preaching what the young Francis Taylor,* then launching his own career at the Philadephia Museum, had told him about his own plans a few months before. Mellon was entranced. He was to tell Theodore Rousseau a few days later that 'Duveen showed me what a government could do with a museum if it wished'.

Mellon also told Rousseau that Joe had hinted very strongly that he had received an ominous diagnosis from his doctors. By an amazing coincidence, Mellon was not only suffering from internal cancer as well but had actually consulted the same specialists. Mellon now asked Rousseau for his opinion as to who were the best American financial minds at devising 'an art trust to hold paintings and sculpture'.

* Later to be Director of the Metropolitan, New York.

Mellon had been brooding over the concept of an American equivalent of the National Gallery for years. He had made up his mind to build and endow a museum of some kind as early as 1927 and had confided the fact to his secretary, David Finley, who lost no time in passing word to Joe. However, it was not until the meeting with Joe at the London National Gallery in 1928 that Mellon definitely decided on an 'American National Gallery'. Several facts conspired to delay his dream.

The Wall Street crash of 1929 and the following slump did not create a suitable climate for a former Secretary of the U.S. Treasury to be seen throwing money about like water. Great care was taken to keep Mellon's Hermitage purchases a secret, while Joe himself was in deep financial trouble.

Joe's indebtedness was enormous, for he had to find the sum needed to pay the balance on the Benson Collection while his own clients, such as Bache and Mackay, were unable to settle their bills. In 1929 Duveens recorded a loss of $900,000 and this rose in the following year to $2,900,000. The next two years were little better and saw Joe struggling to unload much of his stock. He was determined to keep the cream for Mellon but was stuck with two problems, an enormous inventory of second-rate pictures and some superb eighteenth-century French furniture. He had a customer in mind for each group.

Joe had long dreamt of selling the furniture to Mrs Horace E. Dodge, the widow of the automobile manufacturer. He was introduced to her by Dr Valentiner, the Curator of the Detroit Museum, a position which Joe had found for him in 1919. Dr Valentiner was suitably grateful, and whenever someone wished to purchase a work of art for Detroit he usually managed to steer them in the direction of Duveens.

After she was widowed, Mrs Dodge decided to give the Detroit Museum a picture. On her behalf Dr Valentiner chose Matteo di Giovanni's Virgin and Child from Duveens' New York stock. Joe, as a matter of course, wrote to congratulate her on her generosity and invited her to dine in New York. During dinner Mrs Dodge explained her problem. She had inherited all her husband's shares in the Dodge Motor Car enterprise but now she had been offered $100 million for them by the Chrysler Company. Should she accept?

Joe, who, when he wanted a client, did not hesitate to offer advice on any subject, suggested that she would be sensible to accept, and that she should invest the money in 'Liberty Bonds', which carried an exemption from income tax. Mrs Dodge took the advice and became eternally grateful when in due course the slump decimated the holding she had sold to Chrysler. Thereafter she became a firm apostle of the gospel according to St Joe, but she was still not a customer.

In April 1926 Mrs Dodge had bought a villa at Palm Beach from an oil millionaire called Cosden for $4 million. Here Joe had another opportunity. He learned that the villa had some wall decorations by Sert. Again he wrote congratulating her on her taste and letting drop the information that he was presenting the Tate Gallery with four extensions to its premises which were to be opened by royalty. He added that he had decided to emulate her example and commission Sert to decorate the main staircase. However, Mrs Dodge remained seemingly impervious to his attentions.

Then Joe read in his newspaper that Mrs Dodge had decided to marry a small-time actor called Hugh Dillman and that the newlywed couple planned to settle near Detroit in Grosse Point. This was too much for Joe. The thought of that $100 million going to a house in Detroit really moved him to action.

The newly-weds were honeymooning in California. Joe managed to arrange a deal between Dillman's lawyer, Leo Butzel, and Huntington's curator. The Dodges were invited to tour Henry Huntington's mansion, which had been almost completely 'Duveened'. They thoroughly enjoyed the trip, and afterwards Joe and Dillman frequently corresponded by telegram, with Joe always paying for Dillman's replies. Still Anna Dodge Dillman, as she now called herself, remained only a courteous friend, totally uninterested in buying anything.

This situation went on for almost three years. Wherever they went Joe bombarded them with gifts—boxes for the opera, orchids for special occasions, roses for every day. To Mrs Dodge it must have appeared that they were never out of his thoughts. It was an expensive exercise in public relations as Joe practised that 'skill'. His methods may be judged from the code-name he allotted to Hugh Dillman for accountancy purposes. He was called 'Patsy'.

In October 1931, he learned that Anna and Hugh, as they had

now become, were planning a trip to Europe and the Middle East, but their lawyer, the cooperative Leo Butzel, let fall that because of the slump and the fear of adverse publicity Mrs Dodge Dillman was chary of letting it be known that she had money to spend. Butzel wrote: 'Whatever you do, for mighty important reasons, create no publicity with reference to the acquisition by her of a collection. I can give you a number of powerful reasons on the telephone if you want them.'

Butzel dutifully delivered his client in a buying mood. Mrs Dodge Dillman at last opened her collection with the purchase of some French eighteenth-century chairs and a set of Boucher tapestries for $837,500. On Joe's advice they abandoned their plans to see the Middle East and agreed to content themselves with London and Paris.

Joe promised them a sensational tour. He discovered that his client had a weakness for anything connected with Madame de Pompadour, so arranged to have her painted in that role by Sir Gerald Kelly RA. He also laid on private visits to all the major collections and a secret tour of Windsor Castle. A delighted Mrs Dodge Dillman finally surrendered and commissioned him to decorate and furnish her new house from top to bottom, regardless of expense. The deal was to be worth almost $6 million.

Joe paid for the ever-pliant Leo Butzel and his son to sail to England on the *Aquitania* and put them up at the Dorchester, writing to Signor Gigolima, the manager, that they were his honoured guests and were to be granted their every whim. By the same post he wrote to his brother, Ernest, who was anxious for details of the firm's financial affairs:

4th Nov. 1932

I am sending you herewith copy of an invoice covering a sale just made to Mrs Dillman. Whilst the terms of payment provide that the amount is to be paid in instalments over the next two and a half years, nevertheless it is one that can be discounted at our bank . . . The terms have been settled with Mr Leo Butzel—her lawyer, and I cannot stress too much the vital necessity of keeping the transaction confidential. No news whatever of her making such a purchase must leak out. I cannot too strongly emphasise this because there is still bigger business to be done there yet . . . She will not open the house until next year, and to have it ready for opening many things must yet be placed there, such as pictures, porcelains, another tapestry and other items; indeed I have twice gone round the house with her to select the places for each piece yet to be supplied.

You can quite understand that this last deal has largely helped to take us out of trouble, and clears the atmosphere, and one more deal will extricate us entirely . . . If things go better from now on, if only in a small way, I have time by the end of the season, say April, to have everybody paid off, and I am not going to commence anything until everybody is paid. We are not yet out of the wood completely . . .

The 'one more deal' Joe planned was to be with the department store proprietor, Samuel Kress, but it was to be frustrated twice, first by Bernard and then by Joe's bitterest American enemy, the future curator of Mellon's National Gallery, John Walker.

Joe had cultivated Kress since they had met casually at the Battle Creek sanatorium in 1918, but he had found him a difficult man to deal with. Kress had a fetish about his health. He disapproved of the cloud of cigar smoke which at that time almost obscured Joe from his customers. Kress also admired extreme parsimony. Duveen employees were instructed that, when they called on him, they were to park their cars or pay off their taxis round the corner and walk to his entrance, because Kress would be watching from the window and would upbraid them for extravagance should he spot them indulging in luxury.

Kress had calculated to a nicety how long it took to walk from point A to point B in New York. He had timed himself around the city with a pedometer and a stop watch. The drill at Duveens was for an employee to telephone Kress before he left and then time his arrival to coincide with Kress's idea of his probable walking speed. A heavy item was always delivered on a handcart. Again Kress would want to be advised of the delivery man's time of departure, and should the unfortunate fellow arrive within the calculated time he might, if he was lucky, receive a modest tip.

Kress was equally pernickety in his buying. His fortune had come from the astute purchase of cheap goods *en masse* which he then sold through his chain of stores at modest mark-ups. He was used to buying by the hundred gross and could calculate discounts to a fraction of a cent. The thought of paying a large price for one item was totally against his nature.

When he called at Duveens he would select around thirty pictures, inquire the price of each one, and then shoot a series of permutations. 'How much for the lot—cash? How much for the lot minus items 3, 11 and 27?' etc. Joe could not stand his goods being relegated to the status of 'items', nor could he keep pace with the mental arithmetic involved. He would allow Kress to reserve those things he was interested in and leave the negotiations to his accountant, John Allen.

Happily Kress had an Achilles' heel. He had an elegant and knowledgeable lady friend called Mrs Kilvert who collected French furniture. She informed Joe that, provided her hobby was satisfied, then she could bring her lover to the point of decision. Thereafter all sales to Kress included the lady's 'present'.

Kress was extremely sensitive about the relationship, believing that it was a well-kept secret. Since Mrs Kilvert always accompanied him on his buying expeditions, he came to the decision that his major purchases should be made abroad. Mrs Kilvert agreed with him and asked Joe to arrange their visits to Europe. Joe complied and gave them an introduction to BB. Unhappily he omitted to mention to Bernhard that the lady required a percentage.

She made her 'ground rules' plain to BB soon after she and Kress arrived in Florence in 1923. BB disliked her and was unimpressed with her lover. After a brief discussion he slyly suggested that they patronize a dealer called Contini Bonacossi, whom he was sure would be able to accommodate them.

Contini was a former ship's steward who had left his ship in Rio de Janeiro shortly before the outbreak of the First World War. He rapidly became the manager of one of that city's more elegant brothels. He made a considerable fortune, which he invested in postage stamps, then returned to Italy where he began to realize his collection; he reinvested his profits in paintings. The pictures he kept for his own collection were of good quality, but those he put on the market were mostly minor works, generally repainted and heavily restored. His main reputation was as a wholesaler of 'furnishing quality' pictures.

He recognized Kress for what he was and quickly came to an accommodation with the lady friend. He suggested that they collect paintings in the same way as a stamp collector, one example of every Italian artist. He would supply them, frame them identically, and ship them to the States. What was more, he offered an 'after sales service': his 'expert' would visit the collection three times a year and suggest what needed cleaning or varnishing or what could be exchanged for a better example. Kress, who as we have seen found it almost impossible to buy individual items, was delighted with the arrangement and could never thank BB enough for the introduction. Nor could Contini, who over the years sold him almost a thousand second-rate pictures for several million dollars.

Joe tried strenuously to win his errant client back, and thought he had succeeded when, in 1930, Kress agreed to buy several pictures, including the set of Sassetta panels which had belonged to Clarence Mackay, who had been ruined in the depression. Kress sought advice from BB, who advised him against the purchase, and the deal was cancelled. Joe suspected, but could not prove, that BB was receiving a commission from Contini. He was partly right, though it was not until long after his death that Fowles established what really happened. When Contini had offered BB a commission at the beginning of the Kress relationship, BB had airily refused, saying he was not interested, but if it was a matter of principle then he could give a small present to 'my secretary'— Nicky Mariano. Contini honoured the custom until 1939. After 1945, Contini paid BB a regular retainer as a consultant.

The loss of the first major Kress deal was painful to Joe, though Mrs Dodge Dillman's purchases provided some compensation. In 1932 Joe tried to revive Kress' interest and persuade him into making a major purchase. This time Joe was sure that BB would not interfere. He based his confidence on the fact that he knew that the Berensons were drastically short of money. He subtly applied the pressure, asking Fowles to write that business was really bad and that he doubted that they would be able to continue. Mary wrote to her sister Alys in mid-July that she and BB feared the worst from Joe's decision, though they wouldn't know for sure until they met with Louis Levy in September. Mary told her sister they anticipated firing servants, selling their car, and closing I Tatti and moving to Rome to live on the cheap.

She was being rather too pessimistic, but reacting just as Joe wished her to. Eventually the Doris agreement was renewed that November, after six weeks of argument. BB, Nicky and Joe had met in Vienna at the end of September, but BB had returned empty-handed a week later.

BB had had to admit that he had frustrated the Kress purchase of the Mackay pictures as he did not stand to gain from the transaction. He had argued that if Joe was buying back from Mackay then he should have 10 per cent of the buy-back price. Joe had refused. BB was also furious that Joe had not gone ahead with the Hermitage deal. He was, however, in no position to argue. The investments that Louis Levy had written so enthusiastically about had apparently slumped in value. The Berensons were still unaware that their money was tied up in Duveens. Levy, who attended the negotiations, kept quiet.

It was left to Mary and Edward Fowles to patch up a new agreement. Fowles did his best for both parties. He discovered for the first time that Levy had double-crossed the Berensons and invested their $600,000 in the firm while leading them to believe that it was elsewhere and lost in the slump. He persuaded Levy to write and say he had been able to rescue $250,000 from the wreckage and ensured that Levy invested it properly. Fowles funded this sum from the first installment of Mrs Dodge Dillman's money.

Of course this arrangement left the firm with the remaining $350,000, which the Berensons believed was lost forever. Here Fowles exceeded Joe's instructions. On behalf of Duveens he raised BB's annual payment to $100,000 a year. Of this, $60,000 was a retainer and $40,000 on account of what Fowles called 'monies due on contingency'.

However, even this outwardly generous settlement had its price. BB had to agree to waive all future purchasing commissions and to accept a clause stipulating that the contract should lapse immediately on the death of either partner and could be terminated at six months' notice.

BB rarely spoke to Joe thereafter, pouring out his spleen to any who would listen. He did not blame Edward Fowles and wrote to thank him for rescuing something from the impasse. Fowles kept his guard up. When he had exceeded Joe's instructions in agreeing to the new contract he had done so out of respect for Mary. By this time Fowles regarded BB as useful but far from essential, and he had by now grown to dislike and distrust Nicky Mariano, who he believed, no doubt unfairly, was feathering her own nest at Mary's expense.

Fowles was not aware of the peace and order Nicky brought to the chaotic household that I Tatti had become, but his ears were far closer to the marketplace than either Bernard's or Joe's. He knew Nicky was receiving commissions from Contini and from the Baron Lazzaroni, who now supplied Bernard with almost all the pictures which he offered the firm. They were all characterized by an almost fiendish reworking, which gave them the same ominous uniformity. Fowles bought them and put them quietly into store, knowing that if he did not they would finish up with either Wildenstein or Contini. He simply wrote to BB asking that he send no more Lazzaronis.

'Lazzaronis' are one of the modern curator's greatest worries. There are many public galleries, particularly in the United States, which would do well to take a fresh look at any picture of theirs which includes his name in the provenance. A list of his improved and prettified pictures would fill a large volume. One example must suffice: Sebastiano Mainardi's 'Portrait of a Lady', an appealing profile which Joe sold to Mellon in 1923. Mellon was later to return it, and the whereabouts of the picture are presently unknown to the author.

However, a picture with the same title, measurements and attributions surfaced at an exhibition in New York in November 1963; it also had written endorsements as to its authorship by BB, W. R. Valentiner and Van Merle. It had been recently cleaned,* and the young woman had become a mature spinster with a double chin, a less than classic nose, and totally different embroidery and jewellery.

The Fowles settlement formula was agreed to by both parties. Joe was mollified by the death or six-month clause but BB continued to rail to all who would listen to him at the ill-treatment he had been forced to endure. There was no more willing audience than his self-appointed acolyte, John Walker.

During the early thirties John Walker was one of the fringe members of the I Tatti ménage. He had recently graduated from

* Photographs 'before and after' are included among the illustrations.

the Harvard Faculty of Fine Arts and claimed that the university had sent him to study under BB. In fact what had happened was that when he decided to continue his studies in Italy they gave him a letter of introduction to BB. He was not BB's pupil but made himself useful around the place as an aide to Nicky Mariano and helped catalogue books for the library, which arrived by almost every post. The only work of an academic nature he did was to help Mary produce a coffee-table book called *Beautiful Italian Pictures* which, though it was delivered to Yale University Press, was never published.

Mary found that Walker had a natural eye for painting. Walker's charm combined with his ample private income made him a congenial courtier, only too willing to run errands into Florence in his sports car, or to meet some visiting squillionaire at the railway station. He also became a convenient receptacle for the abuse hurled almost daily at Joe.

Walker's sympathies were entirely with BB. He was also deeply disappointed when Yale refused to publish *Beautiful Italian Pictures*, explaining that 'Sir Joseph Duveen had declined to subsidize it as he had Mr Berenson's other works'. From that moment he became a determined opponent of Duveen Brothers, never missing a chance to denigrate the firm's stock or Joe's integrity.

At the time, the only chance Walker saw to serve his adopted master came in December 1932, when he seized the opportunity to torpedo Joe's much-needed deal with Samuel Kress.

After months of negotiations, Kress had agreed to buy a group of nine important paintings from Joe. They included a Madonna and Child attributed by BB to Andrea del Verrocchio and Duccio di Buoninsegna's 'The Calling of St Peter and St Andrew'. Both were offered at cost as Joe was desperate.

Kress wrote to BB as usual, asking for his opinion, not as to their authenticity but as to their value and importance. BB delegated the reply to John Walker, who wrote on his behalf: 'Mr Berenson knows the pictures well. He has not had an opportunity to examine them recently but believes that, should they be as important as Sir Joseph Duveen asserts, then they will undoubtedly have been offered to Mr Mellon'. Walker went on to say that he was a personal friend of the Mellon family—in fact Paul Mellon had been a boyhood companion. He offered to 'determine privately the grounds on which Mr Mellon doubtless declined them'.

Kress, aggrieved that Mellon should have had first choice, turned the deal down. Almost four years later Kress realized that he had been tricked and reopened negotiations. He purchased both pictures at the original 1932 price. He was asked why he had changed his mind and in reply handed John Walker's letter to Joe. Kress presented both pictures to the National Gallery, Washington, at Walker's request.

❧ 20 ❧

Restorations and Reputations

Joe once visited his youngest and rather horsy sister Florrie, who was married to the Paris dealer René Gimpel. As he entered her house, he twitched his nose and remarked, 'Your house, my dear Florrie, smells of the stables'. Florrie retorted, 'At least it's better than the smell of fresh paint on your pictures'.

Joe's craving to rework, and if given the chance to repaint, every painting that passed through his hands was well-known to the trade, who contented themselves by saying that that was the way his American clients wanted them to look. Not only were they refurbished so that they looked as he wished them to look, but he then had them coated in a specially thick carriage varnish, with the result that until modern solvents were developed, it was almost impossible to remedy the damage his restorers caused. The only charitable comment that can be made is that at least he was consistent. He treated his pictures in exactly the same way as he did his furniture. He would obsessively repolish any piece of Chippendale, regild any gilded Louis XV chair, resilver any fine looking glass, even recarve examples of Grinling Gibbons carving if they displeased him.

Bernard did not have this consistency. In his earlier and it must be said less commercial days, he fought shy of restorations; when he made his first famous lists, he would mark any restored picture with the letter 'r' in brackets. He used the same symbol for a picture that had been ruined. To the young aesthete, unless the restoration was reversible, the two categories meant one and the same. Even ambivalent commentators like Kenneth Clark have pleaded that he was innocent and ignorant of the finer or more sophisticated tricks a restorer could produce.

However, Professor Marchig, for many years Wildensteins' chief restorer, who probably worked more closely with Bernard than any other technician, is adamant that Bernard knew all the tricks. 'Bernard knew a great deal about the technicalities of restoration and could spot it at a glance', Marchig recalled. 'No matter how clever the disguise, Bernard's innate sense of style and of the artist's personality could always detect the work of another hand. He was almost infallible'.

On 27 February 1924, BB sent a reassuring letter from I Tatti to a worried American millionaire named Goldman, who had paid Duveens over $250,000 for what he understood to be an original masterpiece by the great Fra Angelico. Mr Goldman had observed that his prize bore distinct signs of heavy restoration and he wished to know if he had the genuine article. Berenson assured him that not only was his work one of the most important of that period, but it was, in fact, remarkably well preserved.

Documents in the Duveen archives show that Berenson was lying. Goldman's Fra Angelico had first been touched up to improve its appearance. It had then been transferred from its original wood (which had split and warped) on to canvas, then back on to new wood. It had then been restored a second time on BB's own instructions. On 26 February 1923, seeing a photograph of the first restoration, he wrote angrily to Edward Fowles demanding that if he still had the picture, it have more restoration work done separately on the figures and landscape.

BB chose not to tell Goldman of the restoration work but it is recorded in Duveens' meticulously kept ledger, which shows that £760 was paid to the restorer.

Today Goldman's painting is not even regarded as a Fra Angelico. It hangs in the Kress Collection in the National Gallery in Washington, labeled as 'attributed to Jacopo del Sellaio'. The catalogue notes that it is 'very much worn, large zones in the landscape and sky repainted'.

The story of Goldman's picture illustrates BB's attitude to tampering with old masters. At what point does restoration—a careful repainting to recapture the original artist's intentions—become 'prettification', perhaps for commercial purposes? There is still much passionate debate over BB's view on this. What is certain is that in his younger days, as a scholar, BB was a purist. No restorer, he said, should add *anything* of his own to the original.

In Goldman's case, the restorer was Joe's redoubtable Madame

Helfer of Paris, whom we have met before. She wholly understood Joe's requirement that pictures had above all to be both bright and pretty. Most of her work can be recognized by a distinct sugariness, and occasionally by her tendency to use one of her young relations, a Mademoiselle Brachet, as a model.

Miss Brachet had almost round eyes and a small but distinctive mouth. She can be recognized in the Duveen repaint of Masaccio's 'Madonna of Humility' (Mellon Collection, National Gallery, Washington), as a dancer in 'The Village Orchestra', attributed to Jean Baptiste Pater in the Frick Collection, and in Mellon's 'Vermeers'—'The Lace Maker' and 'The Smiling Girl', both of which owe far more to Madame Helfer and anonymous nineteenth-century artists than they do to the master to whom they were so ambitiously ascribed. They were 'discovered' by Wilhelm von Bode in his old age when, ruined by the Great War, he consented to advise Joe. 'The Lace Maker' was purchased from a British army officer called Captain Wright, who looted it while with the occupying forces in Hamburg in 1918. Von Bode was allowed to discover it, *after* Madame Helfer had finished with it. He charitably omitted to notice that the lady depicted was using a nineteenth-century style 'bobbin'. Neither Joe, nor Mellon nor the National Gallery of Washington appear to have noticed it either.

Fowles visited von Bode at this time. He noticed that the old man was almost starving and arranged to send him food parcels. He also chided him for his endorsement of some dubious pictures, remarking of a Petrus Christus Madonna he had been offered that 'I would never have believed it was by Petrus Christus if it did not carry your certificate'. Von Bode laughed and replied, 'You don't understand the intricacies of the German language. After a brief description of the subject I say "I have never seen a Petrus Christus like this!" '

Many critics have speculated as to just how much either Joe or BB knew about restoration and have generally come to the conclusion that Joe did not care and BB did not know. In fact they both knew a great deal, but took considerable pains to disguise their knowledge. The trouble was that they did not always agree on how much should be done to restore a picture. Joe was inclined to leave it to his team of restorers, who knew he was keen on prettification, while BB was all too well aware of the effect of overworking an old master. Their different attitudes were well displayed in the case of the Sassetta panels, which also involved Kenneth Clark. But before explaining about Sassetta, it is necessary to tell the story of how Clark came to know first Berenson, and then, through a Leonardo da Vinci painting, Duveen.

While Clark was an undergraduate at Oxford he became friendly with BB's old colleague Charles Bell, by then Keeper of Fine Art at the Ashmolean Museum. Clark mentioned to him that, ever since he was a teenager, he had had a wish to assist BB with a new edition of *Drawings of the Florentine Painters*. Bell, who had maintained a distant relationship with BB although he regarded him as a charlatan, introduced Clark to Mary while she was over in England for a visit in the spring of 1925. Mary, in turn, introduced Clark to her brother Logan, who promptly fell in love with him.

Mary, who liked organizing other people, particularly their emotional attachments, arranged for Charles Bell to bring the young Clark to Florence in September 1925. At her suggestion, BB, who took less than an hour to establish that Clark had at least as fine a mind as his own, invited him to realize his ambition and work with him on the new edition of *Drawings of the Florentine Painters*. After a brief period to consider, Clark accepted.

It was not a happy association. Clark rapidly discovered the falsity of his position. BB admired his pupil's brain, but he wanted a disciple, not a colleague. Logan also made a nuisance of himself, which Clark countered by marrying and bringing his wife out to live with him at I Tatti. This stratagem failed to ease matters, however, and he returned to London, richer by a wife and infant son and a formidable knowledge of the work of Leonardo.

While Clark had been living at I Tatti, BB had made no secret of his relationship with Joe. Every post brought photographs and sometimes paintings for Bernard's opinion—a task he frequently delegated to Mary or Clark. It was through one of Joe's rare brushes with Leonardo that Kenneth Clark earned the acceptance and ultimately the patronage of Sir Joseph Duveen.

On 19 November 1919 a Kansas City dealer called Hug had written to Duveens in New York saying that he had had an opportunity to purchase a picture called 'La Belle Ferronière' by Leonardo da Vinci from the daughter of a distinguished French family, whom a client of his had met and married while serving as an officer with the American army in France during the war. The picture had been certified as genuine by a well-known expert called George Sartias. Because of the pressures generated at that time by Hamilton and Salomon, combined with Uncle Henry's death and other worries, Joe had ignored the letter.

Shortly afterwards the owner of the painting, Mrs Andrée Hahn, had announced that her picture, 'the first Leonardo to arrive in America', was to be sold to the Kansas City Art Gallery for $250,000. The *New York World* had sent a reporter to ask Joe his opinion. He had replied that the lady's picture, which he had never seen, was an obvious copy of a genuine picture of that name in the Louvre. Allegedly for this reason, the sale fell through, and Mrs Hahn brought an action against Joe for frustrating the sale. The issue before the court was not the authenticity of Mrs Hahn's picture but whether the Louvre picture was genuine or not.

The Louvre picture had long been doubted, for it was known that Leonardo began several versions, but was not believed to have finished any of them. As far back as 1907, BB had stated that he could not accept the Louvre picture as genuine.

The case dragged slowly through the courts until September 1923, when Mrs Hahn's picture was taken to the Louvre and the two were compared by a panel of experts including BB, Venturi, Roger Fry, Sir Charles Holmes, then the Director of the National Gallery, London, and several others. It was BB's written opinion to Joe that, though he disliked both pictures, he felt that they were by the same hand. Joe instructed Louis Levy to delay the hearing of the case as long as possible, hoping that Mrs Hahn would collapse under the additional expense.

Mrs Hahn clung tenaciously to her claim, and by 1928 Joe was desperate. Then he learned from Lord Esher that the Royal Collection at Windsor Castle contained a great many Leonardo drawings which had never been properly catalogued and that Owen Morshead, the newly appointed librarian, had neither the time nor the scholarship to do so. Joe mentioned young Kenneth Clark, aged twenty-six, then unknown as a scholar but, Esher was assured, BB's most promising pupil. Clark was offered the job of cataloguing the Windsor Leonardo drawings, which he accepted. While looking through the Royal Collection, he found some minor stylistic evidence that identified Leonardo more closely than before with the Louvre picture, which he passed to BB. When the Hahn case was called in February 1929 BB testified that the Louvre picture was genuine but the Hahn was not. Neither judge nor jury were impressed by BB's equivocation—which today with hindsight seems to have amounted to perjury—and a retrial was ordered.

Considerable pressure was then brought on the Hahns to drop the case. In July 1929 Joe's detectives discovered some damaging facts about the family. Mrs Hahn and her sister had been prostitutes, their father a pimp, and their uncle an antique dealer with convictions for receiving stolen property. The Hahns withdrew their case, Joe paying their costs to date and secret damages of $60,000.

The fate of the Hahn version of 'La Belle Ferronière' continues to be a mystery. It was examined at the National Gallery when Clark was director and Joe a trustee. Both Clark and the Gallery's chief restorer, Helmut Ruhemann, believed it to be genuine.* Their opinion was kept a secret and the painting was returned without comment to a lawyer in Wichita, Kansas, called Leon Loucks. The Louvre version was examined in 1952 and the Louvre declared themselves satisfied that theirs was genuine as well. Perhaps Leonardo did paint two versions.†

Joe had been anxious to put the Hahn case behind him. Emulating his father he donated an extension to the Tate Gallery in 1926, including a special gallery for the work of Sargent.

Up to then, Joe had been a Knight Bachelor; the following year he was rewarded with a baronetcy. Now he aspired to higher things and discussed them with BB in Florence on 2 September 1928. BB wrote the same evening to Nicky Mariano, who was away on holiday, that Joe had asked him for personal advice to help him achieve his ambitions. Joe, he wrote, had asked if he should first become a trustee of the National Gallery or a peer. BB had replied that if Joe became a peer, everything else would follow. Joe also asked if it would be worth contributing to Lord Lee of Fareham's new School of Art Studies at London University and the National

* Ruhemann issued a certificate to this effect to the Hahn family. Clark wrote privately to Joe warning him of this and conceding that he agreed with Ruhemann's verdict.
† An excellent summary of the Hahn case and the picture's history to date was published in an article by Andrew Decker in *Art News* in May 1985.

Portrait Gallery, whereupon BB regaled Joe with the plans he had proposed to Lord D'Abernon about creating a museum and academy for the study of Anglo-Saxon biography.

In the event Joe had to wait five years for his peerage, but he was a Trustee of the National Gallery within six months, a final favour arranged for him by his faithful friend Lord Esher, who found Joe an excellent customer for furniture surplus to his requirements. Joe thanked him profusely: 'I can never sufficiently express my gratitude for your ceaseless favours'.

It was almost the last favour the elderly Esher could arrange, for he was to die within the year. Joe cabled to his widow that her husband had 'held a unique place in my heart. He was the inspiration of whatever success I have had in my career'.

Joe was to find some further inspiration on the board of the National Gallery. It was already graced by Lord d'Abernon and Lord Lee, who had both been on Duveens' list of paid retainers for almost a decade. Joe soon became firm friends with Sir Philip Sassoon too, a rich and extravagant bon viveur—he gilded the gutters and drain pipes of his home and dyed the flowers in each room to match the curtains—but Philip was too rich to be corrupted, unlike the equally colourful Evan Charteris who spent more on corsetry than he did on wine, as Joe quickly found out when he agreed to an arrangement by which he would pay the accounts of Charteris' tailor and wine merchant.

From his new eminence Joe did not forget young Kenneth Clark; first he suggested that Clark replace Charles Bell at the Ashmolean (poor Bell was only fifty-six but had irritated Lord Lee) and then, shortly afterwards, he suggested that Clark should be the joint organizer of a great Italian exhibition scheduled to be held at Burlington House in January 1930. This was originally designed to be a propaganda exercise for the Italy of Mussolini, but Joe saw it as a suitable vehicle to display art as sold by Duveens and briefed Clark to invite many of Duveens' American customers to lend their pictures for exhibition. Clark in his innocence agreed, and invitations were dispatched to Bache, Widener, Mackay, Altman and the Metropolitan. Clark, unaware of the true situation, also invited Carl Hamilton to lend his better pictures.

Joe in his ignorance and Clark in his innocence precipitated an outburst from BB, who saw only too well what would happen if

Burlington House was to show row upon row of 'Duveens'. Berenson wrote a desperate letter to Edward Fowles, begging him to destroy it as soon as he had read it.

He managed to slip around the truth about the restoration, but was adamant that Joe do all he could to prevent the pictures from being sent to London. Despite the ignorance of the critics, just enough of the truth, he wrote, would get out and a serious disaster would ensue.

The particular pictures that Clark was determined to show and Berenson to withhold were a series of fifteenth-century panels by Stefano di Giovanni, called Sassetta. Originally the group had consisted of a magnificent effigy of St Francis surrounded by eight panels depicting scenes from the saint's life. BB owned the St Francis* and Edward Fowles had tracked down seven of the panels, complete with an old frame, and purchased them for a total of $100,000. Joe, thinking more like an interior decorator, had Madame Helfer 'restore' the seven panels on a breathtaking scale. Her bill was $21,350. They were sawed out of the frame and repainted; their colours were changed. A cloak was even added to one figure to balance the composition. The panels were then coated with carriage varnish and reassembled in the wrong sequence so that they would fit round a massive Demotte chimney piece in the Rosslyn New York mansion of Clarence Mackay, who had paid $500,000 for the seven panels without a murmur.

Both BB and Clark wrote appreciative monographs about the series, which Joe had printed on vellum, bound in doeskin and presented to his delighted customer. Clark described them as 'Sassetta's masterpiece' and as 'pictures of the highest quality'.

In the end, however, Mackay's Sassettas were never shown at Burlington House. Clark was persuaded that they were too delicate to travel. No Duveen paintings were shown either.

The Italian exhibition was a tremendous success. Clark became a considerable power amongst the London smart set, sponsored in the beginning by Sybil Colefax, a leading hostess and interior decorator who worked for Duveens on a commission basis. Further support for Clark came from one of Joe's second-string experts,

---

* This single Sassetta is depicted in the frontispiece of *The Bernard Berenson Treasury*, flanked by two other paintings, and is wrongly referred to as a Sassetta triptych.

Tancred Borenius, who arranged for him to give a series of lectures which Borenius then published in the new magazine *Apollo*, which he had founded and which at that time was covertly owned and controlled by Joe. Finally Clark became the protégé of the man who had taken Lord Farquhar's place in Joe's constellation of corrupt public figures, Arthur, Lord Lee of Fareham (mentioned first in Chapter Fourteen).

When Joe drew Lee's attention to the twenty-six-year-old Clark, Lee was Chairman of the Trustees of the National Gallery. In October 1932 Lee, d'Abernon, the corseted Evan Charteris and Sir Joseph Duveen recommended to the Prime Minister that Clark be appointed Director of the National Gallery, but Clark declined on the grounds that he was too young. However, he finally accepted the offer in June 1933, shortly before his thirtieth birthday. He took up the appointment on 1 January 1934, by which time Joe had been created Baron Duveen of Millbank.

The first pictures Clark decided to advise the Trustees to buy were the Mackay Sassettas. His account of the purchase follows:

I knew that seven of the eight scenes from the life of St Francis, by Sassetta, belonged to Mr Clarence Mackay. I had heard that he was in financial difficulties and thought that this might be an opportune moment to secure them. This exercise naturally involved my Trustees and I must now say something about them. In a sense the most eminent was the Prince of Wales, but he did not often come to Board meetings as he was not allowed to smoke . . . The senior trustee was a picturesque old scallywag named Viscount d'Abernon. I liked him because, when director of the Ottoman Bank, he had got into trouble and escaped over the tiles, like Casanova . . . By the time I knew him he was a little deaf and suffered from almost total *extinction de voix*. 'WHAT DO *YOU* THINK, EDGAR?' Philip Sassoon would bellow at him, to which he would reply in an almost inaudible whisper, 'offer half'. He was an amateur dealer, and probably in the pay of Duveen.

Duveen also had a considerable influence with Evan Charteris, the most elegant figure of his time, who for years had been at the summit of the literary *beau monde*. Having practised at the bar he could present a case very persuasively. He was a consummate liar, but always gave one a warning when he was going to tell a lie by delicately patting his moustache with a handkerchief. In contrast with these picturesque but disingenuous characters was Ormsby Gore, industrious, well-informed, combative and tactless. He was at this time Minister of Works . . .

Finally, Lord Duveen, who had been made a Trustee thanks to the influence of Arthur Lee and Lord d'Abernon, from both of whom he had bought pictures at inflated prices. Quite apart from these material benefits, he was irresistible. His bravura and impudence were infectious, and when he was present everyone behaved as if they had had a couple of drinks. He worked entirely by instinct and was incapable of writing a letter or making a coherent statement; and he had rightly seen that, whereas in America it paid him to be very grand, in England he could get further by bribing the upper classes and playing the fool.

I had for some reason decided that the right sum to offer for the seven panels was £35,000. Mr Mackay was said to have paid double, but I saw no reason to behave charitably towards an injudicious millionaire. I persuaded my Trustees to make this offer (which was in line with Lord d'Abernon's 'offer half'), and a letter was sent to Mr Mackay. Weeks passed without an answer and I was instructed to send a telegram. No answer. Another telegram. Still no answer. All this was reported at a Board meeting at which Lord Duveen was present. 'Of course he hasn't answered', he said, with his most expansive smile, 'he never saw the letter'. 'Nor the telegram?' 'Of course not! I know Mr Mackay's butler'. That a trustee of the Gallery should have bribed a vendor's butler not to show him our offer was a bit thick, and even Philip could not suppress a note of surprise. Duveen's stipendiaries shifted uneasily in their seats. 'Send another telegram', said Philip, 'and see that it reaches Mr Mackay'.

Duveen telephoned Clark the next morning, Clark's account continued:

'That Board meeting—I was quite upset. When I got home Elsie said "Joe, you are not looking *at all* yourself." I took a sleeping pill. It did me no harm'. His confidence thus restored, he asked me to go for a walk with him in Hyde Park. Towards the end of the walk (followed by his Rolls) he came to the point. Mr Mackay had never paid for the Sassettas. They were entered in the firm's books at £70,000, but no money had passed. It would have been tactless to ask him how much he had paid for the pictures; clearly it was much less than our proferred £35,000. But his pride was at stake and he could not bear to rewrite the entry in his books. Finally we came to an arrangement by which the price of the Sassettas was £42,000, and it was stated in the press release that the purchase was made possible 'Through the good services of Lord Duveen'.

There is little to add to Clark's account, except for the previous eighteen months the pictures had been in Duveens' basement, not Mackay's house. Clark's letter and telegrams were forwarded to Joe by Mackay's secretary with Mackay's knowledge. Joe did not mention to Clark the fact that it was he who was selling the pictures, as he did not wish to be accused of a conflict of interest. In fact he did not wish to sell them, firstly as he hoped to obtain a far larger price in due course from Andrew Mellon and secondly because Fowles had drawn his attention to BB's dramatic warning of serious disaster at the time of the 1930 Burlington House exhibition.

There was no public disaster such as BB had foretold, but the purchase irritated several of the curatorial members of the staff, who suspected that Clark was little more than another stipendiary of Duveens: they saw Clark as Duveens' unpaid placeman. Nothing could have been further from the truth, for Clark was a millionaire in his own right and regarded Joe with amused contempt.

Clark's insularity—some called it his remoteness—combined with the Sassetta purchase so infuriated the curatorial staff of the National Gallery that they locked Clark out of the library, refused to attend his conferences, and eventually sent him to Coventry. Things came to a head in the autumn of 1937 when Clark called in the Treasury to restore order and reassign certain members of the staff.

Clark now determined to get rid of Joe, whose turn as a Trustee had finished at the end of 1936 and who was now standing for re-election. In his autobiography Clark states that the majority of the Trustees were against his re-election, but that he hastened matters by going direct to the Prime Minister, Neville Chamberlain. Clark told Chamberlain that Duveen used his position at the National Gallery to benefit himself. If pictures from private collections were offered to the Gallery, then his professional instincts were aroused. If they came from rival dealers he was hostile to them; as a result, Clark claimed, the Gallery had lost several fine pictures. Finally—and here Clark produced his master stroke—he said that he had been negotiating with Calouste Gulbenkian for his collection. Gulbenkian had told him that he would not bequeath his collection to the National Gallery if Duveen was a Trustee. Chamberlain accepted Clark's argument. Joe, then in New York, was curtly told by the British Ambassador that the Prime Minister had vetoed the appointment. It broke Joe Duveen's heart.

Clark may well have felt justified in his action. No man likes to be made a fool of. Joe perhaps deserved his come-uppance, but Clark's explanation of his action and his arguments do not stand up to close examination.

First, a majority of the Trustees had not voted against Duveen. In fact he had already been re-elected and Chamberlain had already written to him confirming the fact. Clark went behind the Trustees' backs.

Second, Joe was terminally ill with cancer of the intestines. He had survived a colostomy in 1927 and further drastic surgery in 1930, 1934 and 1935, when he had been given less than a year to live. His condition was known to all the Trustees and to Clark, who had been his guest in New York after the second bout of surgery and who had expressed his sympathy to Lady Duveen.

Third, Joe had not bought a picture since June 1937 and had let it be known that he was putting his affairs in order. All he had done was to pay for a new building for the Tate Gallery, an extension to the British Museum to house the Elgin Marbles, an extension to the National Portrait Gallery, and the cost of redecorating both the Wallace Collection and the Tate Gallery. He had also presented the National Gallery with Hogarth's 'The Graham

Children'* and Correggio's 'Christ Taking Leave of His Mother'. His reappointment as a Trustee had been viewed by most people as a well-deserved reward for his generosity.

Finally, Gulbenkian was a personal friend of Joe's. It is most unlikely that he ever made the stipulation Clark claimed that he did. Not only did he know that Joe was dying and that he would never be able to attend a Trustees' meeting again, but Gulbenkian had never had any intention of bequeathing anything more than a small part of his collection to the National Gallery in London. When Gulbenkian learned of Clark's stratagem from Sir Philip Sassoon he wrote immediately to Joe denying that he had made the stipulation and asking for a plan of the National Gallery in Washington, which is in a sense Joe Duveen's most enduring memorial as he had encouraged Mellon to build it. In the event not one Gulbenkian picture went to London.

The last word belongs to Clark and should come from his written account:

> The effect of my action on those Trustees who were Duveen's friends may be imagined. Philip Sassoon nearly broke the telephone in his rage and did not speak to me again for three months. Even Charteris maintained a dignified silence, saying only 'You do not know what harm you have done'. Needless to say I never saw Lord Duveen again. I had not known at the time that he was already suffering from cancer. The rebuff added to his miseries, and not long afterwards he died. I suppose the moral is 'Never act on principle' or, in Mr Andrew Mellon's immortal phrase 'No good deed goes unpunished'.

* Now in the Tate Gallery.

❧ 21 ❧

End Game

The idea of persuading Andrew Mellon to build a 'National Gallery' in Washington was Joe's major preoccupation during the last years of his life, though the thought of filling it with his own selection of pictures and sculpture had at least an equal priority. He realized only too well that Mellon was primarily a client of his rivals, Knoedlers, but since their joint venture on the Hermitage pictures, Joe and the Knoedler partners, Otto Henschel and Carmen Messmore, had reached an understanding. Neither would interfere in the other's plans and each would do his best to bring their patron up to scratch.

John Walker's memoir, *Self-portrait with Donors*, is dismissive of Joe's role in the planning of the Washington National Gallery. Walker states that Joe had nothing to do with the choice of architect, the location of the gallery, or the materials used to build it; apart from selling Mellon fifty-five overpriced pictures and twenty-three items of sculpture in a block deal, he contributed very little to the gallery's contents in comparison to the 304 works of art Mellon bought from Knoedlers alone, not to mention many other purchases.

This is Walker at his most specious and spiteful. The gallery had been long planned by both men, but events and circumstances described in preceding chapters combined to delay matters. Nevertheless Joe still kept in reserve the group of paintings that he felt was destined for Mellon. The Duveen archives show all too clearly the financial strain this policy caused. They also show that Joe spent considerable time and effort getting the project under way. He had introduced Mellon to his favoured architect, John Russel Pope, way back in 1928 and wrote several times that he would

251

be the best choice. At first Mellon demurred, wanting Charles A. Platt, Junior, whose father had designed the Freer Gallery, but under pressure from both Joe and Kenneth Clark, Mellon changed his mind.

Kenneth Clark came into the picture in January 1934 when Joe commissioned him to prepare a report as to how an American gallery could be modelled on London's National Gallery. He wanted advice on a wide range of matters ranging from lighting to picture storage, staffing levels and draft by-laws. Clark's reports were forwarded by Joe to Mellon and to Pope.

When Kenneth Clark visited the United States for the first time in 1935 it was he who suggested to Joe and Pope that the building be faced with red Tennessee marble and chose a short list of three possible sites from the several available from the government. It is anticipating the narrative, but once Andrew Mellon had given the go-ahead for construction to begin, it was Joe who, in 1936, gave the young Paul Mellon introductions to Clark and the other Trustees of the London National Gallery so that he could study its constitution and administration in detail.

Despite this background work, the project received a major setback in 1934 when the United States Revenue questioned Andrew Mellon's tax returns. They argued that the various charitable trusts he had formed to hold his collection were liable to property taxes. They alleged that his returns were fraudulent and that he had no intention of forming a public collection or building a public gallery. They claimed that his 'trusts' were nothing more than a way of evading tax. As a former Secretary of State, Mellon was impeached.

It was against this background that Mellon invited Joe and Carmen Messmore of Knoedlers for lunch in New York on 29 May 1935. Mellon explained that he was extremely depressed by the allegations, which he was sure were politically motivated by the Democrats. He announced that if he lost the case, he would take himself and his collection out of the country forever. Nevertheless, he assured them both, provided he won, there would be a gallery, and he urged them to continue with the planning. He also urged them to attend his hearing and give evidence on his behalf. Both men agreed to meet his lawyers, Frank Hogan and Donald Shepherd, and agreed on the evidence they would give.

During the afternoon of 14 July 1935, Joe was rehearsing his evidence with one of Mellon's counsel, Paul C. Rodewald, when he was taken ill with an acute internal hemorrhage. He was rushed to the hospital for what was to be his final bout of surgery. The diagnosis was grim. Barring some unforeseen and unlikely remission, he would be lucky to live until Christmas.

Joe refused to accept the verdict. He put himself on a rigorous diet of milk, honey and boiled, shredded breast of chicken. In addition, to sustain his energy, his personal nurse was told to carry a supply of hard-boiled plover's eggs at all times, which the enterprising Bert Boggis managed to obtain whatever the season.

Whether it was the diet, his determination, or an unexpected remission, Joe managed to hold his cancer at bay for a further four years, twice as long as Andrew Mellon, who shared his predicament. Samuel Kress, who was immensely impressed with Joe's fortitude, either from solicitude or because he thought he would be buying cheap before Joe's impending demise, suddenly became a massive customer. During May 1936 he spent $1,240,000, followed by a further $1,500,000 in December and a stupendous $2,300,000 the following March. He was back again on 12 April, spending $897,000 on bronzes, medallions and small objects from the Dreyfus Collection and paintings to the value of $1,448,000.

Bernard learned of these huge purchases but there was little he could do except complain to all who would listen. He had some grounds for complaint, for these pictures and Italian works of art had originally cost the firm under $1 million, and he had sold his 25 per cent share in them to Joe outright in March 1929 for £50,000 ($250,000). If he had waited, his 25 per cent of the profits would have come to almost $1,500,000.

In May 1936 Mellon won his tax case, the U.S. Board of Tax Appeals ruling that his trusts were valid. Joe had never doubted that he would, and despite his infirmity had travelled to Washington the previous October with Pope to select the site for the National Gallery. Mellon met them and, after an argument, deferred to Pope. The gallery today stands on the spot Pope chose. Mellon confirmed his agreement in writing on 23 October 1935, and instructed Pope to start work on 6 February 1936.

While the Appeals Board decision delighted Mellon, it also robbed him of much of the will to fight his illness. Now that the pressure was off, he felt too sick to travel and select pictures for his gallery. What happened then has been hailed by those who did not know as Joe's master stroke. They claimed that Joe rented the apartment below Mellon's, decorated it as a gallery, and hung there all the pictures he hoped Mellon would buy. The truth is slightly different.

David Finley, Mellon's secretary and confidant, was asked by Mellon to travel to New York and make a selection of suitable pictures from which Mellon would be able to choose. These were to be hung in the Corcoran Gallery in Washington. Finley made the trip but, before the paintings left New York, he realized that his boss was too ill to make even the short journey across the city to the gallery. Learning that the occupant of the apartment below wished to leave, he negotiated a sub-lease on Joe's behalf. It was Finley's suggestion and initiative. Joe just paid the bill. The result was Joe's greatest sale ever. Mellon agreed to purchase thirty-nine pictures and twenty-three small pieces of sculpture, the cream of the Dreyfus Collection, for $6,200,000—a net profit of $5 million.

At last, Joe could afford to settle his affairs. He paid all the firm's debts, including the overdraft which his father had first acquired forty years earlier. He established trusts for his wife and daughter and at last paid for the shares which he had acquired from his brothers and sisters. Then he made the first of the two wills that were to survive him.

The first was dated February 1937. It left Duveen Brothers in five equal shares to Edward Fowles, Joe's nephew Armand Lowengard, Bert Boggis, Louis Levy, and his financial comptroller, John Allen. Each was told of the position, and Joe announced that he proposed to retire to Nassau and keep a friendly eye on the business until his death. Armand travelled to New York and took day-to-day charge of affairs.

The scene was now set for the final break with Bernard. During April 1937, in the course of renegotiating the Doris agreement, Levy confided to BB the terms of Joe's will. Bernard saw a way to recoup his fortunes. The loss of what could have been a share of the Mellon profit rankled deeply, and there is no doubt that Levy himself felt extremely guilty about the earlier capital of Bernard's that he claimed to have lost through poor investments.

Bernard proposed that, on Joe's death, he should join the firm as a shareholder and full partner. Levy agreed, and tactfully sounded out John Allen and Armand Lowengard, neither of whom had any objection. They were, of course, relatively unaware of the difficult and protracted quarrels between Joe and his adviser over the years. The three of them would have sufficient voting power to overrule Fowles, who had never been to the United States, and Bert Boggis, who was now with his master in Nassau.

Bernard's motive was to raise the funds he needed to endow I Tatti in order to make it an acceptable bequest to Harvard. He had no intention of stealing a march on anyone; he merely wished to recover, or at least receive, what he believed to be his just reward and thereby benefit his alma mater. Levy, however, had other ideas.

He saw what a power Duveens could become if its assets were properly developed. It could go into real estate, insurance, museum consultancy, even the auction business. He promptly opened negotiations with the American Art Association, then New York's leading auction house, but one which was already beginning to show the tell-tale signs of having been badly managed for too long. They key staff were underpaid and unhappy. He took them into his confidence and arranged what today would be called a management buy-out. The remodelled firm was christened Parke Bernet, and Levy became a member of the board and its legal counsel.

The plan was that, on Joe's death, Parke Bernet and Duveens would merge with Levy as the president and Bernard as the artistic adviser, and with suitable positions for Allen and Armand Lowengard. (In this way he anticipated what nearly happened in 1962 when Mr Peter Wilson of Sotheby's attempted to purchase Duveen Brothers lock, stock, and barrel. Mr Wilson was sent packing but three years later acquired Parke Bernet.)

Levy was in too much of a hurry. Not only did his purely conceptual corporation actually have stationery printed, but he entered into a contract for it to run the United States Fine Arts Pavilion at the 1939 World Fair to be held in Toronto. The future looked promising, but Joe refused to die. He had one piece of unfinished business to attend to, one picture to buy which he had long promised to Andrew Mellon, the picture which Mellon coveted above all others.

The painting was the 'Adoration of the Shepherds' by Giorgione. It belonged to the second Lord Allendale. Bernard had examined it in 1893 and incurred the owner's wrath when he doubted its authorship and ascribed it to Catena. Later he had changed his mind and called it a very early work of Titian. Kenneth Clark had borrowed it for the Italian exhibition he had organized in London in 1930, but as it was extremely dirty Lord Balniel, an excellent amateur scholar, had offered to pay for it to be cleaned. It turned out to be almost certainly by Giorgione and, when hung beside the undisputed touchstone of that artist's work, his 'Tempesta', it was agreed that it was by the same hand. Clark and his colleagues unanimously catalogued it as by Giorgione. After the exhibition Lord Allendale lent it to the National Gallery in London.

Andrew Mellon fell in love with it during his ambassadorship to Britain. In 1933 Lord Allendale offered to sell it to the National Gallery in London for £50,000 but, despite Joe's pleading, the Trustees refused to buy it, although Joe and Mellon each offered £10,000 towards its cost. At that time Allendale refused to allow it to be sold for export. However, he promised Mellon first refusal should he change his mind.

Allendale changed his mind early in 1937 and wrote to Joe. Mellon was desperately ill, on the verge of death, and in no position to make a decision, so Joe, as was his wont, prevaricated with Allendale over the price, which was £63,000. News of the possible sale of the picture reached the ears of a London dealer called Charles Ruck, who wrote to BB asking him his current opinion as to its authorship; he told BB that it was almost certainly on the market and would he or his principals—that is either Duveen, Wildenstein or Contini—be interested in buying it in partnership with him. Ruck believed the price would be £50,000.

Bernard formed a four-man syndicate. He still believed it to be by Titian but the plan was that Contini, Ruck, the new Levy corporation and himself would buy and enter it as the star attraction of a sale at the newly formed Parke Bernet. Two things went wrong. First, Contini covertly offered it to Kress; second, Bernard, mistakenly believing that Edward Fowles was privy to Levy's plans, let the cat out of the bag.

BB had written to discuss Levy's proposals for the 1937 Doris agreement and as an afterthought added that no more than four parties join to buy what he referred to as the Titian. He feared that if Lord Allendale heard of their plans, the price would be driven up over £50,000. BB wrote that the negotiations should be left to Ruck alone.

Fowles realized immediately that he was referring to the Giorgione and, believing that Joe was involved, cabled him for guidance. Mellon had just died but Joe's old competitive spirit was still alive, as was his anger. It took him a matter of hours to wring the full story out of Charles Ruck and preempt Levy's plan by buying it on his own account for the full £63,000 plus £5,000 to Ruck, who remained as the intermediary.

Levy was summarily dismissed from all connections with Duveens and cut out of the will. Allen had his legacy reduced to a nominal 5 per cent, but there was little Joe could do about BB, who had just signed a new retainer agreement—admittedly on six months' notice—at $150,000 a year. Joe decided to embarrass him. He announced the purchase publicly, saying that all 'well regarded' scholars agreed it was by Giorgione and that it was destined for a famous collection. John Walker, who was with BB at the time, wrote his own account of what happened when BB heard the news:

I was with BB when a telegram was delivered, which he showed me. It said, PURCHASED ALLENDALE NATIVITY FOR 60,000 GUINEAS [$315,000] SIGNED, JOE. BB said 'If Duveen paid that much for the picture, he must think it is by Giorgione and it isn't. It is by Titian. Obviously, he thinks he can sell a Giorgione to Mr Mellon, whereas he can't sell a Titian. He is capable of pretending I too think the picture by Giorgione. Please write his son, who is a friend of yours, and tell him my opinion, so there can be no question'. I did; but David Finley told me the picture was never offered to Mr Mellon. Duveen intended it for a new client, a collector BB then knew very little about, Samuel H. Kress. It was sold to Mr Kress with an attribution to Giorgione. BB was furious. Thereafter he would have nothing whatever to do with Duveen Brothers though this meant the termination of his retainer. It was an expensive break; and, as further evidence of his integrity, it should be remembered that at the end of his life, he published the Allendale picture in his revised list of *Venetian Paintings* (1957) as by Giorgione, or as he put it, by 'Giorgione (Virgin and Landscape probably finished by Titian)'. Had he agreed to this attribution twenty years earlier, Duveen doubtless would have continued his large annual payments.

Walker's account must be judged by the reader, bearing in mind that Mellon had died seven weeks previously. Joe still wished the picture to go to the Washington National Gallery. As soon as the news broke that he had bought it, Kress contacted Joe and told him he had been offered the picture by Contini and that he wished to buy it. Joe explained that if the National Gallery in Washington refused it then he could do so. In the meantime Joe wrote to David Finley and said that if the Washington National Gallery would like it they could have it for what it had cost him. Finley replied on 3 December 1937. His letter is an important one in the context of the truth about the end of the partnership, so it is reproduced unabridged:

Dear Lord Duveen,
   Paul Mellon was here yesterday and said he had discussed the question of the Giorgione with David Bruce when they were together at Staunton Hill last week. They both appreciate most deeply your courtesy in giving them the first opportunity to acquire this painting and realise, of course, its enormous importance and desirability for the Collection. They both agreed, however, that it is out of the question for them to consider buying it or to make even this exception to the policy of buying no paintings until the Gallery is built.
   They asked me to tell you this and to say that, as they could not buy it, they would not want you to have the trouble and delay of bringing the painting here for them to see. Indeed, it would be more painful after seeing it, to know that it could not stay here! They both appreciate very much your courtesy in the whole matter and asked me to write at once, so you would not be delayed a day longer than necessary in making your plans for disposing of the picture elsewhere before you go south at the end of this month. I do not need to tell you how grieved I am about this. I have never seen a picture that appeals to me more and it breaks my heart to

know it will not come here. As to Duncan Phillips his heart will be broken into little bits!

How I wish this painting had come to America a year ago— but we must be grateful for all we have.

I hope to see you in New York very soon, and with best regards, believe me.

Most sincerely yours,

David Finley

Joe promptly sold the painting to Samuel Kress for $400,000. Kress announced his acquisition to an astonished art world by putting it in the Christmas display window of his New York store.

BB did his best to spoil the sale. He wrote a series of letters to critics and curators, vilifying Joe and disparaging the painting. The one to Royal Cortissoz, the influential critic of the *New York Herald Tribune*, is typical.

You are acquainted, of course, with the Allendale picture, one of the most fascinating Giorgionesque pictures ever painted. The problem of how to attribute it has preoccupied me for many years. I naturally left no name untried. Finally some ten or twelve years ago, the light dawned on me and I began to see it must be Titian's, perhaps his earliest work, but only half out of the egg, the other half still in the Giorgione formula . . . the longer I looked the more and more I saw in it the emerging art of Titian. It is my deepest conviction that this attribution will ultimately win through.

Bernard's friends had their fling in the newspapers, but Kress, who now knew the full story and therefore the reason for BB's chagrin, was unimpressed. BB had condemned Joe's painting and Joe now knew of the takeover plan with Levy, so Bernard had no alternative but to give the six months' notice that the agreement demanded. The partnership was terminated as from 30 June 1938.

Joe died at Claridges, aged seventy, on 25 May 1939. Kenneth Clark's blackball over his re-election as a Trustee of the National Gallery had robbed him of his wish to live.

His will, drastically altered after Levy's exposure, gave Fowles and Armand Lowengard 90 per cent of the company, with John Allen and Bert Boggis holding 5 per cent each. All the staff were left handsome annuities, while the stock in his basement, though valued at a mere $200,000, eventually generated over $40 million before Fowles sold out to Norton Simon.

Louis Levy was disbarred from practise for his involvement with Duveens, Parke Bernet and certain other dubious company and stock manipulations. He settled down and wrote an account of his time with Duveens, which he gave to his golfing companion, the *New Yorker* humorist Sam Behrman, to knock into shape. Behrman used the manuscript as the basis for a series of articles in the *New Yorker* and then expanded it into a book which was as well received as it was inaccurate.

A month after Joe's death Bernard began a series of written approaches to Fowles, Lowengard and Joe's daughter Dorothy, suggesting that they renew the relationship. The letters, which continued up until the time when the United States entered the war, when Bernard decided to remain in Italy, were answered politely but his suggestion was ignored. When the war ended, Bernard returned to the subject. Fowles, who was by this time sole owner of the firm, kept him at arm's length but on John Walker's behalf negotiated a delicate arrangement.

One of Joe's last suggestions to Mellon's executors had been that John Walker should be recruited as the first Curator of Painting for their new Washington National Gallery. All realized that Walker was more of a courtier than a scholar, but he was rich, he knew the right people, and, from Joe's point of view, it would neatly frustrate Bernard's plan to make Walker the first Director of Studies at I Tatti when Harvard took it over.

Andrew Mellon's will had specifically stipulated that the gallery could only accept donations or acquire works of art which were of at least equal quality to those with which he had endowed it. Walker set himself the self-imposed task of persuading the Kress family to present their collection to the gallery. It was a classic case of covetousness triumphing over ignorance.

There was a problem. Kress would only present his collection *en bloc*. Of the 393 paintings involved, only 131 could possibly be rated as of museum quality. The others—sixteen from Duveens and most of the rest supplied by Contini—ranged from ancient replicas to modern forgeries. Walker was aware of this but he had to sign an affidavit to satisfy the Trustees and the Inland Revenue that they met Mellon's standard.

The matter could be resolved if Bernard could be persuaded to include them in the lists at the end of a new edition of *Italian Painters of the Renaissance*. Edward Fowles was asked to arrange the matter, as hitherto Duveens had always secretly subsidized Bernard's publications.

At first Fowles refused. He had already paid for a new edition of Bernard's *Florentine Drawings*, as he regarded this as a serious and essential piece of scholarship. However, he knew his man. He persuaded Bernard to revise the lists and to include the Kress pictures, but it was the Kress Foundation, not Duveens, who paid for the sumptuously printed three-volume edition. It eventually appeared in 1957 published by Phaidon when Bernard was ninety-two. All his august and brilliant scholarship was retained, while the additions were the work of a group of doting female acolytes who surrounded the elderly sage. Bernard made one personal contribution which related to the star of the Kress Collection, the Allendale 'Adoration of the Shepherds'. It was, he conceded in writing, very largely the work of Giorgione.

Coda

The Second World War had one happy result. It isolated BB from the marketplace. Together with an increasingly ailing Mary he remained at I Tatti even after the United States entered the war, under the benevolent protection of Mussolini's son-in-law, Count Ciano.

When Italy surrendered to the Allies in September 1943 the German army took control of Florence. As an American, a Jew and a well-known anti-Fascist he was forced to hide in the house of a neighbour, the Marchese Filippo Serlupi, who had a somewhat fragile diplomatic immunity as Minister of San Marino to the Holy See. Physically it was a comfortable sanctuary.

This pleasant isolation gave him the time for some rigorous self-analysis, and he did not shirk the task. His diaries and letters show the mental anguish he endured when he re-examined his relationship with the art-dealing world in general and Duveen in particular.

He resolved to make as honourable 'amends' as he could, and to devote much of the rest of his life to teaching and passing on his remarkable gifts.

Admittedly he approached Edward Fowles to try to secure a retainer from the firm and, when his advance was tactfully rebuffed, settled for a handsome stipend from Wildenstein. But—and in fairness to his memory this is an important but—he never dealt again.

A new post-war generation of students and scholars flocked to I Tatti where a now octogenarian BB held court. His main interests now were people as opposed to paintings, and to those with whom he could establish a rapport he was both a generous host and a delightful mentor. Despite what his more immediate disciples have written he took little interest in the updating of his lists, remarking that over time, the actual author of a picture doesn't really matter.

He died at I Tatti on 6 October 1959 at the age of ninety-four. He is buried there in the little chapel in the garden beside Mary and it is their partnership—particularly in those breathless early years when scholarship was foremost in his mind—that is his best memorial.

Appendix I

Heads of Agreement Document, 18 August 1912
WITH Doris

1. Agreement is for five years, that is, to 1 July 1917, subject to mutual right before that date to terminate it on either side by six months' notice, when final account between the parties to be taken.

2. Doris not to be in D.B.'s exclusive employment.

3. Doris to endeavour to secure on most favourable terms for D.B., Italian pictures and works of art; also to report to D.B. on everything he comes across, and to assist in negotiations. Doris free, if D.B. refuse or cannot buy, to introduce and offer goods to collectors, but not to dealers.
   Doris always, as far as possible, to have the first offer made by or through him to D.B. before submitting to or discussing same with other persons.
   If D.B. decline any purchase, they will not mention to anyone that objects have been introduced to them by Doris or anyone else.

4. Doris will advise D.B. on all Italian pictures and works of art where consulted by them, and as far as he reasonably can, he will assist D.B. in all negotiations for acquiring such objects.

5. Doris to supply promptly all provenance, and every possible information concerning such Italian pictures and works of art, their history, their owners, and any dealings or negotiations, as far as Doris has any knowledge or belief concerning same that may have taken place, or any opinions or criticisms that may have been made concerning same, or otherwise.

6. The phrase 'Works of Art' is used in its most comprehensive sense and not with any limitation. It includes
    Pictures
    Bronzes
    Statues
    Furniture
    Tapestries
    Antiques
    Bas-Reliefs
    Majolica
    Jewelry
    Bric-a-brac
    Illuminated Manuscripts
    Curios of any descriptions,
   and more particularly, those which D.B. have in the past dealt in.
   Concerning all works of art, other than Italian pictures, the parties may by mutual consent fix the commission at less than 25%.

7. During this agreement, Doris to have no percentage arrangements with other dealers, the intention being that during this agreement, in all his transactions with other dealers Doris will charge a fixed monetary sum for his advice.
   Neither party shall divulge the fact, or leave anybody to infer that Doris is paid by D.B. on a percentage basis.

8. All Italian pictures and works of art comprehended herein to be entered in 'X' book, open at all times to the inspection of Doris, or of 'X'.
   No fees payable to Doris except in connection with Italian pictures, or other works of art, entered in the said book.
   Regarding works of art other than Italian pictures, these to be calculated on a 25% basis unless specifically and mutually agreed that calculation is to be on another basis, or that said works of art are not to be entered in 'X' Book at all.
   Unless Italian pictures or works of art be entered in 'X' Book, there shall be no claim by or through Doris or the said 'X' concerning any of the percentage fees in respect thereof.
   Entries in 'X' book to be conclusive.

9. Original of said 'X' book to be in D.B.'s possession, preferably in Paris, and D.B. to supply 'X' with half-yearly accounts and copies of all entries made during half year.

10. D.B. to enter in 'X' Book with Doris' approval, all Italian pictures and works of art covered by agreement upon which fees are payable.

11. Any transactions between parties not entered in said 'X' Book to be regulated by private or separate arrangements.

12. Doris to give D.B. his written descriptions or criticisms, or information, or provenances, and particularly when requested by D.B., to furnish written certificates of his own personal opinion or belief in authenticity or otherwise.
    He should also, when requested, state in said certificate his opinion as to value of any Italian picture or works of art.

13. The basis of this Agreement is the very considerable value attached to Doris' opinions and beliefs concerning authenticity, etc.,—also on the fact that D.B.'s dealings are necessarily singular and exceptional, frequently involving not only long credits or return of works of art, but often involving special arrangements regarding various dealings not normally encountered in any other business.

14. Arrangements between parties do not constitute a partnership, but merely provide convenient method for paying fees to Doris. The arrangement hereinafter mentioned for refund by Doris to D.B. is not of a partnership nature, or merely arising from the fact that Doris is to share in profits or losses. The definite agreement is that fees arranged herein are for services rendered and to be rendered by Doris, and must not be referred to by parties or anyone, as commissions or brokerages or otherwise than fees.

15. Doris to surrender to D.B. 75% of any fee or profit on any Italian picture or work of art which he has purchased, and which they may acquire from or through him and enter in 'X' book.
    Doris to inform D.B. of any such facts; the intention being that as Doris would profit from D.B.'s dealings in any picture

or work of art to be entered in 'X' Book, Doris will allow D.B. said percentage on his fee or profit as stated, accounts between parties being adjusted, and regularized in the half-yearly accounts referred to.

16. Regarding Italian Pictures or Works of art entered in 'X' Book, D.B. to pay Doris 25% of their net profits as and when made and realized, Doris following D.B.'s fortunes, D.B. having absolute freedom and disposition of arrangements with customers.

    If D.B. accept return of 'X' picture or work of art from any client, Doris to be debited with whatever amount was placed to his credit in respect to such sale.

    If the amount credited shall already have been paid, Doris to refund same with interest at 5% per annum from date of payment.

    If picture or work of art subsequently resold, Doris entitled to 25% of net profit.

    Should D.B. deem it wise or prudent to sell any 'X' Picture or work of art at a loss, then Doris' fee to be reduced to the extent of 25% of any ascertainable loss.

    If Doris shall have been paid everything due to him in connection with said account, he to refund to D.B. 25% of any such ascertainable loss.

17. Subject to consultation, with the approval of Doris, D.B. reserve right to interest third party in acquiring pictures or works of art in 'X' book, but D.B. not to disclose to such third party Doris' fees.

    If absolutely necessary to disclose the fact then D.B. will only disclose that Doris has received or is entitled to a fee either by a stated or unstated amount, but D.B. to preserve secrecy concerning precise terms and arrangements of this agreement. Any such third party to the transaction to appear in the current half-yearly account.

18. D.B. to keep proper books of account for 'X' book and 'X' Ledger Account.

19. D.B. to render to chartered accountants on 31 August and 28 February yearly, a copy of all their entries in said books down to 31 July and 31 January respectively.

Details of all additions to cost price including travelling to be itemized and recorded, such additions to cost not to include salaries of partners or employees, nor regular office expenses. Interest at 5% per annum calculated half-yearly.

20. Absolute freedom to D.B. to make sales or other disposition of 'X' objects, and in making terms thereunder, as they would do in the ordinary course of their own business, and as if no one else were interested in the transactions.

21. At termination of agreement, or Doris' death, all cash amounts due or to become due to him shall for three years be withheld by D.B., they allowing and paying 5% thereon during that period. The amounts so retained by D.B. for the said three years to be held as reserve against contingencies or debits in connection with dealings in 'X' objects.
'After expiration of three years, any amounts due Doris in respect of cash profits to be immediately paid.
Any amounts still due Doris on uncollected sales to be settled for as received in subsequent half-yearly accounts.
After expiration of said three years, Doris or Executors not to be debited with any losses concerning the return of any 'X' objects; nor are D.B. liable to account for any profits upon sale of 'X' objects sold after expiration of three year period.
If Doris dies all moneys due his Executors to be paid to the First National Bank, New York, or otherwise, as may be arranged. The intention of this clause is that at end of said three years, the account shall be struck absolutely and finally between parties.

22. Secrecy clause binds Executors.
G. and J. to keep original agreement.
Neither party to have copy, even to make note about its terms. Doris to leave with his wife or lawyer, or some other trusted person, whose name from time to time he shall give to D.B., a memorandum concerning agreement, to be opened in the event of death. Such memorandum will state that there is or may be money due to Doris from D.B., and holder of such memorandum is to communicate with 'X'.

Communication about accounts to be dealt with through the accountants only, who are authorized by Doris quite exclusively of everybody to collect anything due from D.B. during Doris' lifetime and after death.

The heirs may not dispute the amount certified by 'X' to be due to Doris.

23. As this agreement is personal between D.B. and Doris, latter not to assign, charge or deal with interest thereunder. Should he do so he forfeits all his interest excepting anything already certified by chartered accountants to be due and unpaid.

Inasmuch as any assignment, charge, etc. would be a breach of requisite secrecy, for every such breach Doris to pay D.B. the sum of £10,000 to liquidate damages, which damages 'X' may and shall deduct from any sum so found to be due and unpaid to Doris.

Thereafter Doris not to be entitled to any fees in respect of any dealings by D.B. in any pictures or works of art contained in 'X' Book or any other works of art, the subject of separate agreement between parties.

24. Agreement ceases if Doris becomes insolvent, D.B. retaining right to set off any sums due them against any sum due from D.B. to Doris.

25. Parties agree that 'X' shall, with or without Doris' request, or in event of Doris' death, be supplied periodically by D.B. with all information and particulars regarding accounts re pictures and works of art mentioned in said 'X' book, and therefore to have fullest possible access to D.B.'s books; the intention being that said 'X' shall investigate and regularize each half-yearly account and adjust all matters in dispute finally. Said 'X' bound to absolute secrecy in connection therewith on anything done under this agreement.

No third party to be consulted or employed by either party with the exception of the said 'X'. If necessary, said 'X' may, at expense of parties, be entitled to take independent legal or other advice under similar terms of observation of secrecy.

26. Neither party to take proceedings against the other upon any difference arising out of agreement. Chartered accountants to

determine all issues and their certificate covering amounts due between parties shall be final and binding.

If either party is sued for payment, chartered accountants to take any necessary proceedings, but not in name of party suing. Chartered accountants to be sole and final arbitrators.

27. Arrangements for substituting other chartered accountants if 'X' unable or unwilling to act.

In event of death or bankruptcy of said 'X' or of his inability or declining or neglecting to carry out the stipulations and provisions of this agreement, general arrangements to be made by the President for the time being of the I.C.A., in London, to substitute other chartered accountants.

28. All expenses relating hereto and to the chartered accountants, etc., to be debited as part of the general expenses in said account.

29. Any notice may be given by D.B. to Doris by sending same through post or leaving same at address above mentioned of Doris, or such other address as he shall indicate to D.B.—and similarly by Doris to D.B. by mailing same or leaving it addressed to them at 21 Old Bond Street, London, or 20 Place Vendôme, Paris.

Such notices shall be deemed to have been received by the parties, seven days after the posting thereof.

30. Agreement construed to be made in England, and according to English law; both parties submit to English jurisdiction.

Appendix II

Letter from Henry to Joe, 3 April 1913

DUVEEN BROTHERS
720 Fifth Avenue New York   20 Place Vendôme
21 Old Bond St. Londres   Paris, le 3 April 1913

HJD

Joseph Duveen Esq.
   NEW YORK

My dear Joe,
   Your letter of 14 March reached me in due course at Monte
Carlo, and this is the first letter I am writing, as I have left everything till I arrived here.
   I want to tell you that we had a most delightful trip, and the
crossing was particularly easy, as the sea was smooth. Our first
days too at Monte Carlo were fine, as the weather was all that
could be desired, but it became very bad later on.
   We arrived here last night rather tired, and Aunt Dora has caught
a cold and is laid up in bed for a few days; nothing very serious,
but I am looking after her carefully.
   It was a strange coincidence that I received your letter recom-
mending me to go to Florence on the very day that I was actually
leaving for that place, for as I found that Berenson was not going
South I had decided to go and see him and learn all there was to
be learned.
   I am very glad I went, for I never spent a more agreeable time

in my life as I did in Florence seeing things with Berenson. It was wonderful. I have no doubt you would like to hear of the greatest picture which I have ever seen in my life. It is the famous work by* which is in the Uffizi Galleries. It is simply marvellous, and no picture in the whole world ever appealed to me more than this does.

The pictures of the Italian School which I saw there are simply wonderful, and so is the Sculpture at the* and the other pictures at the* Palace and the National Palace. They are simply bewildering, and I could have spent weeks there.

RE MARTELLI MARBLES

In regard to the Martelli marbles, they absolutely insisted that I must on no account go to see them, or approach the Martellis in any way, and if I have made a mistake, it was done simply because I did not wish to give them reason to be able to claim later that I had spoilt the business; although all the same I was very sorry not to go there. They gave me proper reasons why I should not, and I must admit they may be right, so I did not force the point.

DESIDERIO BUST

Whilst I was in Florence the matter of the Desiderio Bust was just concluded at £15,000 and £600 expenses to get it out of Italy.

I think that this bust is really a wonderful work of art, and for its size a great purchase, although unfinished it does not alter the fact that it is great. I am only afraid that the nose has never been treated properly, and think it ought to be rightly repaired by a great master in this kind of work.

This bust will be delivered to us very shortly, but of course we do not know when.

* Gaps are in the original.

BARDINI

I also went to see Bardini, and he showed me all over his place. He told me some bare-faced lies, which I enjoyed immensely, but I did not see anything which particularly struck me for Duveen Brothers. He was very anxious to do business with us, and of course asked me about the Martelli marbles and enquired whether I was in Florence after these things. I told him that we were not crazy, and did not want to burn our fingers buying things of that kind, unfinished things, at a mad price.

I did not go to Volpi as I was told it best not to do so, and it is very strange to say but Bardini was rather anxious that I should see him and have a look at the things, and their seeming enmity appears to be only on the surface. For reasons of the Martelli, I thought it best not to go near him.

I had two nights travelling, a good deal for me, as I am more than 44, and I felt it very much.

You can imagine my consternation when I received the news the following day in Monte Carlo of Mr Morgan's death. I can hardly realise that the great man, the great friend is no more.

I am afraid his fortune will not be as large as people anticipate, as I should think he spent very nearly half what he possessed in Works of Art, and if his present possessions figure out at 15 millions pounds sterling I think it will be all he will be found to be worth.

FRANZ HALS

I have cabled you today about this picture. It is simply wonderful, why it is marvellous.

The photograph can give you no idea of what it is, and I think the frame has improved it immensely.

LUINIS

These have now all arrived here, nine of them, just think of that, a roomful, and in fact we are going to exhibit them in a room by themselves.

I have cabled to you today suggesting that you prepare Dr Valentiner to buy them next summer, as they are only suitable for a Museum, and there is no private collector who will buy them.

Ernest is having them mounted in rather a novel and artistic manner, of which I approve very much.

LYDIG SALE

Under the present circumstances, we should go slow, in fact very slow, until things are more in our way. I therefore hope you are not buying very much there.

WILDENSTEIN SOFA

I have seen this, and I agree with Louis and Ernest that at £7,000 this sofa is no purchase for Duveen Brothers.

They have explained to you all about the colour and quality, but they did not mention to you that the back and seat has on each side six inches of modern stuff with flowers and motives woven in. As you know this is considerable and shows in the front on the back and seat, and will discolour in no time. We must not buy this Sofa, especially at this price.

I think that if Wildenstein had left this Sofa in its original state, and had done nothing to it, we would have bought it at a fair price, and could have done something with it. As it is it is no good today.

He spent £800 on a old Sofa Frame, which is really very good, but it does not help us, as the modern parts spoil it.

SELIGMANN CHAIRS

I have seen these chairs which came from Warings, and I cannot agree with Louis and Ernest in not buying them. I believe the 7 pieces are worth to buy £5,000, and furthermore they should be bought.

Ernest has since changed his opinion about them, and seems to agree with me that they are a bargain.

I have been through Seligmann's Stock, that is to say the stock belonging to Arnold Seligmann, but there is nothing amongst it that Duveen Brothers can make any money out of.

The old Stock belonging to the old Account is all put away, and will be sold by auction later on.

RE MORGANS

I will write to the Morgan family by next mail, that is to say I will write to Mrs Morgan and family, and also to Mr Jack Morgan.

I had already cabled on Tuesday my condolence to Mrs Morgan in New York, and also to Mr Jack Morgan.

I now enclose my card, and should like you to send a magnificent wreath, with simply the word 'FRIEND' standing out in red flowers, that is to say of course providing if wreaths of flowers are permitted. Whatever it is, do something charming.

Naturally we are anxious to know what you are doing, as you can appreciate business here is at a stand-still, and it is the same everywhere. Your silence about the Harrington pictures does not look very promising, nor have I heard anything settled about the Frick matter. You can quite understand that this news interests me.

MR A.

I am writing him tomorrow further about the Titian, but I want to tell you that Berenson is not going to write him direct. I have urged him to do so, but he declined under the circumstances to write until he had seen Mr A. I cannot entirely disagree with

Berenson in this decision, although I tried to make him write: however it was no use.

Of course I missed the picture here, as it left yesterday, for which I am sorry. From all accounts I hear it is something marvellous.

I am very grieved to hear that you have lost the sale of the 2 Mainardis to Mr A. I do not know how this occurred, and there is something I cannot appreciate in it. They were so beautiful and so sensible. Let me know what was the objection Mr A. had to them.

RE DECORATORS

I cabled you from Montecarlo that the decoration of important houses of our clients must be kept entirely under our direction, that is to say, if we introduce Allom or Carlhian to our clients who are having this work done, any interviews which take place between the client and the Decorator should be held in our presence. We ourselves should discuss every detail from an independent point of view. Perhaps even it would be well to discuss sometimes for the mere sake of discussion, and with a view to showing our client that we are the master and that we know our business. We do not want it to appear as if the Decorator is in any way the master, and we should always keep the whip-hand. Whenever I have allowed the Decorator to go his own way, and arrange directly with the client, I have always found it to be a mistake.

Besides by doing this you will always be kept 'au fait', and you will always be called in to decide matters, and you will see what strength you retain in the house.

Moreover, it would be a good plan to find fault whenever necessary with some serious point, and thus show the interest you have at heart for your client. Do not let the Decorator be the master, as Allom was at Mrs H's* house, and did as he pleased. You will regret this, if you do permit it.

* Arabella Huntington.

Your remark about Mr F.* telling you that you would be kept busy for years is very nice indeed, and I only hope it is true. It certainly is good news.

The only point to which I would draw your attention once more, is that in offering objects to Mr F. for his new house you should not start out with things of enormous price for him, as he is not accustomed to the idea of Objects of Art of great value, and you only frighten him for the sum total. Be well aware of this, please. You would do far better in offering him a few good things, even if at a lower rate of price, and then change them later on for more expensive objects. Please remember what he told you in regard to the Rose du Barri Set.

DUKE

The visit of Mr Duke was certainly very nice. Your remark that he wanted to buy sang de boeuf and other collections 'en bloc' means nothing in regard to this man. He has a way of asking the prices of everything that is shown him. I am curious to know what was the outcome of the intended trial of the Boucher pictures for the Ball-room. These people are very difficult.

In regard to his remark with reference to the 4 Tapestries which are now going into Mrs Widener's house, this was made by him for the sake of comparing prices. You must understand that the tapestries were shown to him when they were here, but as they only wanted two I was not inclined to separate them, whilst you had them reserved for your other client: besides he would not pay the price.

NEW BUILDING

It is very encouraging to hear the good news regarding our New Building, and the new people who are coming in.

I think Ben has a great chance of tackling some of these people,

* Frick.

who are at present unknown to him, and such people are bound to come in.

In regard to the visit of Mrs James, I am rather sorry I was not in New York, as she is a very wealthy woman in her own right, having a lot of Standard Oil millions.

Here again you must try and get Allom in, but keep on top, be master. I will take this matter in hand myself in the fall, but for Heaven's sake keep her in touch with yourself, do not turn her over to Allom entirely, or you will be sorry afterwards.

I smile when I read your news about Mrs Blumenthal, as they are using you very nicely for the Lydig Sale, and keeping a good competitor out of the market for the things they want. I consider they are pretty smart, as Seligmann is not there, and she herself wanting to leave for Europe.

I notice Leopold Hirsch was with you, and I do hope you were very careful in your conversation with him, and that you measured your words, for he is a very dangerous man and much less a friend of yours than you think.

I am very sorry indeed that you have taken him to Mr A., and you will regret this. You know very well he could not have got in there, and why need you have taken him to Mr A. I am very much annoyed about it, and I will remind you of this later in your life, when you will have seen what has become of the visit of this man to Mr A. and you will then say I was right.

RE LORD M.*

I have had a conversation with Ernest about this, and he explained to me very satisfactorily the position of affairs. It appears that they are much more difficult now in the selection of their puchases than formerly. However Ernest is quite satisfied that he will be able to do business with them next May, but he has to be careful what he offers to the lady, and I can see that he is right. No doubt he has written you more fully about this, and there are certain things which he wants you to return here for them. I should certainly not return things here which are not wanted in Europe.

* Michelham.

You may rest assured that Ernest will do all he possibly can to sell to these people.

FINANCES

I fully agree with all you say in this relation, but it is very difficult for a firm like ours to live up to this, seeing that we are practically always in the market, and are also selling on long credit. We have no other course but to make dates of payment for periods with our clients, and then keeping milking them, otherwise the game cannot be carried out.

I see no reason at all why you should be in such tremendous haste to come back to Europe, when there is no business over here, as everything is at a stand-still. I should certainly advise you to stay as long as you can in New York, as I believe you have business there which would carry you on to 7 May.

As far as I am concerned I am very sorry I have left New York, feeling as I do well and ready for work, and now that one of the main businesses for which I was preparing myself, has been cut off. It is certainly much more agreeable to be in a 'live' house, than in a dead one, for this house seems to me like a slaughter house, and I do not see a soul in the place. We have always something to do in New York.

As you know we are not in the humour to go out buying right and left, for conditions do not warrant so doing, and our object is to try and make money.

CARPACCIO

I think £35,000 for the Carpaccio is a mad price, and then you must consider that we have about half a dozen commissions which would have to be paid to different people, for instance there is Mr Kann, Mr Agnew and Mr Berenson, and then what is left for us? What are you going to sell this picture for? I therefore do not at all agree that we should buy this picture at £35,000.

I am enclosing you two cables which I have received from the Morgan family in answer to my own cables, and have decided not to write any more letters, after receiving these charming replies.

I also send you the original cables which I sent to Mrs Morgan and family and Mr Jack Morgan.

RE MR RYAN

I was delighted to see that you have concluded some business with this gentleman. The 2 marble figures I had myself tried in the room, but had no chance at the time, as the house-keeper asked me to take them out again, without seeing Mr Ryan. In fact I never have had a real interview with him concerning these, so I am more than pleased with the outcome of this.

When he called to see me in our house, he promised to have a look at the Renaissance things on his next visit, and it certainly is gratifying, as he has kept his word to buy something in place of the 17th century Marble Italian Bust which he returned.

MR LEHMANN

I notice from your letters that you propose showing the marble bust which we lately bought in Florence to Mr Lehmann. Allow me to tell you that you are making a great mistake: because firstly these people will not give the price which you expect to get from others, viz Mr A. or Widener, and secondly I telegraphed Mr A. about it, as you will have seen from the copies of telegrams I sent to you from Florence, and therefore you must not show it to Mr Lehmann, or if you do, you must ask him an impossible price. However I believe it is far better not to show it to him at all. Mr A. is too important a client, more important now than ever. I think you are making a grave mistake in showing Mr A. too many things. It would be better far to put some of the things away, and not show him everything. You are not carrying out the original policy we decided on in regard to him.

Let him be hungry and enquire for beautiful things, and he appreciates our things because we only show him the very finest.

I am writing this particularly because I really cannot understand how you have missed the sale of these two Mainardis. He told me before I sailed that he was very interested in them, as he wanted portraits, and after my interview with Berenson I am more and more convinced that it was possibly a mistake to have shown them to him at the time you did, when we had been telling him that there were further pictures being shipped.

MR ARTHUR LEHMANN

I observe the visit of Mr Arthur Lehmann, the cousin of Mr Philip Lehmann, and I think he is well worth taking in hand. He is a very good friend of mine, and you will find him rather a quicker buyer than his cousin, when you have his confidence. I advise you to take a lot of trouble with him, as he has plenty of money. This gentleman is married to the daughter of Mr Lewisohn, and his father-in-law has bought tapestries from us before, and you have a great chance of getting in with Mr Lehmann Senior, who is an enormously rich man, and is buying 16th Century objects from Seligmann. This is a very important affair, and if properly handled may bring good results.

My advice to you in selling to people like this, is to first of all gain their confidence, and as they do not know anything about works of art, the idea is to educate them to appreciate the fact that they are getting things from us at the *proper value*. Give Mr Arthur Lehmann books on tapestries, and show him the way and wherefore these things are so valuable, and in this way you will obtain his confidence.

I enclose you herewith a page of The Daily Telegraph of 1 April, containing articles with reference to the Morgan treasures. We think the interview with Mr Locket Agnew is charming.

I have no further news now, believe me.*

* No signature in the original.

Chronological List of Some Events
in the Lives of the Partners

1820   Birth of Joseph Henoch Duveen
1839   Birth of Isabella Stewart
1843   Birth of Joel Joseph Duveen
1853   Birth of Henry Duveen
1860   Jack Gardner marries Isabella Stewart
1865   Birth of Bernhard Valvrojenski (later Berenson)
1869   Joel Duveen marries Rosetta Barnett and Joseph is born
1874   'Ivan Lermolieff' article published
1875   Bernhard Berenson arrives in America
1877   Henry Duveen arrives in America
1879   Joel Duveen visits America
1884   Berenson enters Harvard
1887   Berenson sails for Europe
1890   Berenson in London
1891   Mary Costelloe goes to live in Florence with Berenson
1894   *Venetian Painters of the Renaissance* published; Henry Duveen
       and Berenson meet in New York
1895   Venetian Exhibition at New Gallery in London; Isabella Stewart
       Gardner and Berenson come to a formal arrangement
1898   Death of Jack Gardner; Berenson meets Godfrey von Kopp
1900   Mary Costelloe marries Bernhard Berenson; Death of Collis Hun-
       tington
1905   Hainauer Collection purchased by Duveen
1906   Death of Rodolphe Kann; George Barnard purchases Abbey de
       Parthenay stones and meets Joe Duveen
1907   Arabella Huntington comes to Paris; Berenson purchases I Tatti;
       Joel Duveen donates Turner wing to Tate Gallery
1908   Joel becomes Sir Joseph and dies
1910   Henry and Joe lease corner of Fifth Avenue; Customs troubles

1912   Berenson-Duveen contract signed
1913   Arabella Huntington marries her nephew-in-law, Henry E. Huntington
1914   Cloister Museum New York opened; I. S. Gardner buys a pair of kings
1917   BB meets Joe Duveen in Paris and inspects Schickler Collection
1919   Death of Henry Duveen; Joe Duveen becomes Sir Joseph; Deaths of Lord Michelham and William Salomon; Carl Hamilton arrives in Paris
1922   Edward Fowles and BB meet in Berlin to renegotiate contract; Sir Joseph asked to value Dreicer Collection for probate
1923   Death of Boutron and Demotte
1924   Death of Isabella Stewart Gardner
1925   Kenneth Clark visits I Tatti
1926   Sir Joseph donates extension to Tate Gallery; Mary travels to London to ask for monies due from Duveen; X accounts brought up to date
1927   Jules Bache lunches at I Tatti; Sir Joseph created a baronet
1928   Andrew Mellon and Sir Joseph visit the National Gallery in London together; New agreement signed between BB and Duveen
1929   Hahn case; Sir Joseph becomes a Trustee of the National Gallery in London
1930   Italian Exhibition at Burlington House organized by Kenneth Clark
1932   Doris agreement renewed; BB, Nicky Mariano and Sir Joseph meet in Vienna
1933   Duveen created Baron Duveen of Millbank
1934   Kenneth Clark becomes director of the National Gallery; Death of Andrew Mellon
1938   End of Berenson-Duveen partnership
1939   Death of Lord Duveen of Millbank
1959   Death of Bernard Berenson
1971   Death of Edward Fowles

Bibliography

Archives

Isabella Stewart Gardner letters, Fenway Court, Boston, Mass.
Berenson-Richter letters, Zurich, Switzerland.
Berenson Diaries, Harvard University.
Berenson unpublished mss, Harvard University.
Berenson-Fowles correspondence, Metropolitan Museum, New York.
Berenson-Duveen X ledger, Metropolitan Museum, New York.
Duveen Archives, Metropolitan Museum, New York.
Huntington Collection, Pasadena.

Works by Bernard Berenson

Venetian Painters of the Renaissance, Putnam, New York, 1894.
Lorenzo Lotto, Putnam, New York, 1895.
Florentine Painters of the Renaissance, Putnam, New York, 1896 (reprints and additions from 1909 on paid for by Duveen).
Central Italian Painters of the Renaissance, Putnam, New York, 1897 (1909 edition onward subsidized by Duveen).
North Italian Painters of the Renaissance, Putnam, New York, 1907 (subsidized by Duveen).
(The books on Florentine, Central and Northern painters were last published as a 3-volume set by Phaidon in 1968, and subsidized by the Kress Foundation, Duveen having refused to continue the subsidy after the 1932 editions.)
Drawings of the Florentine Painters, John Murray, London, 1903.
Study and Criticism of Italian Art, George Bell and Sons, London, 1901, 1902, 1916.
(These volumes included various essays and articles which first appeared

in art journals, and in the 1901 volume, Berenson's famous critical catalogue of the exhibition, 'Venetian Painting, Chiefly Before Titian' at the New Gallery, London, February, 1885.)

Venetian Painting in America, George Bell and Sons, London, 1916 (subsidized by Duveen).

Three Essays in Method, Clarendon Press, Oxford, 1926.

Sunset and Twilight, Hamish Hamilton, London, 1964.

Sketch for a Self-Portrait, Hamish Hamilton, London, 1949.

Rumour and Reflection, Constable, London, 1952.

Selected Letters, edited by McComb, Harvard, 1965.

Catalogues of the Hamilton, Mackay and Bache Collections for their owners.

'A Sienese Painter of the Franciscan Legend', *Burlington* magazine, September, 1903.

Other Works

Behrman, Sam. *Duveen*. Hamish Hamilton, London, 1959.

Berenson, Mary. *A Self-Portrait from her Letters and Diaries*. Edited by Barbara Strachey, Gollancz, London, 1983.
    Unpublished biography of Bernard Berenson (Strachey papers).

Catalogue of Italian Paintings in the National Gallery, 1892.

Census of Pre-19th Century Italian Paintings in North American Public Collections. Harvard, 1972.

Clark, Kenneth. *Another Part of the Wood*. John Murray, London, 1974.

Douglas, Robert Langton. *Duveen Sculpture in Public Collections in America* (privately printed in an edition of 500, New York.
    'A Forgotten Painter', *Burlington* magazine, May 1903.
    Fra Angelico. George Bell and Sons, London, 1900.
    History of Siena. John Murray, London, 1902.

Duveen, J. H. *Confessions of an Art Dealer*. Longmans Green, London, 1935, 1936.
    The Rise of the House of Duveen. Longmans Green, London, 1957.
    Unpublished history of the firm in the Duveen Archives.

Fowles, Edward. *Memoirs of Duveen Brothers*. Times Books, London, 1976.

Gombrich, Ernest. *Meditations on a Hobbyhorse*. Phaidon, London, 1963.

Hendy, Sir Philip. *Catalogue of the Paintings in the Isabella Stewart Gardner Collection*. Boston, 1931.

Italian Paintings in the Walters Art Gallery, 2 volumes. Baltimore, 1976.

Lermolieff (*see* Morelli).

Metropolitan Museum, New York. *Catalogue of Italian Paintings: Florentine School.* 1971 Venetian School, 1973 (Federico Zeri).

Morelli, Giovanni. I have used the 2-volume collected work *Italian Painters, Critical Studies of their Works*, which includes the original 'Lermolieff' article, which first appeared in what Professor Wollheim describes as 'an obscure German periodical:' Vol. 1 *The Borghese and Doria Pamfili Galleries in Rome*; Vol 2 *The Galleries of Münich and Dresden.*
Published in English, translated by Constance ffoukes and with an introduction by Sir A. H. Layard, London, 1892 and 1893.

Pater, Walter. *Studies in the History of the Renaissance.* Macmillan, London, 1873.

Marius the Epicurean. Macmillan, London, 1885.

Pearsall Smith, Mary (*see* Mary Berenson).

Richter, Irma and Gisela, editors. The Richter-Berenson correspondence. Circulated in mimeographed form in 1969. The originals are in the Zurich Art Gallery. It was meant to be a companion to *Italienische Malerei der Renaissance im briefwechsel von Giovanni Morelli und Jean Paul Richter 1876–1891*, Baden Baden, 1960

Samuels, Ernest. *Bernard Berenson: The Making of a Connoisseur.* Harvard University Press, 1980.

Shapley, Fern Rusk. *Paintings from the Kress Collection*, 3 volumes. Published for the National Gallery, Washington, Phaidon 1966, 1968, 1973.

Secrest, Meryl. *Being Bernard Berenson.* Weidenfeld & Nicolson, London, 1980.

Sprigge, Sylvia. *Bernard Berenson.* Allen & Unwin, London, 1960.

Walker, John. *Self-portrait with Donors.* Atlantic Monthly, New York, 1974.

Wollheim, Richard. *On Art and the Mind.* Allen Lane, London, 1973.

Valentiner, Professor. *Duveen Pictures in Public Collections in America.* New York, 1941. Begun by Bernard Berenson in 1935 and finished by Valentiner.

Zeri, Federico. *See* Metropolitan Museum, New York, *Catalogue of Italian Paintings.*

Index of Paintings

The purpose of this index is to enable the reader to see at a glance the present whereabouts and current attribution of the principal paintings discussed in the text. These attributions often differ from those proposed by Berenson and Duveen, for a variety of reasons. Although in some instances they undoubtedly intended to deceive, they also sometimes sincerely over-estimated or indeed under-estimated the quality of their pictures. Attribution always has been and always will be a difficult business, and scholars often disagree violently about the authorship of paintings. The current attributions given here are those which would, I believe, be generally, though not all of them universally, accepted today. They are not meant to express a personal judgement.

ARTIST	TITLE	PRESENT LOCATION	CURRENT ATTRIBUTION	PAGE
ANGELICO, Fra	Annunciation	Detroit, Mrs Edsel Ford	Fra Angelico	194
ANGELICO, Fra	Entombment	Washington, National Gallery of Art	Attributed to Jacopo del Sellaio	239
BALDOVINETTI	Madonna and Child	Washington, National Gallery of Art	Pseudo Pier Francesco Fiorentino	184
BELLINI, Giovanni	Portrait of a Young Man	New York, Metropolitan Museum of Art	Jacometto Veneziano	184
BELLINI, Giovanni	Madonna and Child	Boston, Isabella Stewart Gardner Museum	Giovanni Bellini	182
BELLINI, Giovanni & TITIAN	Feast of the Gods	Washington, National Gallery of Art	Giovanni Bellini & Titian	196–7
BELLINI, Giovanni	Madonna and Child with Saints	New York, Metropolitan Museum of Art	Giovanni Bellini and Workshop	182
BELLINI, Giovanni	Madonna and Child	New York, Metropolitan Museum of Art	Workshop of Giovanni Bellini	201
BENVENUTO di Giovanni	Adoration of the Magi	Washington, National Gallery of Art	Benvenuto di Giovanni	196
BONIFAZIO Veronese	Holy Family with SS John the Baptist and Elizabeth	Boston, Isabella Stewart Gardner Museum	Bonifazio Veronese	74
BORDONE, Paris	The Child Jesus Disputing in the Temple	Boston, Isabella Stewart Gardner Museum	Paris Bordone	74
BOTTICELLI, Alessandro	Death of Lucretia	Boston, Isabella Stewart Gardner Museum	Botticelli	73
BOTTICELLI, Alessandro	Madonna of the Eucharist	Boston, Isabella Stewart Gardner Museum	Botticelli	85

293

Index

Abdy, Sir Robert, 212–13
Agnew, Sir Geoffrey, 82
Agnew, Lockett, 84, 281, 283; makes enquiries regarding authenticity of pictures and bust, 84
Agnew & Sons, Thomas, 68, 69, 73, 82, 85, 98, 205, 213
Aldington, Richard, 48
Allen, John, 224, 254, 255; reduced legacy of, 259
Allendale, Lord, 63
Allendale, Lord (second), 255–57; offers to sell painting to National Gallery, 257
Altman, Benjamin, 26, 102, 107, 117, 136, 244; Collection, 26, 134
Altoviti, Bindo, 83, 84
American Art Association, 182–83, 255
André, Jean, 155
Angelico, Fra, 91, 194
Antoine de Bourbon, Prince, 191
Ariosto, Ludovicio, 137
Arnold, Matthew, 42
Art Institute of Chicago, 83
Ashburnham, Lord, 73
Astor, Jacob, 165

Bache, Jules, 184, 203, 228, 244; his initiation into world of Italian Renaissance art, 203; personality, 203; makes many purchases, 204–05; influenced by daughter, 204–06; deception practised on, 209; purchases Crivelli painting, 211; many paintings bought from Joseph Duveen, 214–15; decimation of fortune, 215; stratagem employed by, 216; cooling of relationship with Joseph Duveen, 216
Bache, Kitty, 207–08ff.; marriage to Gilbert Miller, 212
Bachnitz, Kurt, 215